W9-BZZ-713

THE HOUSE OF GOD

THE HOUSE OF GOD

Sacred Art and Church Architecture

R. KEVIN SEASOLTZ

HERDER AND HERDER

1963
HERDER AND HERDER NEW YORK
232 Madison Avenue, New York 16, N.Y.

Nihil obstat:
Patrick A. Barry, V.F.
Imprimatur:
† Robert F. Joyce
Bishop of Burlington
June 25, 1963

Library of Congress Catalog Card Number: 63–18161

Printed in the United States of America

CONTENTS

Introduction

It is a sign that the liturgical revival has come of age that it can afford to discuss art and architecture. For a generation or so most promoters of this revival have avoided, almost to excess, any profound involvement with the arts of the Church, lest their central concern, the holiness of God's People at worship, should be compromised.

Such a misunderstanding is hardly possible now. No one could reasonably suggest that the liturgy is a matter of externals, of only peripheral interest to the real life of the Church; it is too evidently the primary action of a People committed to praying and praising God. Thus it becomes possible to give sacred art, music, and architecture the attention they have always deserved.

The attention is deserved because all the sights and sounds, the spaces and the forms, are signs in the whole complex of signs that constitutes the public worship of the Church. It is possible for the worshipers to assemble out of doors, in a place uncovered by roof, unenclosed by walls, as it is possible for the words of holy rites to be uttered without melody or musical accompaniment. But this possibility does not lessen the significance, in the complete meaning of that word, of the sacred place of worship and of the disposition and content of that place.

Even negatively, the need to study church architecture and design from the viewpoint of worshipful activity is evident, especially when the issue of communal participation is faced. A church where seeing and hearing are impossible is an impediment to real worship. A church with a misdirected focus of attention is a distraction from worship. A spatial arrangement designed exclusively for watchers and hearers rather than for doers frustrates the liturgy which "of its nature demands that all who are present should participate, each one in his own proper manner."

In the past few years those with a genuine concern for sacred architecture have shown a fresh and sound feeling for the church structure as the place of community worship. Architects have sought a "liturgical brief" from those expert in the theology, history, law, and pastoral science of Christian worship. In other fields similarly related to the liturgy, notably sacred music, progress has been much slower in the direction of understanding the liturgy as community action and life. All the more credit to architects, artists, and artisans. Their new churches and new works, as well as writings in books and magazines, reveal a sincere desire to search for the true meaning of a church and to achieve its chief purpose, that is, to be a room in which the Christian assembly may celebrate the Eucharist.

This making or remaking of a church to satisfy its very purpose is of course an aspect of the form–and–function tension. Who would build a school or library, a hospital or, for that matter, a kitchen without first satisfying every legitimate function the structure is to serve? Yet it has been a new awakening to reconsider the church building in such a light, so often had it been romanticized as the (static) house of God, the finger pointing to heaven, the visible expression of prayer, the (museumlike) tribute of beauty to God.

Perhaps this fresh and dynamic concentration on a church's function has appeared to disparage or destroy the equally sound concept of the church as sign and symbol of religious reality. Rather, it seems to me, balance and proportion have been restored. Negatively, nothing must be added to the church structure which will be incompatible with its holy function. Positively, the church must be built for the act of worship of God, worship in which every Christian has a vital part, with all else secondary—and with the proper roles of the several participants and the relative liturgical values of the different rites and services recognized.

Without being archtraditionalists, some have felt that this simplicity of purpose leads to barrenness and rejection of the beautiful rather than to simplicity of design. A ready answer is that the function, far from being a constraint upon design, is a challenge to do well and beautifully what needs to be done for fitting worship.

A fuller answer to this difficulty, why form seems a little neglected in this current attention to liturgical purpose, may be proposed. First, there is the fear of error, for example, that the invention of a new iconography might not be consonant with biblical or theological development or that the spirit of this age of Christian faith might not be caught in greater embellishment or more elaborate decor. Next, there is a proportion to be recovered and past errors to be redressed. Too often the form has betrayed the function: the magnificent cathedral of Toledo, to mention a form that is good and great, is totally unsuited for Catholic worship by any considerable number of people; and we have enough (sometimes beautiful) choir galleries that have obscured and frustrated the choir's function, too many (perhaps elegant) "altar rails" that have divided priest and people without providing a table for the eucharistic meal.

Above all, we must insist that a church's purpose does have priority and that its function is to house the People of God at worship. If the liturgical brief is well drawn—as it surely is in the present volume by Father Seasoltz—no least disservice will be done to beauty of form.

There are, of course, adequate summaries of rubric and decree already in existence. Indeed it may be said that we have quite enough specific ecclesiastical law on sacred architecture. What is needed is principle and interpretation, the sense and meaning behind (and above) the directives. What is needed is exposition of the doctrine and norm combined with some vision of the future. Again, such is the present work of Father Seasoltz, awake to every development of our time, breathing the vitality of the Church's renewal.

Thus it becomes a pleasure to recommend this book, in the first place, to architects and designers and builders, to artists and artisans and church decorators; many of them are already deeply committed to a revival of church building in the light of the church's primary function and purpose. Similarly, this book has an obvious audience in the individual pastors and priests and in the members of building committees and commissions, who desperately need such a study if they are to provide theological, liturgical, and canonical guidance for the artist and the professional. Less obviously, because in this country at least lay men and lay women are denied a role in the building of churches—other than that of providing the funds—Father Seasoltz has written a book which can be recommended to all parishioners who appreciate their true interest in the building of the parish church and who seek to understand its function in common worship. With this recommendation goes the hope that a better understanding of the church structure may increase the understanding of the Church as the Body of Christ, as the People of God, so that all the people may have a greater role in the act of worship and indeed in the building of the sacred house of that worship.

FREDERICK R. MCMANUS

Foreword

The progress which has recently been made in promoting a better understanding of the liturgy and the increased active participation of the layman in the Church's worship have prompted theologians and architects to give serious consideration to the design and appointment of church edifices. If we are to have churches which fulfill the demands of a pastoral liturgy, there must be intelligent collaboration between patrons and architects, but such collaboration will be effective only if both patrons and architects are well informed about the nature of the Christian community and its worship. A church edifice derives its meaning from the Christian assembly and the functions which the people fulfill.

Contemporary liturgical research indicates quite clearly that many concepts of church design, once thought to be valid, are no longer applicable to present needs. From time to time ecclesiastical legislation has been enacted to facilitate the erection of church buildings worthy of the functions which take place within, but in general the laws are only skeletal. Unfortunately, the extant legislation has all too often been interpreted as in a vacuum, with little or no reference to the theology of worship. This legislation, as well as the general rubrics which direct the execution of Christian worship, constitutes a part of the Church's canon law and as such must be interpreted by the principles taken from Roman law. To interpret the legislation in the light of Anglo-Saxon law is to violate the nature of the directives. One must keep in mind, then, that Roman rubrics do not always mean precisely what they seem to say to the Anglo-Saxon mind, but they must always be interpreted in the light of that sound theology of Christian worship which should form the basis for the formulation of all rubrics.

The present work is an attempt to examine and interpret the more important current canonical legislation with regard to church building and sacred art. The discussion throughout is based on a historical, theological, and pastoral concept of a church as a house of God and His people. The work is not intended to be an exhaustive study but is designed to give priests and religious, architects and artists, and those laymen who are patrons of the arts, a fundamental understanding of the liturgical requirements of ecclesiastical architecture and sacred art.

R. KEVIN SEASOLTZ

PART I

SACRED ART

1

The Concept of Sacred Art in *De Arte Sacra*

An attempt to define the concept of sacred art is at first disconcerting, for in the abundant literature on the subject one finds the terms "sacred art," "religious art," "liturgical art," and "Christian art" used interchangeably. Although the various authors who have attempted to clarify the distinction in these terms are not in agreement,[1] it seems that at least the concept of sacred art is quite clear in the Church's legislation on the subject.[2] For example, in the Instruction *De Arte Sacra*, issued by the Sacred Congregation of the Holy Office on June 30, 1952, sacred art is de-

[1] Cf. Pie-Raymond Régamey, *Art Sacré au XX Siècle?* (2nd ed.; Paris: Editions du Cerf, 1952), English adaptation, *Religious Art in the Twentieth Century* (New York: Herder and Herder, 1963); Justus George Lawler, "The Idea of a Christian Art," *Thought*, XXIV (1949), 309–20; Sister Mary of the Compassion, "Sacred Art and Stylism," *Journal of Arts and Letters*, II (1950), 69–70; J. A. Jungmann, "Liturgy and Church Art," *Pastoral Liturgy* (New York: Herder and Herder, 1962), pp. 357–368.

[2] Cf. Pius XII, Encyclical Letter *Mediator Dei*, Nov. 20, 1947: *Acta Apostolicae Sedis, Commentarium Officiale* (Romae, 1909–), XXXIX (1947), 521–95 (hereafter referred to as *AAS*); Holy Office, instruction *De Arte Sacra*, June 30, 1952: *AAS*, XXXXIV (1952), 542–46.

fined in terms of its function: "It is the function of sacred art, by reason of its very definition, to enhance the beauty of the house of God and to foster the faith and piety of those who gather in the church to assist at the divine services and to implore heavenly favors."[3]

Sacred art is always religious art because its theme is religious. Both materially and formally, it is subordinate to a specifically religious end. If the subordination is only material, the work will not be truly religious. For example, one may deal with a religious subject by painting a Madonna in a manner that has nothing religious about it. There are many painted and sculptured Madonnas which are fine works of art, but their artistic quality bears much more on the merely human theme of motherhood than on the religious theme of divine maternity. Religious art requires that both the material subject and the formal content of the work be religious.[4] Such work will be specifically Christian when it is guided by the deposit of revelation and the truths of theological wisdom.[5]

Religious art is not necessarily liturgical art. Liturgical art requires not only that the work have a religious theme but also that it take its inspiration from the liturgy, so that it might serve the Church in its divine worship.[6]

The liturgy, which centers about the Mass and the sacraments, may be defined as the worship which the Mystical Christ offers to the heavenly Father. It is characteristic of

[3] *Ibid.*, 542.

[4] Cyprian Vagaggini, *Theological Dimensions of the Liturgy*, trans. Leonard J. Doyle (Collegeville, Minnesota: The Liturgical Press, 1959), p. 33.

[5] Lawler, *art. cit.*, p. 309.

[6] Kilian McDonnell, "Liturgy and Sacred Art," *Sponsa Regis*, XXXI (1960), 159.

the liturgy "to be an action, a communitarian action of an assembly in which the members all have a role to play, . . . an action whose whole meaning is to have the mystery of Christ relived by those who take part in it."[7]

The liturgy is essentially symbolic, since the Mass and the sacraments, which are its core, are essentially symbolic.[8] The function of a symbol or sign is to point to something else. It does not contain in itself its essential meaning, but derives its meaning from that to which it points.

The Mass and the sacraments have this in common with other signs, that they take their meaning from that to which they point. But they differ from other symbols in that they also contain that which they signify. The Eucharist, for example, points to a triple reality. It points to a reality in the past: Christ's death; it points to a present reality: the giving of Christ-life, grace; and it points to a future reality: the life of the glorified Christ in which men will share after His second coming. As a sacred sign, the Eucharist points to all these realities, but since the Eucharist is an effective sign, doing what it signifies, it also renders these realities present.[9]

The symbolic world of the liturgy is a supra-temporal world, in which both the past and the future are rendered present. The liturgy contains historical realities, but it transcends the space-time limitations of such realities.[10]

The laws of symbolism which govern the liturgy are also

[7] Vagaggini, *op. cit.*, p. 35.
[8] Cf. Romano Guardini, "The Symbolism of the Liturgy," *The Church and the Catholic and the Spirit of the Liturgy*, trans. Ada Lane (London: Sheed and Ward, 1935), pp. 162–70.
[9] McDonnell, *loc. cit.*, pp. 158–59.
[10] *Ibid.*, p. 159.

the laws which govern liturgical art. Like the sacraments, liturgical art is a sign which points to something beyond itself and from this reality it takes its meaning. It points to the mystery of Christ.[11]

Understood in this sense, liturgical art is identical with sacred art as it is described in the Instruction *De Arte Sacra.* It is art dedicated, proximately or remotely, to divine worship. From the outset it should be clear that, as a craft, sacred art does not differ in any way from profane art, but it differs essentially from profane art in its content, in the dignity with which this content must be expressed, and in its end which is the service of the liturgy. In short, sacred art includes all the arts when they put themselves at the service of the Church and its divine worship.[12]

In the Code of Canon Law, both canons 1164, § 1, and 1296, § 3, speak of the "laws of sacred art." Before an attempt is made to clarify what is meant by such laws, it should be noted that sacred art is art, and as such is subject to the rules of art in general. These norms are not superimposed by some external authority, but rather they are deduced from the very nature of art. So it is with sacred art. There are norms which are deduced from its very nature. But there are also ecclesiastical laws on the subject of sacred art which have been expressly formulated by the Church through the centuries. Under the direction of the late Cardinal Celso Costantini, the ecclesiastical legislation on art was collected in a small corpus and published in a special

[11] Cf. Mark Barron, "The Sacramental Character of Christian Art," *Liturgical Arts,* XXVII (1959), 32–34.

[12] J. B. O'Connell, *Church Building and Furnishing* (Notre Dame, Indiana: University of Notre Dame Press, 1955), p. 31.

issue of *Fede e Arte*, the official organ of the Central Commission for Sacred art in Rome.[13] In this collection, one finds an orderly arrangement of the pertinent acts of the popes from St. Gregory the Great (590–604) to Pius XII (1939–1958), the decrees of the councils, the prescriptions of the Code of Canon Law, and the acts of the various Roman Congregations and Commissions. Since much of the legislation contained in the collection is concerned with special episodes in the history of the Church, it is of greater interest and value to the historian than to one attempting an exposition of the Church's present legislation on sacred art. Consequently, a detailed analysis of these documents in a historical fashion is not necessary here. Since much of the former ecclesiastical legislation on sacred art is incorporated in the present Code of Canon Law, the discussion here will be confined to the appropriate canons in the Code and the post-Code legislation which is pertinent.

THE HOLY OFFICE INSTRUCTION, *DE ARTE SACRA*

Undoubtedly the most important piece of legislation on sacred art promulgated in recent years is the Instruction issued by the Supreme Sacred Congregation of the Holy Office on June 30, 1952.[14] Since the Instruction was meant to be a summary of the ecclesiastical legislation on sacred art which was in force at the time of its publication, it will serve as a point of reference for the discussion here.

As has been noted above, the opening paragraph of the

[13] *Fede e Arte*, V, Nos. 10–11 (October–November, 1957).
[14] *Loc. cit.*

Instruction defines sacred art in terms of its function: "It is the function of sacred art, by reason of its very definition, to enhance the beauty of the house of God and to foster the faith and piety of those who gather in the church to assist at the divine services and to implore heavenly favors."[15] The Instruction then repeats the same idea in a negative manner by recalling St. Pius X's remarks on sacred art from his *Motu Proprio* on liturgical music, *Tra le Sollecitudini:* "Nothing therefore should have place in the church which disturbs or even merely diminishes the piety and devotion of the faithful, nothing which might reasonably be considered in bad taste or be the cause of scandal, nothing above all which might be unworthy of the house of prayer and the majesty of God."[16]

This essentially pastoral attitude of the Church toward sacred art is verified throughout the centuries. For example, the Instruction *De Arte Sacra* cites the action of the Second Council of Nicaea (787) in condemning the Iconoclasts and confirming the cult of sacred images.[17] It also mentions Session XXV of the Council of Trent (1545–1563), which issued laws on Christian iconography, as well as the norms of Pope Urban VIII (1623–1644) providing for the execution of the decrees of the Council of Trent concerning sacred images. The Council of Trent had concluded its exhortation to the bishops with these words: "Let bishops exercise

[15] *Ibid.*, p. 542.

[16] *Acta Sanctae Sedis*, XXXVI (1903–1904), 329 (hereafter cited as *ASS*).

[17] Joannes Dominicus Mansi, *Sacrorum Canonum Nova et Amplissima Collectio* (Paris, 1901–27), XIII, 378, 379, 414, 415 (hereafter cited as Mansi); *Codicis Iuris Canonici Fontes*, cura Emi Petri Card. Gasparri editi (Romae, postea Civitate Vaticana: Typis Polyglottis Vaticanis, 1923–39), I, 2–3.

much diligence and care concerning these matters, that nothing disordered may meet the eye, nothing distorted and confused in execution, nothing unbefitting and unbecoming, since sanctity belongs to the house of God."[18] Pope Urban VIII repeated the same pastoral ideas expressed by the Council of Trent: "Let those objects which are exposed to the gaze of the faithful be neither disordered nor unusual in appearance, and let them engender devotion and piety."[19]

The Instruction *De Arte Sacra* then proceeds to list the canons of the present Code of Canon Law which gather all the ecclesiastical legislation on sacred art under summary headings:

Canon 485 mentions the reverence that is due to the church as the house of God.

Canon 1161 defines the church as a sacred building dedicated to divine cult. As a public edifice, it should be available to all the faithful for the public exercise of divine worship.

Canon 1162 asserts that no church may be constructed without the permission of the local ordinary.

Canon 1164 declares that the area above and below the church may not be used for profane purposes. It also legislates that in the building of a church the laws of sacred art and the forms received from Christian tradition are to be observed.

Canon 1178 emphasizes that churches must be kept clean.

[18] Conc. Trident., sess. XXV, *de invocatione, veneratione et reliquiis sanctorum, et sacris imaginibus.*

[19] *Bullarum Diplomatum et Privilegiorum Sanctorum Romanorum Pontificum Taurinensis Editio* (Augustae Taurinorum, 1857–1872), XV, 171 (hereafter cited as BR(T)).

Canon 1261 forbids the introduction of superstitious practices into the worship of the Church.

Canon 1286 and canon 1269 are concerned with the reservation of the Blessed Sacrament.

Canon 1279 forbids unusual pictorial images to be exposed for veneration in church without the permission of the ordinary.

Canon 1280 requires the written permission of the bishop for the restoration of all art treasures.

Canon 1385 requires ecclesiastical approbation for the printing of devotional pictures.

Canon 1399 forbids the printing of devotional pictures which are foreign to the mind of the Church and its decrees.

The Instruction makes explicit mention of the prescriptions of two canons: canon 1261, which obliges ordinaries to be vigilant lest anything foreign to the faith or not in harmony with ecclesiastical tradition be introduced into divine worship; and also canon 1399, n. 12, which prohibits the production of all images which are foreign to the mind and the decrees of the Church. Lest there be any doubt, however, that contemporary art has a legitimate place in the liturgy, the Instruction recalls first of all the words of Pius XI on the occasion of the inauguration of the new Vatican Gallery of Paintings: "Open wide the portals and tender sincere welcome to every good and progressive development of the approved and venerable traditions, which in so many centuries of Christian life, in such diversity of circumstances and of social and ethnic conditions, have given stupendous proof of their inexhaustible capacity of inspiring new and beautiful forms, as often as they were investigated, or studied and cultivated under the twofold light of genius and faith."[20]

The Instruction then adverts to the words of Pius XII in *Mediator Dei* on the place of contemporary art in the liturgy:

It is eminently fitting that the art of our times have a free opportunity to serve the sacred edifices and sacred rites with due reverence and with due honor, so that it too may add its voice to the magnificent hymn of glory which men of high talent have sung throughout the past centuries of the Catholic faith. Nevertheless, in consciousness of Our office, we cannot but deplore and reprove those images and forms recently introduced by some, which seem to be deformations and debasements of sane art, and which at times are even open contradiction to Christian grace, modesty, and piety, and miserably offend true religious sentiment; these indeed are to be totally excluded and expelled from our churches as "in general whatever is out of harmony with the holiness of the place." (Canon 1178)[21]

After reasserting the foregoing points, the Instruction *De Arte Sacra* proceeds to enumerate a number of directives of its own, first concerning architecture and then concerning descriptive art. Rather than analyze each of these directives separately, it will suffice to give a general treatment of the present controversy over sacred art, at the same time pointing out the appropriate legislation as occasion arises.

Historical Background of the Present Controversy

With the passing of the baroque style of religious art in the last century, there was no genuine style of sacred art to

[20] AAS, XXIV (1932), 356; AAS, XXXXIV (1952), 543.
[21] AAS, XXXIX (1947), 590–91; AAS, XXXXIV (1952), 544.

take its place, as is clear from the history of art.[22] In the nineteenth century, sacred art attempted to imitate past styles of art, and so to give birth to a devoted academicism which naturally rendered a vital art difficult, if not impossible. Although the nineteenth century witnessed a serious deterioration in sacred art, the same period also saw the development of a new style of profane art. Man, his person, his works, especially the great moments of his life—these were the subjects for the artists to dwell upon. The profane artists, however, were frequently trained in schools of modern materialism; consequently, they were often opposed to the truths of revelation. Likewise, those Christians who were taken up with devout academicism, with the production of lifeless copies of artifacts from past ages, were opposed to the efforts of their contemporary profane artists. For the first time in the history of Christianity, then, there was a rupture between religion and art: what was called "sacred" art was really not art, and was rejected by true artists; what was called "profane" art was in general true art and often religious art, but it was not admitted to the service of the liturgy.[23]

In the nineteenth century, sacred art lost contact with contemporary art. This rupture is the principal reason why the twentieth century is heir to so many problems in the sphere of sacred art.[24]

The present century is without doubt striving seriously to restore and create sacred art worthy of the name. This attempt, however, has been rejected and suspected by many

[22] Hermanus A. Schmidt, *Introductio in Liturgiam Occidentalem* (Roma: Herder, 1960), p. 686.
[23] *Ibid.*
[24] *Ibid.*

within the Church, with the result that much misunderstanding has arisen. One of the most difficult problems is the lack of communication between profane art and sacred art. For example, many modern artists, even Catholics, have been trained in principles of esthetics which alienate them from the Christian religion. Cubism and surrealism seem to be based on philosophies which are more or less opposed to Christianity. Artists trained in these schools naturally have difficulty in expressing valid religious themes. Likewise, most Christians, brought up in the tradition of academicism, are not equipped to judge what is good sacred art. To many, approved sacred art means imitations of old styles; nothing new is admitted. Consequently, in many areas, the only sacred art which is recognized is that which is imbued with stylistic principles of former periods. Artistic creations, then, are mere copies of what has been made before. Although the taste of the common people is frequently corrupt, it is nevertheless often said to be the only valid judge of what is reputable.[25]

It is obvious, then, that there is sharp controversy in the field of sacred art. The twentieth century, nevertheless, has witnessed at least the birth of a new and truly sacred art, but like every new child, it must be nourished, trained, encouraged, and developed.

It seems that the birth of this new sacred art goes back to France and the dedication of three French churches in the last decade: the church at Assy en Haute-Savoie, consecrated on August 4, 1950; the Dominican oratory at Vence de la Côte d'Azur, consecrated on June 25, 1951; and the church at Audincourt, consecrated on September 16, 1951.

[25] *Ibid.*, p. 687.

These churches are the works of artists who are among the most celebrated designers of this age. They are without doubt bold experiments, but no one can truthfully deny their simple beauty. Following their dedication, sharp controversy arose throughout Europe. In the abundant literature on these churches, writers attempted to give some solution to such difficult questions as the relation between art and liturgy, sacred art and tradition, and sacred art and the inspiration of the artist. In view of the controversy which found its way into both learned journals and the daily newspapers, the intervention of ecclesiastical authority was deemed necessary. On April 28, 1952, the French hierarchy issued its norms on sacred art. Somewhat later, the Sacred Congregation of the Holy Office promulgated its Instruction *De Arte Sacra*.[26]

Type of Sacred Art Forbidden by the Church

Since the Holy Office phrased its Instruction *De Arte Sacra* in general terms and refrained from exercising judgment upon specific works of art, this directive has been the subject of abundant commentary and has also given rise to numerous misunderstandings and generalizations. Although the Instruction has been accused of being hostile to contemporary art in general, there is no question of this either in the text itself or in the commentaries which were written by Cardinal Celso Costantini in *L'Osservatore Romano*.[27]

[26] *Ibid.*, p. 688.

[27] Celso Costantini, *L'Osservatore Romano*: "Competenza della Santa Sede," July 25, 1952; "Modernità e Tradizione," July 27, 1952; "Dell'Architettura Sacra," July 30, 1952; "Epurazione Artistica delle Chiese," August 1, 1952; "Circa l'Arte Figurative," August 3, 1952; and "Per la Cultura Artistica del Clero," August 13, 1952.

Unfortunately, much of the Instruction is expressed in negative terms, and, in order to arrive at some positive conclusions, one must analyze the key concepts individually. In the pages which follow, the writer will attempt to clarify the various categories which are forbidden by the instruction: (1) art which disturbs the devotion of the faithful; (2) art which expresses distorted forms or confused conceptions; (3) art which is unusual; (4) art which is not in accord with the approved usage of the Church, and (5) art which is corrupt, errant, or debased.

First of all, the Instruction frowns upon art which disturbs or diminishes the devotion and piety of the faithful.[28] This is quite understandable, since "the only purpose of sacred art is to give the faithful the greatest aid in turning their minds piously to God through the works it directs to their eyes and ears."[29] However, one must be careful in deciding what really disturbs piety and devotion. A person may be surprised when he is confronted with a work of art having strong vigorous lines, but this does not necessarily mean that his spiritual life will be upset.

> Modern pictures and statues, whose style is more adapted to the material in use at the present day, are not to be condemned out of hand. On condition that these modern arts steer a middle course between an excessive realism on the one hand and an exaggerated symbolism on the other, and take into account more the needs of the Christian community than the personal taste and judgment of the artist, they should be allowed full scope if with due reverence and honor they put themselves at the service of our churches and sacred rites.[30]

[28] *AAS*, XXXXIV (1952), 544.

[29] Pius XII, Encyclical Letter on Sacred Music, Dec. 25, 1955, ad II: *AAS*, XXXXVIII (1956), II.

[30] *Mediator Dei*, Nov. 20, 1947: *AAS*, XXXIX (1947), 590.

If sacred art is to foster the devotion and piety of the faithful and to serve for their instruction, it must be first of all intelligible. One must bear in mind, however, that sacred art is wholly intelligible only to those who are fully initiated into the truths of the Faith.[31] For example, the tympanum at Vézelay can be admired by a tourist for its artistic qualities, but it will yield its full meaning only to the Christian who is living the paschal mystery of which it is so powerful a symbol.[32] Since the majority of the faithful have never been educated in any truly artistic culture, one must not be too hasty to assume that their piety is disturbed by something new. Rather than reject good sacred art because it is new or modern, one should strive to educate the faithful, so that they will understand and appreciate art that truly expresses the richness and the beauty of Christian revelation. "It would seem that there must be clear evidence that a given work of art, and not other causes, is directly disturbing or lessening the devotion of numbers of souls before it becomes necessary to remove it from a church."[33]

It is important to keep in mind that what is accepted as devotional in one part of the world might well be repelling in another, because the style of art varies considerably from country to country and from culture to culture. Such variation certainly does not merit condemnation. This has been emphasized in two letters of the late Cardinal

[31] Jacques Maritain, *Art and Scholasticism* (New York: Charles Scribner's Sons, 1930), p. 111.

[32] Peter Hammond, *Liturgy and Architecture* (London: Barrie and Rockliff, 1960), pp. 159–160.

[33] Anthony Lauck, "Modern Art, Sacred Art: Rome Speaks," *Creative Art*, ed. Sister Esther Newport (Washington, D.C.: The Catholic University of America Press, 1955), p. 13.

Peter Fumasoni-Biondi, written when he was the cardinal prefect of the Sacred Congregation for the Propagation of the Faith. In a communication on June 1, 1935, to Archbishop Paolo Marella, Apostolic Delegate in Japan, after Pope Pius XI had received a picture done in Japanese style, the Cardinal noted: "An art which is at once thoroughly Catholic and distinctively national will be a concrete and effective proof that the Church is not identified with or bound to any particular form of culture, but that it welcomes whatever it finds that is good and beautiful in all peoples."[34]

Following an exhibition of Congolese art in Leopoldville, the same cardinal wrote on December 14, 1936, to Archbishop G. B. Dellepiane, the Apostolic Delegate in the Belgian Congo, as follows: "The Catholic Church is neither Belgian, nor French, nor English, nor American, but Catholic. It is Belgian in Belgium, French in France, English in England. In the Congo, it must be Congolese. In the construction of sacred edifices and in the making of articles of devotion, it must carefully take into account the lines, colors, and other elements of Congolese art."[35] African art is certainly among the most abstract and least imitative arts in the world, and yet in its proper place it functions well as sacred art.[36]

Moving along to the second classification of art forbidden by the Instruction *De Arte Sacra*, one finds the rejection of

[34] *Sylloge praecipuorum documentorum recentium Summorum Pontificum et S. Congregationis de Propaganda Fide necnon aliarum SS. Congregationum Romanorum ad usum missionariorum* (Civitate Vaticana: Typis Polyglottis Vaticanis, 1939), No. 193.
[35] *Ibid.*, No. 203 bis.
[36] Lauck, *loc. cit.*, p. 19.

"distortion" or "confused conceptions" in sacred art.[37] To distort something means to pervert its true meaning or to twist it out of its normal shape. One must not be too hasty in condemning works of art on the ground that they are distorted. On April 8, 1952, several months before the promulgation of the Instruction *De Arte Sacra*, Pope Pius XII in an address to a group of Italian artists referred specifically to four great works of art: the mosaics of Rome and Ravenna, the bronze and stone façade of the cathedral of Orvieto, the windows of the cathedral at Chartres, and the bronze doors of Ghiberti in Florence.[38] Since the Pontiff called these works "artistic masterpieces" and "Bibles of the people," it seems safe to assume that they are acceptable as sacred art. Yet if one examines these works carefully, he will find a certain degree of distortion.

For example, above the main door of the cathedral at Orvieto, there are three bronze angels which have an uncommon unction and grace about them, but their beauty is enhanced by the elongation of their necks. Certainly this is distortion. Likewise, in the mosaics at Rome and Ravenna, the artists have frequently taken liberties with color and color contrasts which distort the natural blending of the colors. But this distortion has brought out new richness in color harmony. Distortion is perhaps most evident in the stained-glass windows of the cathedral at Chartres, where proportion is frequently sacrificed to attain balance. In view

[37] *AAS*, XXXXIV (1952), 544.

[38] Pius XII, Discourse of April 8, 1952, to the artists of the VI Quadriennale d'Arte in Rome, *Discorsi e Radiomessaggi di Sua Santità Pio XII*, XIV (Civitate Vaticana: Typis Polyglottis Vaticanis, 1952), 50.

of the great quality of these works of sacred art, it is obvious that distortion is not always wrong, but often it is a valid means of attaining design.[39] The degree to which an artist may distort his subject is dependent on a number of factors: for example, the contribution distortion makes to the strength and quality of the work, the attractiveness attained, and the power of the work to edify the faithful. In short, each case must be judged separately. Distortion in itself is not always wrong, but is often a licit means of achieving artistic effect.

The third type of sacred art to which the Holy Office objects is that which is "unusual."[40] Canon 1279 forbids that unusual images be placed in churches unless they have been approved by the ordinary of the place. Some might conceive of this prohibition as applicable to all images executed in a modern style, but this is surely out of the question. It has already been shown that art is primarily a matter of iconography. Certainly every original work of art is unusual in so far as it is different from every other work in its style and treatment. Pope Urban VIII condemned unusual art;[41] yet during his pontificate something quite unusual was added to St. Peter's Basilica in Rome, namely, Lorenzo Bernini's canopy over the papal altar. It was executed in a baroque style quite unusual for the time.[42] The word "unusual" both in Pope Urban's directive and in the Instruction *De Arte Sacra* obviously refers to what is novel in formal content, not to what is contemporary in the matter of style.

The next category of sacred art which is rejected by the

[39] Lauck, *loc. cit.*, pp. 14–15.
[40] *AAS*, XXXXIV (1952), 545.
[41] *BR*(*T*), XV, 172.
[42] Lauck, *loc. cit.*, pp. 15–16.

Instruction from the Holy Office is that which is "not in accord with the approved usage of the Church.[43] The type of art which is included here is quite clear from the action of the Holy Office on several occasions. On April 8, 1916, representations of the Blessed Virgin clothed in priestly vestments were specifically condemned.[44] Likewise, representations of the Holy Spirit in human form were rejected by a response of the Holy Office on March 16, 1928.[45]

Included in the final category of sacred art forbidden by the Instruction *De Arte Sacra* are those works of art which are "corrupt," "errant," "deformed," or "debased." Although no conscientious artist would intentionally create a work which would fall within this category, nevertheless certain works of art must be classed here because they deviate from the truth. It would seem that surrealistic art must be included here, for it carries with it a look of deterioration, illusion, and decay, which indicates a perverted attitude toward life on the part of the artist.[46] Such art implicitly distorts the Christian doctrine of creation and redemption.

A different kind of distortion is found in the sentimental commercial art which still clutters so many churches.[47] It seems, for example, that an image of a completely humanized Christ who is no longer the God-man but only the man worthy of human approval is just as much a denial of the divinity of Christ as the heresy of Arius. Such works are actually an enemy of the faith. They are certainly to be

[43] AAS, XXXXIV (1952), 545.
[44] AAS, VIII (1916), 146.
[45] AAS, XX (1928), 103.
[46] Lauck, *loc. cit.*, p. 17.
[47] Cf. Maritain, *op. cit.*, pp. 112–13.

condemned along with those works which are severely frowned upon by the Holy Office because they are "second-rate" and "stereotyped." "Let them [the ordinaries] severely forbid second-rate and stereotyped statues and images to be multiplied and improperly and absurdly exposed to the veneration of the faithful on the altars themselves or on the neighboring walls or chapels."[48] Such art makes the faith a laughing-stock for unbelievers, sets obstacles in the way of those who are seeking the faith, and not only warps the artistic taste of the faithful but also militates against any true appreciation of the greatness and immensity of the realities of the faith. In short, such art debases and degrades the faith. In this regard, the decree of the Holy Office prohibiting novel forms of worship and devotion should be cited:

Long ago the Sacred Council of Trent (Sess. XXV, *De invocat., venerat., et reliquiis Sanctorum et sacris imaginibus*), after declaring that the worship of the saints and the use of their images to obtain favors from God is legitimate, solemnly warned the Bishops that, if they found that any abuses were creeping in or had crept into these holy and salutary practices, they must take great care to eradicate them, so that no images that are theologically false and might be an occasion of dangerous error to the unlearned be set up; that all superstition in the invocation of saints and in the use of sacred images be removed; . . . and finally that nothing inordinate, nothing distorted or hasty, nothing profane, nothing unworthy be observed . . .

Unfortunately, however, so many grave warnings and injunctions of the Supreme ecclesiastical Authority have thus far failed to obtain full obedience. In fact, as everyone knows, these new forms of worship and devotion, often enough ridiculous, usually useless imitations or corruptions of similar ones which are already legitimately established, are in many places, especially in

[48] *AAS*, XXXXIV (1952), 545.

these recent days, being daily multiplied and propagated among the faithful, giving occasion to great astonishment and to bitter aspersion on the part of non-Catholics.

Again and again, therefore, this Sacred Congregation of the Holy Office, which is charged with the guardianship of the purity and integrity of faith and morals, by express mandate of His Holiness, by Divine Providence Pope, Pius XI, earnestly appeals to the zeal and pastoral solicitude of the Bishops who have the care of souls throughout the Catholic world, and charges them in conscience to urge at last the strictest observance of the aforesaid admonitions and injunctions, by firmly abolishing abuses which have already arisen, and taking the most diligent precautions lest any new ones come into vogue.[49]

Reference has already been made to the words of Pius XII in *Mediator Dei* to the effect that modern art should "steer a middle course between an excessive realism on the one hand and an exaggerated symbolism on the other."[50] It seems, then, that a semi-abstract art is the ideal medium for sacred art. Symbolism grapples with ideas, it is intellectual. If one wishes to avoid shallowness in art, a certain degree of symbolism and abstraction is necessary, for the more charged with symbolism a work of art is, the richer, the more profound will be its meaning.[51] Religious art began with the representation of God by means of abstract symbols which were devoid of any sentimental appeal. Purely abstract symbols gave way to anthropomorphic forms which were still symbols rather than figurations, but, as the centuries went on, these anthropomorphic forms de-

[49] S.C.S. Off., decree on new forms of worship or devotion not to be introduced, May 26, 1937—*AAS*, XXIX (1937), 304.

[50] *AAS*, XXXIX (1947), 590.

[51] J. P. Kenny, "Reflections on Contemporary Religious Art," *America* (February 25, 1961), pp. 699–700.

preciated into sentimental, humanized representations of the divine. It was undoubtedly for this reason that St. Thomas Aquinas recommended the use of lower rather than higher forms of existence as symbols of the divinity, "especially for those who can think of nothing nobler than bodies."[52]

If what claims to be sacred art makes no demands upon the human intelligence, it has distorted the truth of Catholicism by emptying it of its content. A purely representational art cannot fully convey the mysteries of faith. As an example, one may cite Guido Reni's "Crucifixion." Although it is often acclaimed a Renaissance masterpiece, from the point of view of sacred art it is little more than the figure of a handsome athlete hanging on a cross. The work communicates very little of the mystery of God-made-man dying for the salvation of the world. The function of sacred art is not to convey what a person or thing looks like, but rather its function is to serve as a symbol of the faith.[53]

The place of purely abstract art in sacred places is more difficult to justify because it is often unintelligible to the faithful and is in grave danger of succumbing to total subjectivism. The world of Christianity is objective; it is not a vague pantheism, but rather pivots about real historical people and events. Nevertheless, some wholly non-figurative art may be quite satisfactory in sacred places. For example, such art may well evoke a mood which stimulates prayer and devotion. This effect has been brilliantly achieved in stained glass in many of the modern churches in Switzer-

[52] *Summa Theologica*, i. 1. 9.
[53] Kenny, *loc. cit.*, p. 700.

land, Germany, and France.[54] It should be obvious, then, that in this whole sphere of sacred art one must be careful not to generalize; the prudent critic will judge each work of art on its own merits.

CONSTRUCTIVE EFFORTS TO PROMOTE GOOD SACRED ART

In order that genuine sacred art may be put at the service of the Church and its liturgy, work of a constructive nature is essential. To encourage the development of such work, the Holy Office concluded its instruction with a brief treatment of the qualities of those who are to be appointed to the Diocesan Commission for Sacred Art, the artists who are to execute sacred art, and the patrons who promote sacred art.

Diocesan Commission for Sacred Art

The first mention of a Diocesan Commission for Sacred Art is found in the document instituting the Central Commission for Sacred Art in Rome. It was issued by the Secretariate of State on September 1, 1924.[55] The text urged ordinaries to establish diocesan or regional commissions for the promotion of sacred art. In 1947, Pius XII in his encyclical *Mediator Dei* spoke of commissions for sacred art as already existing in the various dioceses.[56] He also men-

[54] As examples, one might cite the church of St. Kilian in Schweinfurt, St. Maria Königin in Cologne, St. Kolumbakapelle in Cologne, the Dominican convent chapel at Vence, the church of the Sacred Heart at Audincourt, and the work of Paul Stöckli of Stans in various Swiss churches.

[55] Cf. text published in *Il Monitore Ecclesiastico*, Series 4, VI (1924), 332–34.

[56] *AAS*, XXXIX (1947), 562.

tioned them in his encyclical *Musicae Sacrae Disciplina*, and intimated that such a commission should be found in every well-organized diocese.[57] Even more recently, the 'Instruction on Sacred Music and the Sacred Liturgy" issued by the Congregation of Rites on September 3, 1958, declared that "there should be a commission for sacred art established in every diocese."[58]

The document issued by the Secretariate of State in 1924 enumerated four tasks of the commission for sacred art. The members should compile an inventory of the art treasures in the diocese. They should aid in the organization and administration of diocesan museums. They are to pass judgment on the designs for new buildings and to examine plans for restoration, expansion, and decoration of church property. Finally they are to educate the faithful in matters of artistic taste and culture by writing articles and by giving lectures on sacred art.

Appointed by the local ordinary, the members of this commission may be either laymen or clerics. Since they function merely as administrative aids to the bishop, they serve only as consultants or advisors and may be removed at the will of the bishop.[59] What is most important is that the members themselves should have an intelligent understanding and appreciation of sacred art and also a thorough knowledge of the Church's laws on sacred buildings and furnishings.

In order that the local ordinaries may with greater assurance seek and receive from the diocesan commission for sacred art advice which is in perfect harmony with the prescriptions of the Apos-

[57] AAS, XXXXVIII (1956), 24.
[58] AAS, L (1958), 663.
[59] James A. O'Donohoe, "Administrative Aids to the Bishop," *The Jurist*, XX (January, 1960), 25–27.

tolic See and the end of sacred art itself, they should see to it themselves that those appointed to the commission not only are experts in art but also firmly adhere to the Christian faith. They should have been brought up in piety and should gladly follow the precise principles defined by ecclesiastical authority.[60]

Artists and Sacred Art

It is obvious that ecclesiastical legislation of itself cannot produce sacred art. No art is possible without artistic ability, which can only be a gift from God.[61] However, artistic talent alone does not suffice for the execution of sacred art, because sacred art is a very special art requiring not only artistic genius but also religious inspiration and moral discipline.[62] The Instruction *De Arte Sacra* did not expressly exclude atheistic artists from the execution of sacred art; it merely provided that: "Works of painting, sculpture, and architecture should be entrusted for their execution only to men who are outstanding for their technique, and who are capable of expressing sincere faith and piety, which is the purpose of any sacred art."[63] The French hierarchy expressed the same idea in the directive on sacred art promulgated in April, 1952, when they declared that artists who work for the Church "should know how to steep themselves in the Christian spirit; otherwise they are unfitted for their task."[64]

[60] *AAS*, XXXXIV (1952), 545.

[61] Johannes Wagner, "Liturgical Art and the Care of Souls," *The Assisi Papers* (Collegeville, Minnesota: Liturgical Press, 1957), p. 72.

[62] Celso and Giovanni Costantini, *Fede e Arte*, I (Turin: Società Editrice Internazionale, 1946), p. 23.

[63] *AAS*, XXXXIV (1952), 545.

[64] "Directive of the French Hierarchy on Sacred Art," April 28, 1952, No. 3. Cf. the text of the directive in *Nouvelle Revue Théologique*, LXXIV (1952), 958–59.

Since the dedication of the church at Assy and the chapel at Vence, the question has been asked whether an artist with no faith can build and decorate churches and treat Christian themes validly.[65] Certainly the question is very complex and cannot be answered simply, for there are arguments both for and against religious art executed by artists who have no faith. In an attempt to offer a solution to the problem, the arguments on both sides of the question will be weighed briefly.

Those who would reject religious art executed by atheists claim that a wholly religious work requires an artist who is himself a religious person. They assert that the man who would reach God must believe, for faith is the principle of every religious act. They maintain that this is especially true if a man's art is to bring others closer to God, as is the case with sacred art. They further insist that if the external honor which works of sacred art render God as "the noble handmaids of the liturgy"[66] is to be in harmony with the liturgy and not a discordant lie, it must represent that interior act of religion which springs from faith. Finally, they hold that without faith, the artist cannot undertake the execution of sacred art as a Christian. The valid function of sacred art will be only a pretext for him, and the form which he expresses in his work will be only accidentally what the Church requires.[67]

These claims, however, seem to over-simplify the case.

[65] The history of this question is treated in detail by William S. Rubin, *Modern Sacred Art and the Church of Assy* (New York: Columbia University Press, 1961).

[66] *Mediator Dei, AAS*, XXXIX (1947), 591.

[67] These arguments have been summarized by Pie-Raymond Régamey, "The Modern Artist and Religious Art: Christian Possibilities in Artists without Faith," *Cross Currents*, I (Spring, 1951), 55.

The very fact that non-Christians and non-believers have executed sacred art which is not only satisfactory but actually of outstanding quality is sound reason for not rejecting the artifacts without further consideration.[68] It is true that there is a great danger of subjectivism in the execution of sacred art. More and more, contemporary artists seem to revel in domains which are morally dangerous. When they undertake the execution of artifacts with religious themes, they frequently emphasize the tragic and sinful aspects. Without faith, despair is almost inevitable.

Furthermore, one should bear in mind that those who serve the Church by their art pursue not a particular human end but rather one that is divine. Consequently, the "more they live their faith, the more spiritual their inner life becomes, the more deeply rooted they are in the Church, the higher do they rise above human limitations and the conventions, opinions, and special interests of particular social groups; so that with a fuller understanding of the pure spirituality and universality of the action of God on their souls, their art and their thoughts are purged of all human narrowness, to be henceforth concentrated upon the boundless love which is and acts on earth as in Heaven."[69]

It is true that faith is the principle which ideally should unite the artist with the members of the Church for whom sacred art is executed. Without faith, it is difficult for the artist to understand the needs of the community he attempts to serve.[70] But faith in the artist is certainly no assurance that the sacred art which he executes will be worthy

[68] Bonnard, Chagall, Leger, Lipchitz, Lurçat, and Matisse are among contemporary non-believers who have produced satisfactory sacred art.

[69] Maritain, *op. cit.*, p. 105.

[70] Régamey, *loc. cit.*

of its place in the church. Frequently, faith, as it exists in many people today, includes large areas of personal error, ignorance and ambiguity.[71] Faith often appears as a negative obedience, concerned with not going counter to the Church's directives, rather than with producing a vital familiarity with the life of the Church. Religious themes in art frequently are caught up in mere sentimentality because the faith of the artist is often little more than a mixture of mediocre devotion, anemic ideas, and a piety which is utterly lacking in quality and depth.[72]

It should be clear that faith operates on two distinct levels: one on the profound level where the work of art will take on the value of worship to the degree that faith has produced it, the other on the level of experience where the quality of faith in the artist himself is not so important as the presence of faith in the works which he makes. Certainly a religious work of art does not necessarily require the artist to be religious except in the sphere of his art. The truly religious artist is one who imprints a religious character on the works which he makes. The great artist is always intuitive. Although genius does not produce faith, the analogy between mystical inspiration and the inspiration of artists is too profound for one not to be immediately prejudiced in favor of the artist. Since every true artist is inspired, it seems that both by nature and temperament he is predisposed and prepared for spiritual intuitions, even though he may not have faith.

In the creation of sacred art, what matters is not so much the presence of faith in the artist's heart as the presence

[71] Cf. Hyacinthe Paissac, "L'athéisme des Chrétiens," *Supplément de la Vie Spirituelle*, I (May 15, 1947), 5–28.
[72] Régamey, *loc. cit.*, p. 57.

of faith in his creative powers. That faith can exist in an artist's creative powers without being at the same time in his heart has been verified in recent times by the design and execution of truly sacred art by various non-believing artists.

The fact that artists may not have supernatural faith is not of itself sufficient reason to exclude them from the execution of sacred art. But like all artists who turn their hands to church art, they must have a sense of reverence and humility. They must grasp the meaning of what is "sacred." If the artists themselves are unable to give assent to the truths of revelation, at least they should have an intellectual knowledge of those truths which are expressed in sacred art. In this sense, sacred art presupposes in the artist a genuine theological culture.[73] Sacred art is a language, not a decor, and like all languages it is usually mastered slowly and laboriously, and its normal school is the liturgy.[74] If the artist attempts to design a church, he must grasp the meaning of the *Civitas Dei* assembled in hierarchical order, and he must understand what the meaning of active participation really is. The task of the artist will naturally be easier if he himself knows how to share with priest and assembled community in the common worship of God.[75]

Any artist who works for the Church needs deep humility, for he does not execute a work of sacred art primarily for his own gain or glory; he works for and under the guidance of the Church.[76] He must realize that his commitment does not make his work easier but rather frequently curbs its di-

[73] Maritain, *op. cit.*, p. 113; also O'Connell, *op. cit.*, p. 53.
[74] Hammond, *op. cit.*, p. 159.
[75] Wagner, *loc. cit.*, pp. 72–73.
[76] O'Connell, *loc. cit.*

rection.[77] He must learn the mind of the Church by a theological and liturgical formation; he must understand Christian tradition and "the laws of sacred art"; and he must be loyal both to the letter and the spirit of liturgical prescriptions.[78]

Patrons of Sacred Art

In the majority of cases today, the patrons of sacred art are clerics. They may be ordinaries, pastors, religious superiors, or the members of cathedral or conventual chapters. Since sacred art plays such an important part in the external cult of the Church, it is essential that these clerics should have the discernment necessary to select work which is worthy of the Church. To remedy faulty judgment on the part of the clergy, the Instruction *De Arte Sacra* urges the the education of clerics in the matter of sacred art: "Care should be taken that aspirants to sacred orders in schools of philosophy and theology be educated in sacred art and formed in its appreciation, in a way adapted to the ability and age of each one, by masters who reverence what our ancestors cherished and established, and comply with the precriptions of the Holy See."[79]

Since the Instruction speaks specifically of seminarians, the obligation to train the candidates for sacred orders falls first of all upon the rector. It seems that in every house of formation the rector should provide that at least a few lectures with slides on sacred art be given annually, and there should be an ample collection of fine reproductions

[77] Maritain, *op. cit.*, pp. 56–57.
[78] O'Connell, *op. cit.*, p. 54.
[79] AAS, XXXXIV (1952), 545–46.

and books on sacred art available in the seminary library.[80]

It is not unusual, however, that laymen are the patrons of sacred art. Sometimes they subsidize the building of churches and chapels or they promote the creation of sacred art by their financial assistance. At other times they are appointed to the diocesan commissions for sacred art or to the board of directors of liturgical conferences. Laymen may also be patrons of sacred art by reason of the fact that they are members of the administrative board, the *consilium fabricae*, which is constituted in some places.[81] Frequently, laymen are appointed to those positions in which they become patrons of sacred art simply because they are competent to judge sacred art. If they are not themselves adequately trained, both the Code of Canon Law and the Instruction *De Arte Sacra* direct the patrons to consult experts.[82]

As part of the educational program which the Holy See recommends for the patrons of sacred art, the diocesan commission on sacred art might well compile a brochure of directives for church building and furnishings. After the Council of Trent, Charles Borromeo drew up a collection of such directives for the clerics of his diocese.[83] In 1946, by order of and in cooperation with the Liturgical Commission established by the Catholic bishops of Germany, Theodore Klauser, the then Rector Magnificus of the University of Bonn, composed a list of directives for the building of a

[80] Lauck, *loc. cit.*, p. 23.

[81] Cf. canons 1183, 1184.

[82] Canon 1164, § 1; *AAS*, XXXXIV (1952), 544.

[83] *Acta Ecclesiae Mediolanensis*, cura et studia A. Ratti (Mediolani, 1890–92). *Instructionum Supellectilis Ecclesiasticae Liber II*, II, 1503–1588; *Regulae et Instructiones de Nitore et Munditia Ecclesiarum, Altarium, Sacrorum Locorum, et Supellectilis Ecclesiasticae*, II, 1589–98.

church.[84] Reference has already been made to the directives promulgated by the French hierarchy in 1952.[85] The diocesan liturgical commission of Superior, Wisconsin, has issued a series of church building directives, which not only incorporate the concrete letter of the law but also the liturgical spirit.[86] This series might well serve as a model for other dioceses.

Legislation of itself will not produce good sacred art. Example is usually the best teacher. Consequently patrons should take great care in furnishing churches and chapels so that only first-class works of sacred art find a place there. Likewise in building new edifices, they should patronize only the best among those artists who are equipped to execute sacred art.

It may be said that a church or a chapel is a mirror of the priest who is in charge. The church may be simple and even poor, but if it is free from sentimental art and furnished in good taste, it will not only reflect the care and artistic culture of the priest but it will also edify the people and cultivate in them a sense of what is truly "sacred."

SUMMARY OF THE LAWS OF SACRED ART

The foregoing articles of this chapter have summarized in their essentials the pronouncements of the Church on sacred

[84] An English translation of the directives may be found in *Orate Fratres*, XXIV (Dec., 1949), 9–18.

[85] *Loc. cit.*

[86] Cf. William Wenninger, "A Diocese Directs," *Worship*, XXXII (February, 1958), 192–96. The present writer is grateful to Fr. Wenninger for providing him with a complete text of the directives.

art. In order to draw some concrete conclusions from what has been said, the following principles may be stated:

1. *Sacred art is a dedicated art.* Its first law is the glory of God; its second, the salvation of souls. In its innermost essence, therefore, sacred art is a pastoral art. Since it is bound to the Christian community, it must have continuity despite all changes which may take place in man and in his thought.[87]

2. *Sacred art must give witness to the truth.* In other words, it must be orthodox. It must represent genuine Catholic dogmas and morals. It should aid in the Catholic formation of intelligent worshippers. Hence it must not foster superstitions.[88] Like the liturgy itself, it must present first things as first things and subordinate things as subordinate.[89]

3. *Sacred Art must spring from authentic Christian inspiration.* As Pius XII noted in *Mediator Dei*, "artists and architects must have both the skill and the will to find in religion the inspiration of methods and plans best adapted to the exigencies of divine worship."[90] Consequently, sacred art must never be sentimental or overly emotional. Reserved in its portrayal of sacred doctrine, it must never descend to an overemphasis of the gaudy, the ornamental, the petty, or the ostentatious. This rules out all stereotyped commercial imitations which masquerade under the name of sacred art.

4. *Sacred art is social in character.* It is art at the service of the community. Consequently, it is not simply the ex-

[87] Wagner, *loc. cit.*, p. 71.
[88] Cf. canon 1279, § 3.
[89] Wagner, *loc. cit.*, p. 72; O'Connell, *op. cit.*, p. 33.
[90] *AAS*, XXXIX (1947), 591.

pression of the artist's own subjective intuition or inspiration. It must enable the people to experience the grandeur of God and the dignity that is proper to the Christian community and its worship.[91] All art must necessarily be subjective to a degree, since it is the product of the artist's own experience and appraisal of reality; nevertheless, this subjectivity must not be stressed to the detriment of what must be portrayed objectively. To serve the community, sacred art must be universal in its appeal. It must serve the needs of the faithful for whom it is executed. Although it is impossible to please all the members of a community at all times, the artist must remember that, in general, sacred art is intended for the public and not for a coterie of esthetes. As Pius XII noted in *Mediator Dei,* one of the qualities demanded of all that pertains to the liturgy is a "universality which, while respecting legitimate local customs, manifests the unity of the Church."[92]

In keeping with its social character, sacred art must also be intelligible. Since it has a didactic function,

> It should reveal its message clearly and quickly. It must have an expressive value, without which it ceases to be true art. To say as much is not superfluous in our own day when all too often, among certain groups, the work of art is not sufficient in itself to render the thought, to externalize the feelings, to lay bare the soul of its author. Yet the moment it needs to be explained in verbal terms, it loses its value as a sign and serves only to afford the senses a physical joy rising no higher than their own level, or else it affords the mind merely the pleasure of subtle and useless play.[93]

[91] Wagner, *loc. cit.*

[92] *AAS,* XXXIX (1947), 588.

[93] Pius XII to the First International Congress of Catholic Artists on September 3, 1950, *Discorsi e Radiomessaggi di Sua Santità Pio XII,* XII, 128.

When artists work in the sanctuary, they must remember that they are not working in a locked cenacle, and so their work must be capable of being understood by the body of the faithful without the necessity of long and learned explanations.[94]

5. *Sacred art must be executed in accordance with liturgical law and the spirit of the liturgy.* This conformity will go a long way in procuring sacred art which is worthy of the house of God.

6. *Sacred art is subject to ecclesiastical control.* This follows immediately from the definition of sacred art. Once art enters the Church, it must accept control beyond that enforced by the laws of esthetics. Ecclesiastical authorities, however, must be competent in their judgment and direction. Lacking such competence, they must consult experts.

7. *Artists who turn their hand to sacred art must have a solid theological and liturgical formation.* Such a formation is not to be presupposed in artists merely because they are practicing Catholics, nor must non-Catholics be automatically excluded from working on sacred art simply because they are not members of the Church. Those artists should be commissioned who are outstanding for their technique and who are capable of expressing sincere piety and faith.

If sacred art is faithful to these principles, it will not only give pleasure because of its beauty, but it will also give glory to God and assist the faithful in raising mind and heart to God within the context of the liturgy.

[94] Directive of the French Hierarchy on Sacred Art, No. 5, *loc. cit.*

2

Sacred Art and Tradition

In canon 1164, § 1, the Church legislates that "the forms received from Christian tradition" are to be preserved in the construction and restoration of churches, and in canon 1269, § 3, it notes that "ecclesiastical tradition" is one of the norms which should govern the design of sacred furnishings. These general norms appear for the first time in the Code of Canon Law. Prior to the promulgation of the Code, authors had written treatises on sacred furnishings, but none of them ventured to set forth general norms on sacred art and architecture such as the ones contained in the above mentioned canons.[1] Although the term "tradition" appears in both of these laws, canonists have made little or no commentary on the word, which is difficult to analyze and even more difficult to define. In view of the important role which tradition plays in sacred art and architecture, an attempt will be made to clarify the term as it is used in the context of the above mentioned canons.

[1] Cf. St. Charles Borromeo, *Instructionum Supellectilis Ecclesiasticae Liber II, Regulae et Instructiones de Nitore et Munditia Ecclesiarum, Altarium, Sacrorum Locorum, et Supellectilis Ecclesiasticae, loc. cit.*; F. X. Wernz, *Ius Decretalium* (Vol. III, 2d ed.; Romae, 1908), III, nn. 501 sqq.; Petrus Gaspari, *Tractatus Canonicus de Sanctissima Eucharistia* (Paris, 1897), cap. v, *De Sacris Utensilibus*, nn. 653 sqq.

THE CONCEPT OF TRADITION IN CANON 1164, § 1, AND CANON 1296, § 3

There is no doubt that sacred art must be traditional. First of all, it must be traditional in the sense that its intellectual content must be in conformity with the preaching and teaching of the Church. Just as tradition is the rule of faith for the believer, so it is the rule of making for the artist. If the artist is to be truly traditional, therefore, he must appreciate especially the fact that the tradition of the Church is dynamic, that it is pulsing with life. Since the sacred arts are the servants of the liturgy, it is essential that the artist have an intimate knowledge and understanding of the preaching and teaching of the Church as it is contained in the liturgy. As Pius XII stated in his allocution to the First International Congress of Pastoral Liturgy:

> It would be difficult to find a truth of the Christian faith which is not somehow expressed in the liturgy, whether it is the readings from the Old and New Testament in the Mass and the Divine Office, or the riches which mind and heart discover in the psalms. The solemn liturgical ceremonies are, besides, a profession of faith in action. They express the great truths of faith concerning the inscrutable designs of God's generosity and His inexhaustible goodness to men, concerning the love and mercy of the heavenly Father for the world, to save which he sent his Son and delivered him to death. Thus, the Church in the liturgy abundantly dispenses the treasures of the "deposit of faith," the truth of Christ.[2]

Without an intimate and dynamic knowledge of the Church's preaching and teaching, the artist who attempts to execute sacred art cannot express what is essentially implied in the liturgy. Without tradition to guide him, there is a

[2] *AAS*, XXXXVIII (1956), 713, and *The Assisi Papers* (Collegeville, Minnesota: The Liturgical Press, 1957), p. 225.

real danger that he will seek beauty for its own sake and use the liturgy as a mere occasion for artistic expression.[3]

The artist must first of all be concerned with those truths expressed in the Church's official worship through which divine life is communicated to men. The liturgy is the expression of an intense experience in which man approaches God and God gives audience to man. When this is realized and truthfully expressed, the manifestation of truth is also beautiful. This is what Romano Guardini meant when he wrote:

> The Church has not built up the *Opus Dei* for the pleasure of forming beautiful symbols, choice language, and graceful, stately gestures, but she has done it . . . for the sake of our desperate spiritual need. It is to give expression to the events of the Christian's inner life: the assimilation, through the Holy Ghost, of the life of the creature to the life of God in Christ; the actual genuine rebirth of the creature into a new existence; the development and nourishment of this life, its stretching forth from God in the Blessed Sacrament and the means of grace, towards God, in prayer and sacrifice; and all this in continual mystic renewal of Christ's life in the course of the ecclesiastical year. The fulfillment of all these processes by the set form of language, gesture, and instruments, their revelation, teaching, accomplishment and acceptance by the faithful, together constitute the liturgy. . . . Here truth is at stake, and the fate of the soul, and real—yes, ultimately the only real—life. All this it is which must be revealed, expressed, sought after, found, and imparted by every possible means and method; and when this is accomplished, lo! it is turned into beauty.[4]

It is essential that the artist who turns his hand to sacred art must be aware of the dynamic aspect of sacred tradition. In contemplation he must "look reflectively to the historical

[3] Javier, "Living Tradition," *Liturgical Arts,* XXVII (1959), 32.
[4] Romano Guardini, "The Spirit of the Liturgy," *The Church and the Catholic and the Spirit of the Liturgy,* p. 185.

past, synthesize it in the present, and give it back to posterity enriched by an ever-increasing depth of spiritual activity."[5]

WHAT FIDELITY TO TRADITION DOES NOT MEAN

Perhaps the role which tradition plays in sacred art will be clarified if it is shown what fidelity to tradition in sacred art does not mean. First of all it does not mean the adoption of any particular style, as if certain styles were more Catholic or more religious than others.[6] Just as the Church has never canonized any system of philosophy or theology nor adopted any rite or style of music to the exclusion of others, neither has it imposed upon its subjects any particular style of sacred art. As Celso Costantini wrote in *L'Osservatore Romano:* "All styles are admissible, provided they are conformable to this fundamental principle that a church must be, and must appear to be the house of God. . . . Nowadays one can see churches whose construction was inspired by a new style—for one can truly say today that there is a new architectural style—and which fully satisfy the requirements of worship, of a fresh appreciation of artistic beauty, and of an enlightened economic sense."[7]

[5] Javier, *loc. cit.*

[6] The word "formae" as it appears in canon 1164 § 1, should be translated "forms," not "styles." T. Lincoln Bouscaren mistranslates the word as it appears in the context of the Instruction *De Arte Sacra—Canon Law Digest*, III (Milwaukee: Bruce, 1954), p. 510. In place of "traditional Christian styles of architecture," the translation should read: "forms received from Christian tradition."

[7] "Del'Architettura Sacra," *L'Osservatore Romano*, July 30, 1952, p. 1.

Furthermore, fidelity to tradition does not mean "archeologism." The Church is a living organism, and its liturgy is vital. It does not adopt or retain what is old merely because it is old. As Pius XII wrote concerning liturgical usages, "an ancient custom is not to be considered better, either in itself or in relation to later times, just because it has the flavor of antiquity."[8] Archeologism forgets that the life of tradition transcends variable styles and themes; tradition lives on in the eternal truths which know no change.[9] The artist must assimilate what is good from the spirit of his time, not merely because it is modern, but because it is something good, something better than what he was able to express before. In adopting what is good in contemporary thought, church architects, for example, are at present manifesting a greater appreciation of the value of simple lines and plain surfaces, and they are discarding what is superfluous, over-ornate, pretentious, or fake.[10]

Finally, fidelity to tradition does not mean a canonization of what is customary merely because it is customary. The liturgy involves two classes of elements: divine elements, which cannot be changed by men, since they have been instituted by Christ, and human elements, which can undergo variations according to the exigencies of time and circumstances.[11] Throughout history a variety of liturgical rites has arisen, and liturgical institutions, forgotten in the course of time, have frequently been restored or reclaimed. This is but a proof of the Church's vitality. Furthermore, the variations in the human elements of the liturgy reveal the

[8] *Mediator Dei,* November 20, 1947: *AAS,* XXXIX (1947), 545.
[9] Régamey, *Art Sacré au XXᵉ Siècle?* pp. 125–26.
[10] O'Connell, *Church Building and Furnishing,* p. 44.
[11] Cf. *Mediator Dei: AAS,* XXXIX (1947), 541–42.

Church's wise pedagogy in nourishing in the faithful a sense of Christ.[12]

Because of the human element, the liturgy of the Church has a history all its own, with periods of greater and lesser splendor. Human accretions to the liturgical rites have at times necessitated liturgical reforms. It was this fact which prompted St. Pius X to write as follows in 1913: "A long period of years must pass before the liturgical edifice, which the mystical Spouse of Christ has formed in her zeal and understanding to proclaim her piety and faith, may again appear splendid with dignity and harmony, as cleansed of the accumulations of age."[13]

Looking back upon the history of the liturgy, one notes certain moments when the Supreme Pontiffs gave decisive directions to the liturgical movement among the Christian people. It is sufficient to recall the names of St. Gregory the Great, Gregory VII, Innocent III, St. Pius X, and Pius XII. Reform and restoration of the Church continue to the present day, and they will continue till the end of time. The Church is at once a divine mystery and a human structure. Where there are human beings, there will always be failures, and where there are failures, there is a need for restoration and renewal.[14] Throughout change, the sacred tradition of the Church remains unchanged, although it often gets out

[12] Cardinal Gaetano Cicognani, "Opening Address to the First International Congress of Pastoral Liturgy," *The Assisi Papers*, p. 3.

[13] Motu propr., *Abhinc duos annos*, October 23, 1913: *AAS*, V (1913), 449–50.

[14] For a discussion of the place of restoration and reform in the Church, cf. Congar, *Vraie et fausse reforme dans l'Église* (Paris: Editions du Cerf, 1950); also, Hans Küng, *The Council, Reform and Reunion* (New York: Sheed and Ward, 1961).

of proper focus. Reforms and restorations are part of the teaching and preaching of the Church; as such they form part of the Church's dynamic tradition, upon which artists and architects must draw for the inspiration they need to execute truly sacred art.

From what has been said, it is obvious that tradition is something quite different from traditions or customs. One should note, too, that tradition is only partly embodied in the Church's rubrics. Tradition is prior to the rubrics both logically and in time. It supplements the rubrics and should be used as a basis for their interpretation. Like the rubrics, customs or traditions arise, change, and die. They may be good or bad, genuine or false, universal or only national. Traditions are frequently dated, but the truth of tradition continues.[15]

SUMMARY

If the artist who turns his hand to sacred art is to be faithful to the tradition of the Church, he must have grasped profoundly what the Church really is, what its mission is, and what its teaching is. There is no doubt that great artistic tasks have been evoked by the present-day "awakening of the Church in men's souls,"[16] by the liturgical reforms of the popes, and by the ideal of active participation by the faithful in the liturgy. If artists are to be successful in accomplishing these tasks, they must be animated by the same liturgical spirit. St. Augustine summed up Christian

[15] O'Connell, *op. cit.*, p. 47.
[16] Guardini, *The Church and the Catholic and the Spirit of the Liturgy*, p. 11.

freedom while inculcating Christian duty: "*Ama et fac quod vis* . . . Love, and do what you will."[17] These words might well be paraphrased for the artist who seeks to work for the Church: "*Vivas cum Ecclesia et fac quod vis*. . . . Live with the Church, and do what you will."[18]

[17] *In epistolam Johannis ad Parthos, Tractatus*, X, 8: *PL*, XXXV, 2060.

[18] Wagner, "Liturgical Art and the Care of Souls," *The Assisi Papers*, p. 73.

PART II

THE BUILDING OF A CHURCH

3

The Mystery of the Church Edifice

The seventh chapter of the Acts of the Apostles gives an account of St. Stephen's discourse before the Sanhedrin following his arrest. St. Peter and the other apostles had taught that Christ was the Messias, but like Christ, they still observed the whole Jewish Law. On the contrary, St. Stephen proclaimed the temporary nature of the Law, which was fulfilled and replaced by the New Covenant.[1] He spoke of the prophecies concerning the destruction of the Temple, which was superseded by the spiritual temple of Christ's Body, and said: "The Most High does not dwell in houses made by men."[2]

Later, St. Paul proclaimed the same idea at Athens in the midst of the Areopagus: "The God who made the world and all that is in it, that God who is Lord of heaven and earth, does not dwell in temples that our hands have made."[3] At Athens, Paul "was repelled at finding the city so much given over to idolatry,"[4] and when he appeared before

[1] Cf. Matt. 5:17; 19:7–8.

[2] Acts 7:48; cf. F. J. Foackes, "Stephen's Speech in Acts," *Journal of Biblical Literature*, XXXXIX (1930), 283–86; M. Simon, "St. Stephen and the Jewish Temple," *Journal of Ecclesiastical History*, II (1951), 127–42.

[3] Acts 17:24.

[4] Acts 17:16.

the Areopagus, he proclaimed the emptiness of idols and the inaneness of the pagan temples.[5]

The situation at Jerusalem was totally different from that which Paul found at Athens. The temple built for the glory of the true God was not the dwelling place of idols. The Jews accused Stephen of "speaking evil against the holy place and the law. We have heard him say that the Nazarene, Jesus, will destroy this place and will alter the traditions which Moses handed down to us."[6] But within a short distance of the temple, Stephen affirmed that God did not dwell in places made by human hands.

These two accounts of Paul and Stephen in the Acts touch upon one of the fundamental truths of Christianity. The religion taught by Christ is not tied down to an edifice built by human hands, but is rather built up by God himself. In proclaiming the originality of Christianity as opposed to paganism and Judaism, Paul and Stephen defined the universal character of the religion taught by Christ.[7]

In spite of the proclamations made by Stephen and Paul, there do exist buildings called churches; the churches, chapels, and oratories, however, do not constitute a negation of the truth proclaimed by Stephen and Paul. It is the purpose of this chapter to analyze the mystery of a church, to trace the development of a place of worship throughout the Old Testament, and to define the relation between the edifices for worship under the Old Law and the the church as it exists in the present economy of Christianity.

[5] Acts 17:22–31.

[6] Acts 6:13–14.

[7] François Louvel, "Le mystère de nos églises," *La Maison-Dieu*, LXIII (1960), 5–6; cf. Johannes Quasten, "The Conflict of Early Christianity with the Jewish Temple Worship," *Theological Studies*, II (1941), 481–87.

THE PRESENCE OF GOD IN THE OLD TESTAMENT

During the period of the patriarchs, there was no temple. Abraham was a nomad, and wherever he happened to be, there he adored the true God. In making the covenant, God had told Abraham, "Walk in my presence and be perfect."[8] The command was simply a matter of living in God's presence and of modelling oneself after the Lord. It was a preview of the later precept of the gospel, "Be you perfect as your heavenly Father is perfect."[9]

Nevertheless, the book of Genesis notes that Abraham built an altar to Yahweh and there invoked his name.[10] From these texts one may conclude that at the time of the patriarchs there were special periods set aside for prayer. Although Abraham always walked in the presence of God, he could not always offer sacrifice. Consequently, he set aside special periods for prayer. Adoration must be rooted in man's heart, but there must also be times for its expression.[11]

Just as there must be a time for prayer, so also there must be a place. In the era of the patriarchs, the place was not very important. Abraham built an altar successively at Sichem and in the Valley of Clear Seeing,[12] at Bethel and Hai,[13] and at Hebron by the valley of Mambre.[14] The places of dwelling became the places of sacrifice, and since God

[8] Gen. 17:1.
[9] Matt. 5:48.
[10] Gen. 12:6–8; 13:4–5; 13:18.
[11] Louvel, *loc. cit.*, p. 6.
[12] Gen. 12:6–7.
[13] Gen. 12:8.
[14] Gen. 13:18.

appeared to Abraham at these various places, they became important marks in the history of salvation, and afterwards became holy places.[15]

The religion which Moses proclaimed was closely linked with the religion of the patriarchs, for both stemmed from divine revelation. Whereas God spoke immediately with the patriarchs, he delegated Moses to speak to Israel in his name. Although he manifested his presence to all the people, as he did when he appeared on Sinai in lightning, thunder, and smoke,[16] when he led them by a pillar of fire,[17] when he descended on the tabernacle,[18] when he intervened at the uprising against Moses and Aaron,[19] and the rebellion by Core's band,[20] yet only rarely did he communicate his commands directly to the people, as he did when he gave the decalog.[21]

God made the covenant with Israel as a whole, not with the individual tribes. Israel's election, however, did not imply that God had rejected other peoples. Although Yahweh was Israel's God, he was not a national God; consequently, he continued to guide and protect other tribes, other nations.[22]

With Moses, there is the appearance of a priesthood,[23] a ritual of sacrifice,[24] and above all the ark of the covenant

[15] Louvel, *loc. cit.*, pp. 6–7.
[16] Exod. 19.
[17] Exod. 13:21; 14:19; Num., 9:17.
[18] Exod. 40:34.
[19] Num. 14:10.
[20] Num. 16:19.
[21] Exod. 20; cf. G. R. Berry, "The Glory of Yahweh and the Temple," *Journal of Biblical Literature*, LVI (1937), 115–17.
[22] Paul Heinisch, *History of the Old Testament*, trans. William Heidt (Collegeville, Minnesota: The Liturgical Press, 1952), p. 111.
[23] Exod. 28, 29; Lev. 8–10.
[24] Exod. 25:23–30; Lev. 2–8; 10:1; Num. 16:6; 17:11.

and the sacred appurtenances that accompany it.[25] The ark, howerever, is not stationary; it accompanies and organizes the wanderings of the Israelites. Nor is the ark the dwelling place of God. It is the sign of his presence in the midst of his people. "I will dwell in the midst of the Israelites and be their God; and they shall know me for the Lord God that rescued them from the land of Egypt, so as to abide among them, their Lord and their God."[26] God, then, is present everywhere—in Egypt, on Mt. Sinai, in the wilderness, and in Canaan.[27]

The Book of Numbers states that three tribes of the Israelites were to camp to the east of the ark, three to the south, three to the west, and three to the north.[28] In the center of this great quadrangle, the tribe of Levi surrounded the tent in which rested the ark, the symbol of God's presence in the midst of His people. As the Israelites moved about, the ark, too, was moved about, and God was, so to speak, made a nomad among nomads.[29] This divine nomadism was to last from the time of Moses up to the time of David, who would triumphantly lead the ark, the symbol of God's presence, into Jerusalem.[30]

Three short conclusions may be drawn concerning the presence of God during the exile:

1. Just as in the age of the patriarchs, so also during the

[25] Exod. 25–29.

[26] Exod. 29:45–46.

[27] Cf. Congar, "The Presence of God at the Time of the Exodus and in the Lifetime of Moses," *The Mystery of the Temple* (Westminster: The Newman Press, 1962), pp. 3–19.

[28] Num. 1:52–2:34.

[29] Louvel, *loc. cit.*, p. 8; cf. M.-J. Lagrange, *Le judaisme avant Jésus-Christ* (Paris: J. Gabalda, 1931), p. 446.

[30] II Kings 6.

exodus, God dwelt with those who believed in Him and who trusted in Him.

2. Since men need visible signs to attain the invisible, the ark became the principal sign of God's presence in the midst of His people.

3. God's presence, however, was not confined to a determined place. The ark was placed beneath a tent, where it was always prepared to go with the people of God.[31]

The Israelites worshipped God in many places: at Shechem,[32] Shiloh,[33] Gilgal in Ephraim,[34] Bochim,[35] Bethel,[36] Mizpah in Benjamin,[37] Mizpah in Gilead,[38] Gilgal near Jericho,[39] Gibeon,[40] Bethlehem,[41] Gibeah of God,[42] Ophrah,[43] Dan,[44] and Ramah.[45] The law did not restrict the offering of sacrifice to one place;[46] it could be offered wherever God had made a place holy by a theophany or a favor. The most important place for cult, however, was normally the sanctuary where the ark was reserved.[47]

It was David who brought the ark to Jerusalem. He sensed the impropriety of housing the ark in a tent and

[31] Louvel, *loc. cit.*, p. 8.
[32] Jos. 8:30; 24:1; 26.
[33] Jos. 22:9; Judg. 18:31; 21:19–21; I Kings 1–4.
[34] I Kings 7:16.
[35] Judg. 2:1–5.
[36] Judg. 20:18–28; 21:2–4; I Kings 7:16.
[37] Judg. 21:1; I Kings, 7:5.
[38] Judg. 11:11.
[39] Jos. 4:20; 5:10.
[40] III Kings 3:4.
[41] I Kings 16:1–5.
[42] I Kings 10:5.
[43] Judg. 6:24; 8:27.
[44] Judg. 18:30–31.
[45] I Kings 7:17.
[46] Exod. 20:24–26.
[47] Heinisch, *op. cit.*, p. 149.

laid plans for the erection of a temple. When Nathan informed him that this task was reserved for his successors,[48] David was content to make preparations by collecting funds and materials, by purchasing the site, and by erecting an altar in Jerusalem.[49]

The formula with which the author of the Book of Kings recounts the building of the temple has a special solemnity which emphasizes the importance of the event. "It was in the four hundred and eightieth year after the Israelites left Egypt . . . that the building of the Lord's house began."[50] The account is an architectural description, but it reveals the love with which the author speaks of the temple. It climaxes with the dedication. "The whole of the Lord's house was wreathed in cloud; . . . his own glory was there, filling his own house. Where the cloud is, cried Solomon, the Lord has promised to be; it is true, then, the house I have built is to be thy dwelling, thy throne forever immovable."[51] Solomon had built the temple with the materials of the earth and the elaborate plans of men. But God ratified the work of the builders and chose the temple for his earthly dwelling place by a manifestation analogous to that of the Exodus.

After affirming God's special presence in the temple, Solomon suddenly exclaimed in the course of his dedicatory prayer: "Folly it were to think that God has a dwelling-place on earth. If the very heavens and the heavens that are above the heavens cannot contain thee, what welcome can it offer thee, this house that I have built."[52] From this

[48] II Kings 7:4–16.
[49] II Kings 24:18–25; I Par. 22, 28.
[50] III Kings 6:1.
[51] III Kings 8:10–13.
[52] III Kings 8:27.

prayer, it is clear that God did not actually dwell in the temple, because He could not be enclosed in the narrow confines of a sanctuary. The temple was only the privileged place for prayer: the meeting place of God and his people.[53]

Numerous texts of the Old Testament and especially the Psalms speak of the grandeur of the temple and the joy of Israel marching toward the house of God. But there are other texts which speak of the temple, but not in the same vein of enthusiasm. For example, after David had resolved to build the temple, God sent the prophet Nathan to David with this message:

> Dost thou think to build a house for me to dwell in? House was never mine, since I rescued the sons of Israel from Egypt; still in a tabernacle, a wanderer's home, I came and went. This way and that the whole race of Israel journeyed, and I with them; now to this tribe, now to that, I gave the leadership of the rest, and never did I reproach any of them for not building me a house of cedar.[54]

There is no doubt that the temple changed the relationship between God and his people.[55] The solemn transfer of the ark marked the end of an epoch, for God no longer appeared as a nomad in the midst of nomads but rather as a king in a palace, a king whom no one sees except his servants, a king dwelling in the privacy of his own apartment.[56]

Four centuries after the dedication of the temple, the Jews returned from exile and reconstructed the destroyed edifice, but again a prophetic voice was raised against the project:

[53] Louvel, *loc. cit.*, *La Maison-Dieu*, LXIII (1960), 8–10.

[54] II Kings 7:6–7; cf. J. L. McKenzie, "The Dynastic Oracle: II Sam. 7," *Theological Studies*, VIII (1947), 187–218.

[55] III Kings 8:1–8.

[56] Louvel, *loc. cit.*, p. 10.

Thus says the Lord, Heaven is my throne and the earth the footstool under my feet. What home will you build for me, what place can be my resting place? Nothing you see about you but I fashioned it, the Lord says; my hand gave it being.[57]

In two particularly important circumstances, David's resolution to build the temple and its reconstruction years later, the word of God was raised against the project. On both occasions, however, the project was realized and, so it seems, with God's blessing. The apparent contradiction is one of the mysteries of divine pedagogy.[58] God accepted the construction of the temple and he made it a place of grace. Although pilgrimages continued to be made to Israel's older places of sacrifice,[59] the temple at Jerusalem gradually became Israel's principal place of cult. The temple was the great place for prayer; it was there that the faithful went periodically on pilgrimage; it was in the temple that they assembled, just as of old they assembled about the ark of the covenant. They went forth to Jerusalem and its temple from regions far and wide. For ten centuries the temple played an important role in the history of Israel. In fact it is unlikely that the history of Israel would have been the same without the temple. It is sufficient to observe the reverence and esteem of Christ, his Mother, and his apostles to understand that the temple was a source of blessing for Israel.[60]

Yet without ceasing, God tried to arouse the conscience

[57] Isa. 66:1–2.

[58] Louvel, *loc. cit.*

[59] E.g., Mizpah, where Saul was chosen (I Kings 10:17); Gilgal, where Saul was proclaimed king (I Kings 11–14); and Hebron, where David was anointed king (II Kings 2:4; 5:1–3) and where Absalom arranged the festival which began his revolt (II Kings 15:7).

[60] Cf. Luke 2:41–51; Matt. 23:16–22; Mark 11:17.

of Israel to a mission higher than that of a mere ritual cult. The invectives of the prophets against those who placed a blind trust in the temple are less a criticism of the temple than an invitation to return to the essential truth of religion: "Seek Yahweh and you will live."[61] The temple required of those who approached it a ritual holiness, but, according to the prophets, God sought a holiness which sprang from within. Although the temple seemed to be the property of the Israelites, since it was located at Jerusalem, the prophets nevertheless announced that all the nations would come there to adore the God of the whole earth.[62]

In the divine plan, the capture of Jerusalem by Nabuchodonosor, the destruction of the temple, and the exile of the chosen people also played essential roles. The prophets had announced many times that God would abandon the temple.[63] Finally in 588 B.C., what seemed to be an extravagant oratorical hypothesis became a reality, for Jerusalem was captured, the temple was razed, and the Israelites went into exile far from their own land. For half a century they lived in a foreign land. After the first exiles returned to Judea, they had to wait twenty years for the reconstruction of the temple, a project which was finally completed in 515 B.C. For seventy years, then, Israel lived without a temple.

Before the destruction of Jerusalem, Ezechiel had described the departure of Jahweh.[64] In fulfillment of these prophecies, the glory of God left the temple, not because the enemies of Israel came in, but because idols had invaded

[61] Cf. Jer. 5:31; 6:13; Os. 4:4–10; Mic. 3:11–12; Bar. 2:26; Isa. 8–9; 22:8; 28:7–15.

[62] Congar, *op. cit.*, pp. 200–228; Louvel, *loc. cit.*, p. 12.

[63] E.g., Ezek. 8:6; 24:20–21.

[64] Ezek. 10:4–5; 10:18–19; 11:22–23.

the courts of the temple. God freely left the temple just as He had freely come of old. He did not abandon his people, but rather went with His people into exile. Far from Jerusalem and its temple, God remained with those who suffered and hoped. Although Jeremias had prophesied the destruction of Jerusalem and the exile of the Israelites, he had also foretold a new alliance of God with His people: "I will implant my law in their innermost thoughts, engrave it in their hearts; I will be their God, and they shall be my people."[65] It was God's intent that the new Jerusalem should be founded on justice and righteousness.[66] Ezechiel prophesied a new temple, where the glory of God would dwell, but not until he had first announced a new covenant:

> I mean to set you free from the power of the Gentiles, bring you home again from every part of the earth. And then I will pour cleansing streams over you to purge you from every stain you bear, purge you from the taint of your idolatry. I will give you a new heart and breathe a new spirit into you. . . . You shall be my people and I will be your God.[67]

From a study of the period of the exile, one may deduce the following conclusions:

1. The temple at Jerusalem was subject to destruction. In spite of its ruin, however, God did not cease to watch over and guide His chosen people.

2. Although God is always everywhere, He is especially with those who suffer and trust in Him. While the Israelites were far from the promised land, God was "for them a sanctuary."[68]

[65] Jer. 31:33–34; cf. also Isa. 1:26; 4:2–6; 28:16–17; Soph. 3:11–13; Jer. 7:3–7; 33:14–16.
[66] Cf. Isa. 1:26; 54:14; Jer. 33:15; Bar. 5:4.
[67] Ezek. 36:24–28.
[68] Ezek. 11:16.

3. During the exile, God prepared a holy people, a people who were purified, a people who loved God and were animated by the spirit of love which they shared with one another.[69]

THE SYNAGOGUE

Although the synagogues are not mentioned in the Old Testament, they cannot be passed over in silence, for they were actually one of the most important institutions in the centuries immediately before Christ. In the exilic literature of the Old Testament, there are indications that the dispersed Israelites gathered together,[70] and one may suppose that some of these meetings served for religious purposes. After the return of the exiles to their own land, the scribe Esdras called the people together and had the Scriptures read to them. When the solemn reading was finished, however, there was no offering of sacrifice. Instead the people took a vow to carry out the sacrifices when the city had been rebuilt and the temple reconstructed. Although there is no proof that there were synagogues during the exile, nevertheless, the predominant opinion today is that they originated in Babylonia during the exile as a substitute for the services in the temple.[71]

During the diaspora, a whole network of synagogues covered the Holy Land and extended over the breadth of the

[69] Louvel, *loc. cit.*, pp. 12–13; Congar, *op. cit.*, pp. 94–96.
[70] Cf. Ezek. 8:1; 14:1; 33:30.
[71] Roland de Vaux, *Ancient Israel: Its Life and Institutions,* trans. John McHugh (New York: McGraw-Hill Book Company, Inc., 1961), p. 343; Giuseppe Ricciotti, *The History of Israel,* trans. Clement della Penta and Richard T. Murphy (Milwaukee: The Bruce Publishing Company, 1955), II, 67; Heinisch, *op. cit.*, p. 316.

world where the Jews were dispersed. In most cities where Jews resided, there was at least one synagogue, and in the larger cities there were several.[72]

The synagogues were erected so that the faithful Jews would have a place to assemble. They came together regularly because they knew that God dwelt with them in a special way as a united people. On the one hand, the Jews assembled in the temple because it was constructed as a sacred edifice, but, on the other hand, the dispersed Jews constructed synagogues because they sought to be a united people.[73]

The ritual in the synagogue was in no way opposed to the cult in the temple, nor did it interfere with the great annual pilgrimage to Jerusalem. There is no doubt, however, that the worship of the synagogue gained in importance after the reconstruction of the temple; for then the people realized that the temple, as it was rebuilt, failed to realize the hopes expressed by Ezechiel and, in fact, was not even the equal of the older temple.[74]

The synagogue worship fostered the eschatological expectation, sown by Ezechiel, of a true and lasting worship, an eternal sacrifice. When the people recalled God's great deeds in the work of their salvation, they did not praise them as a final accomplishment, but rather recalled them as a pledge and a foreshadowing of those far greater works which God would accomplish in the future. This accounts for the increasing decline in the importance of the temple ritual, even after it had been restored. It is true that the eschatological hopes of the chosen people were expressed

[72] Heinisch, *op. cit.*, p. 394.
[73] De Vaux, *op. cit.*, pp. 343–44; Louvel, *loc. cit.*, p. 14.
[74] Ag. 2.

in ritual, but it was not the ritual of those Jews who did not accept this expectation. It was rather the ritual of the synagogue, of those small pious communities which were preparing for the kingdom to come.[75]

THE CHURCH BUILDING IN THE NEW TESTAMENT

From the time of Moses to the coming of Christ or from the time of the ark to that of the new covenant, the chosen people were a people apart. Moses had led them into the desert and separated them from other nations. The believers were separated from non-believers especially by the observance of food ordinances, the sabbath rest, and circum cision.[76] The coming of Christ, and more precisely the mission of the Holy Spirit, inaugurated a regime of dispersion. There was geographic dispersion: the new Christians lived not only in the towns where up till now there had been only Jews, but also in every place where the gospel was preached. There was ethnic dispersion: in the Church of Christ there was neither Jew, nor Greek, nor barbarian, nor free man. St. John could truly write that the Church was composed of men of every race, every language and every nation.[77] The first Pentecost, that of Mount Sinai, had created a people separated from other peoples, but the new Pentecost tossed the seed of the gospel to every wind and carried the word of God to all parts of the world. Although the converts to the new Church belonged to various nations,[78] they

[75] De Vaux, *op. cit.*, pp. 289–343.
[76] Cf. I Macc. 1:5; 1:43; 2:34–38; Tob. 1:11; Jth. 12:2; Dan. 1:8.
[77] Apoc. 5:9–10.
[78] Acts 2:5–11.

nevertheless formed a single people, the people of God. They were not united by social origin, geographic location, or common language, but only by the Spirit of God. Ezechiel had prophesied that God would assemble the men of every nation through the gift of His Spirit.[79] The unity attained by the Holy Spirit was, and still is, a true organism in spite of world-wide dispersion. The people of God are a single body. "For in one Spirit we were all baptized into one body, whether Jew or Gentile, whether slave or free; and we were all given to drink of one Spirit."[80]

Although St. Paul developed the concept of the Church as a body, he was accustomed also to employ another figure —that of the temple. In the first letter to the Corinthians, written sometime between 54 and 57 A.D., he asked: "Do you not know that you are the temple of God and that the Spirit of God dwells in you? . . . The temple of God is holy and you are this temple."[81] A little further on in the sixth chapter of the same epistle, he wrote: "Do you not know that your members are the temple of the Holy Spirit, who is in you, whom you have from God, and that you are not your own? For you have been bought at a great price. Glorify God and bear him in your body."[82] Several years later in his letter to the Ephesians, Paul wrote:

> You are built upon the foundations of the apostles and prophets with Christ Jesus himself as the chief cornerstone. In him the whole structure is closely fitted together and grows into a temple holy in the Lord; in him you too are being built together into a dwelling place for God in the Spirit.[83]

[79] Ezek. 36:22–38.
[80] I Cor. 12:12.
[81] I Cor. 3:16–17.
[82] I Cor. 6:19–20.
[83] Eph. 2:20–22.

House of God, building, holy temple—these terms call to one's mind the temple of Jerusalem. But the temple St. Paul spoke of is not built of inert stones, nor is it built only of men of good will, but rather of those who are members of Christ through baptism.[84]

St. Peter also spoke of the community of the faithful as a temple. In his first letter, written about 62 A.D., he advised his readers:

> Draw near to him, a living stone rejected indeed by man but chosen and honored by God. Be you yourselves as living stones, built thereon into a spiritual house, a holy priesthood, to offer spiritual sacrifices acceptable to God through Jesus Christ. . . . You are a chosen race, a royal priesthood, a holy nation, a purchased people, . . . you who in time past were not a people, but are now the people of God.[85]

St. Paul spoke of "living stones." He chose the term while speaking at the time of a building which is constructed, and then of a body whose members are organically united. St. Peter's language is more descriptive. He spoke of the Christian people as a temple living unto the living God, and those living stones which enter the living building are grafted on to the living cornerstone which is Christ.[86]

The texts of St. Paul and St. Peter cited above were drawn up while the temple of Jerusalem was still in existence and when no one suspected that it would shortly be destroyed.

[84] Cf. Louvel, *loc. cit.*, pp. 15–16; L. Cerfaux, *The Church in the Theology of St. Paul* (New York: Herder and Herder, 1959), pp. 145–155; J. M. Boyer, "In aedificationem corporis Christi: Eph. 4:12," *Estudios Biblicos*, III (1944), 311–342; G. B. Ladner, "The Symbolism of the Biblical Cornerstone in the Medieval West," *Medieval Studies*, IV (1942), 43–60.

[85] I Pet. 2:4–10.

[86] Cf. Louvel, *loc. cit.*, p. 16; Cerfaux, "Regale Sacerdotium," *Revue des Sciences Philosophiques et Théologiques*, XXVIII (1939), 5–39.

Both Peter and Paul were loyal to the temple. Their letters do not contain even the slightest criticism of the temple. In comparing the Christian community to the temple of the Lord, they were not referring to the transitory character of the Jerusalem temple, but rather, in a long line of prophets, they announced simply that God would dwell with His people. And at the same time, under the inspiration of the Holy Spirit, they described the Church which had been born from the side of Christ on Calvary. They described this Church in concrete terms as a body, as a temple. It springs wholly from Christ; it is wholly animated by His Spirit; and through this Life it develops into a splendid structure which is the dwelling of God.

The Church is wholly of Christ, and "in Christ dwells the fulness of the Godhead bodily."[87] This is what St. Paul wrote to the Colossians, at the same time anticipating what St. John would later say in his gospel, "The Word was made flesh and dwelt among us."[88] The term which St. John used to express the dwelling of the Word among men (ἐσχήνωσεν ἐν ἡμῖν) recalls the sojourn in the desert and the dwelling of Yahweh with His people: the Word was made flesh and *He pitched his tent and camped among us.* The Godhead, however, is wholly in Christ, for He is at one and the same time God and man. When one looked upon His body, one saw both God and the dwelling-place of God.[89] Never before had God dwelt in this way among men—neither in the ark nor in the temple. In Christ, in His body, united to His body, men saw their God.

This was all in fulfillment of the prophecy of Nathan.

[87] Col. 2:9.
[88] John 1:14.
[89] I John 1:1–3.

David sought to construct a temple, but the Lord told him, "You want to build me a house; it is my God who will build you a house."[90] In Hebrew, the term building (*bait*) can designate either a dwelling or a dynasty. God promised David a house, i.e., a dynasty. When the descendants of David ruled no longer, they recalled the old prophecies and looked forward to the "Son of David" whom God had promised. When the angel Gabriel greeted Mary, he repeated word for word the promise God made to David.[91] With the coming of Christ, hope was fulfilled, for the Son of David was the Son of God. He was the true house of God, the temple of the Most High. The temple of Solomon did not contain God, but in Jesus resided the fulness of the divinity. Christ and Christ alone merited fully the title, "Temple of God." The Gospels record explicitly the testimony of Christ, "Destroy this temple and in three days I will build it up again."[92] Although neither the Jews nor the apostles understood Christ's words, St. John affirmed that "he spoke of the temple of his body."[93]

The true temple of God, then, is not a material edifice. It is the Body of Christ, the physical body which the apostles had seen and touched. It is the mystical Body of Christ which is the Church.[94]

The destruction of the temple at Jerusalem in 70 A.D. did not change or add anything to what the apostles had said. The veil of the temple had been rent after the death of Christ on the cross. The Christians knew for some time

[90] II Kings 7:11–16.
[91] Luke 1:32–35.
[92] John 2:19.
[93] John 2:21.
[94] Louvel, *loc. cit.*, pp. 17–18; Charles Journet, *L'Église de Verbe incarné* (Paris: Desclée & de Brouwer, 1952), II, 44–47; 303; 961–65.

before the destruction of the temple that the true temple of God is the Body of Christ. Nevertheless, the destruction of the temple at Jerusalem was a providential sign, foretold by Christ, which marked the end of an epoch. The temple at Jerusalem disappeared just as the Church was beginning to spread throughout the world. In other words, the material temple fell just as the spiritual temple started to rise. The symbol gave place to the reality.[95]

After Christ's ascension, it was necessary for the new Christians to assemble. According to the Acts of the Apostles, they gathered regularly to listen to the word of God and to share in the breaking of the bread. Christ had promised His disciples that he would be in the midst of those who gathered in His name.[96]

For the early Christians, the actual place of assembly was of little importance, for they knew that God dwelt not within the walls of a building but within the assembly of the faithful. Nevertheless it was convenient to have a place for meeting. The last supper was not celebrated in an arbitrary place but in an "upper room," carefully chosen so that it was large enough to accommodate the community of Christ and his apostles, and so situated that the ritual of the meal could be freely expressed. Motivated by a need for a place of assembling, the early Christians had designated places for meeting. For several centuries they used private dwellings, especially those of the wealthier Christians. These are the so-called "house-churches."[97] It seems that it was not until the fourth century that they built special

[95] Louvel, *loc. cit.*, pp. 18–19.

[96] Matt. 18:20.

[97] F. van der Meer and Christine Mohrmann, *Atlas of the Early Christian World* trans. and ed. Mary F. Hedlund and H. H. Rowley (London: Nelson, 1958), p. 29.

churches in which to worship.[98] Since the early Christians did not build designated places of cult for such a long time after the foundation of the Church, one may conclude that church buildings are not of divine institution but only of ecclesiastical origin. The church building came into existence because there was a need for the Christian community to assemble. The need of the Christians to assemble is of divine law, but the church building itself is only an ecclesiastical institution.[99]

CONCLUSIONS

From the foregoing discussion of the mystery of the church, four general conclusions may be deduced concerning the church edifice:

1. Church buildings of the New Law are not a replica of the temple at Jerusalem. Those who constructed the Jerusalem temple sought to construct a house of God, but the church buildings of the New Law are built primarily that the people of God may assemble and so themselves become the temple of God. It is only because the churches are the houses of the people of God and because the people of God are the living temple of God that one may say that churches are the house of God, for only Christ and the community of the faithful united to Him constitute the temple of God.[100]

2. Like the synagogues, church buildings had their origin in the people's need to assemble. Christian cult is similar

[98] *Ibid.*
[99] Louvel, *loc. cit.*, p. 20.
[100] *Ibid.*

to that of the synagogue in that it consists in listening to the word of God and in the chanting of psalms, but it is greater than that of the synagogues in that it centers around the Eucharist. The term "church" designates both the assembly of the faithful and the building where they gather, just as the term "synagogue" designates the community of the Jews and their place for cult.[101]

3. Since the church buildings are at the service of the Christian community which has need of them, they should be so designed that they will serve the community well. Church buildings are essentially functional: the size of the building should be determined by the size of the community which will meet there, and the plan of the building should be determined by the functions which ought to take place there.

The Christian community assembled in each particular church, however, must realize, under the penalty of failing in its Christian vocation, that it is but a part of the whole Christ, the Mystical Christ, the Church of Christ. The Church rests on Christ as the cornerstone, and it comprises not only the Christians on earth but also those in heaven and in purgatory. Although the church buildings are at the service of the local community, they must assist the assembled Christians to go beyond the building so that they may contemplate the fulness of the Church.

Granted that the church building itself has a pedagogic, a symbolic, and an artistic value, nevertheless, the true temple of God is made up of the Christians and not of the edifice. The community which is assembled and the action

[101] *Ibid.*, pp. 2–21.

which is celebrated are of greater importance than the place.

4. Even if the Blessed Sacrament is not reserved there, churches are of themselves holy places, because the grace of God is manifested there, the Church prays there, the Eucharist is celebrated there, and the Body of Christ is given there in nourishment. Churches are sacred because they are constructed to help man place himself in the presence of God and in communion with his brothers.[102]

[102] *Ibid.*, p. 22.

4

The Development of the Church Edifice

THE PRIMITIVE CHURCH

In the Acts of the Apostles, it is clear that after Pentecost the Apostles continued to frequent the temple, but for the celebration of the Eucharist they went to their own places of worship, which were usually the private houses of wealthy Christians.[1] They probably assembled in that part of the house, above the ground floor, which is commonly referred to in the New Testament as the "upper room." It was there that Christ gathered with his Apostles for the Last Supper;[2] it was there that the Apostles assembled before Pentecost;[3] and it was there that Paul celebrated the Eucharist at Troas.[4]

A number of the houses where the early Christians gathered are specifically mentioned in the Acts of the Apostles and in St. Paul's epistles. For example, mention is made of the house at Jerusalem belonging to Mary, the mother of Mark,[5] of the house of Tyrannus at Ephesus,[6]

[1] Cf. Acts 2:46.
[2] Luke 22:12.
[3] Acts 1:13.
[4] Acts 20:7.
[5] Acts 12:12.
[6] Acts 18:7.

of the house of Philemon at Colossae,[7] and of that of Aquila and Prisca on the Aventine in Rome.[8] There is also archeological evidence that the early Christians gathered in the house of Senator Pudens in Rome, in the area of the present church of St. Pudentiana.[9]

In referring to their places of worship, the early Christians usually associated the two concepts of church and house. For example, Tertullian (ca. 160-ca. 235) spoke of the *domus Dei*,[10] Hippolytus (235) spoke of the οἶκος τοῦ θεοῦ,[11] Clement of Alexandria (ca. 150-ca. 215) wrote of the Οἶκον κυριακόν,[12] and Eusebius (ca. 260-ca. 340) referred to the *domus ecclesiae*.[13] In the *Didascalia*, the church is described as "locus in parte domus ad orientem versa."[14] The apocryphal *Recognitiones Clementinae* narrates that a certain Theophylus, a rich magistrate of Antioch, converted his

[7] Col. 4:15.

[8] Rom. 16:3–5; I Cor. 15:19.

[9] Van der Meer and Mohrmann, *Atlas of the Early Christian World*, p. 29; Horace Marucchi, *Elements d'archéologie chrétienne*, III (Paris: Desclée, Lefebvre et Cie, 1900), p. 9; Mariano Armellini, *Le Chiese di Roma dal secolo IV al XIX* (Roma: Typografia Vaticana, 1891), p. 192.

[10] *De idolatria*, 7—*Migne, Patrologia Latina*, I, 745 (hereafter referred to as *PL*). One must not take the expression *domus Dei* to mean God's dwelling place, for at the time of Tertullian the Eucharist was not regularly reserved in church. The expression was used to refer to a true *house* dedicated to cult. Cf. Raymond Lemaire, *L'Origine de la Basilique Latine* (Paris: Vromant, 1911), p. 83. For a complete list of the third-century house-churches in Rome, cf. Van der Meer and Mohrmann, *op. cit.*, p. 29.

[11] *Commentarium in Daniel*, 1, 20—*Die grieschischen christlichen Schriftsteller der ersten drei Jahrhunderte*, I, 32 (hereafter referred to as *GCS*).

[12] *Stromata*, 3, 18—*Migne, Patrologia Graeca*, VIII, 1212 (hereafter referred to as *PG*).

[13] *Historia Ecclesiastica*, 7, 30; 8, 13; 9, 9—*GCS* IX (2), 714.

[14] *Didascalia et Constitutiones Apostolorum*, ed. F. X. Funk (Paderbornae, 1905), II, 57.

own house into a church: "domus suae ingentem basilicam ecclesiae nomine consecravit."[15]

The early Christians were accustomed to meet in homes. The ancient houses, especially those of the patricians, would have been quite easily converted into churches. Usually the house was made up of two main sections, the *atrium* and the *peristylium*. The *atrium*, normally given over to the servants and their work, was rectangular in shape, without columns, and covered only on its four sides. In the center was a pool, the *impluvium*, which served to collect the rain coming through the opening in the roof. Surrounding the *atrium* were the servants' quarters. At the far end of the court was a vestibule, the *tablinum*, which opened out into a second court, the *peristylium*. The latter was larger than the *atrium* and was flanked on all sides by a colonnade. This section of the house was the family dwelling. Leading from the *peristylium* were the private rooms of the members of the family, the study, and the dining room. At the far end, opposite the *tablinum*, was the *oecus* or *osedra*, the family sitting room.[16]

Little is known of the exact manner in which these houses were converted into churches, but the house-church uncovered at Dura-Europos gives evidence that, by the middle of the third century, the *domus ecclesiae* had de-

[15] *Recognitiones Clementinae*, 10, 71—*PG*, I, 1453. *Pseudo-Clementines* is the title of a comprehensive novel whose protagonist is Clement of Rome. The real author is unknown. *The Ten Books of Recognitions* are available in their entirety only in the Latin translation of Rufinus.—Johannes Quasten, *Patrology* (Westminster, Maryland: Newman, 1951), I, 61.

[16] Cf. Jerome Carcopino, *Daily Life in Ancient Rome*, ed. Henry T. trans. E. O. Lorimer (New Haven: Yale University Press, 1940), pp. 22–51; Mary Johnston, *Roman Life* (Chicago: Scott, Foresman and Company, 1957), pp. 73–81.

veloped certain simple but recognizable forms to satisfy the practical needs of the Christian community.[17] Opening off the central courtyard of the edifice at Dura-Europos, there was a large room for meetings, a baptistry for the initiation of new Christians, and another room in which to hold the *agape*; upstairs there was a room for the priest's lodging, and rooms which probably served for the instruction of catechumens. The church at Dura remained essentially a house, indistinguishable from the other houses uncovered in the town. Such a house-church definitely marks a stage in the evolution of church architecture, since in large parts of Syria the normal church of the fourth century was patterned after the type of house-church uncovered at Dura.[18]

As Lassus remarks, with reference to the fourth-century Syrian churches, the basilica did not constitute the church, but the church was constituted by a group of rooms, of which the basilica was just one. Other examples of these Syrian churches are the small church of Qirk Bizzé in Northern Syria and the larger Julianos Church at Umm al-Jema in Southern Syria, both dating from the early fourth century, and both the product of architectural traditions that go back well into the third century.[19]

[17] Noële-Maurice Denis-Boulet, "Le leçon des églises de l'antiquité," *La Maison-Dieu*, LXIII (1960), 24; Van der Meer and Mohrmann, *op. cit.*, pp. 71–72; Emile Mâle, *The Early Churches of Rome* (Chicago: Quadrangle Books Inc., 1960), pp. 42–43; P. Kirsch, "La 'domus ecclesiae' cristiana del III sec. a Dura Europos in Mesopotamia," *Studi dedicati alla memoria di Paolo Ubaldi* (Milano: Società editrice "Vita e Pensiero," 1937), pp. 73–82; and John Ward Perkins, "Constantine and the Origins of the Christian Basilica," *Papers of the British School at Rome*, XXII (1954), 79.

[18] J. Lassus, "Syrie," *Dictionnaire d'archéologie chrétienne et de liturgie*, XV(2) ed. Fernand Cabrol, Henri Leclercq, and Henri Marrou (Paris: Letouzey et Ané, 1951), XV(2) 1855 (hereafter referred to as *DACL*).

[19] *Ibid.*, figs. 11001, 11002.

What is known with certainty about the early Syrian churches can only be surmised for other parts of the early Christian world. In Rome, however, there is documentary evidence to show that a number of churches arose on the site of buildings which had belonged to distinguished members of the pre-Constantinian Christian community.[20] An exceptionally well-preserved example is the third-century house beside the present Roman church of San Martino ai Monti. The site was identified as the *titulus Equitii* by René Vielliard,[21] although in recent years serious doubt has been cast upon this identification.[22]

The ancient *titulus* functioned much the same as a parish church, and since the building next to San Martino shows no trace of any architectural alteration during the fourth century, it would seem to indicate, *a priori*, that the old house churches served the needs of the community for a long time before being replaced by specially constructed church buildings. Even if the house beside San Martino ai Monti is the original *titulus*, it is unlikely that the central hall, a rectangular room divided into two aisles by a row of brick piers, was built as a church,[23] or that it was used as a place of meeting by the persecuted Christians, since it opened directly into the street. The same objection applies to the room beneath the Roman church of San Clemente, which is often cited as a forerunner of the Christian basilica, despite the fact that it also opened on to a public street.

[20] A list of these early churches and the owners of the sites upon which they were built may be found in Van der Meer and Mohrmann, *op. cit.*, p. 29.

[21] René Vielliard, *Les origines du titre de Saint-Martin aux Monts à Rome* (Roma: Pontificio Instituto di Archeologia Cristiana, 1931).

[22] Perkins, *loc. cit.*, Appendix, p. 89.

[23] Cf. Vielliard, *op. cit.*, p. 26.

As at Dura-Europos, the Christians must have met in rooms withdrawn from the traffic of the street.[24]

As the Christian communities grew in size, they may have enlarged one of the rooms of an already existing house, as was the case at Dura, or they may have taken over the entire house of a private citizen, as the Christians of Antioch are said to have done by the third-century author of the *Recognitiones Clementinae*.[25]

The term *titulus*, followed by the name of the owner of the dwelling, indicated those houses in Rome where the early Christians assembled. The walls of a number of such houses which accommodated the primitive Church are still in existence. Besides the remnants discovered at San Martino ai Monti and San Clemente, there are also remains at Santi Giovanni e Paolo, Sant' Anastasia, Santa Cecilia, Santa Sabina, Santa Prisca, and San Crisogono. Although it was not always possible for the early Christians to own property in common because of their lack of legal security, it seems quite certain that these titular churches were corporately owned by the Christians even before the time of Constantine,[26] and that they were used exclusively to satisfy the religious needs of the Christian community.[27]

[24] Perkins, *loc. cit.*, p. 80.

[25] 10, 71—*PG* I, 1453.

[26] Cf. the decree of Aurelian concerning the controversy over the church property between the Christians at Antioch and Paul of Samosata, their deposed bishop: Eusebius, *Historica Ecclesiastica* 7, 30—*GCS* IX(2), 714, 4–7; and also the decree of the Emperor Gallienus to Dionysius of Alexandria: *ibid.* 7, 13—*GCS* IX(2), 666, 14–23.

[27] J. P. Kirsch, *Die römischen Titelkirchen im Altertum* (Paderborn: F. Schöningh, 1918), pp. 118–26; *Die Stationskirchen des Missale Romanum* (Freiburg im Breisgau, 1926), "Die christlichen Cultusgebäude in der vorkonstantinischen Zeit," *Festschrift zum*

On occasion the early Christians probably had to erect new buildings to serve as churches, and such buildings naturally would have included a large room for the celebration of the liturgy. As yet, however, there is no archeological evidence to indicate that this was the case previous to the victory of Constantine. On the basis of evidence available at the present time, one is probably justified in concluding that until the victory of Constantine the house-church was the only form of meeting place used by the Christians.[28]

Mention need only be made of the erroneous though rather common belief that the liturgy was regularly celebrated in the catacombs during the persecutions. As a matter of fact, the cemeteries exercised little or no influence on the development of the Christian church edifice, except insofar as they increased devotion to the martyrs. Since the catacombs were public places, well-known to the pagan authorities, they did not serve as hiding places for the Christians nor would they have been safe places for the celebration of Mass. The narrow passageways, the humid atmosphere, and the presence of decaying corpses would scarcely have recommended the catacombs as healthful places for an assembly. Whatever services were held there were of an exceptional character, such as a funeral or a memorial celebration. The anniversary service was regularly held in a small chapel, *cella memoriae* or *cella martyris*,

---

elfhundertjahrigen Jubiläum des deutschen Campo Santo in Rom, ed. Stephen Ehses (Freiburg: Herder, 1897), p. 19; Lemaire, *L'Origine de la Basilique*, p. 85; Denis–Boulet, "Le leçon des églises de l'antiquité," *La Maison-Dieu*, LXIII (1960), pp. 26–7; Hartman Grisar, *History of Rome and the Popes in the Middle Ages*, trans. Luigi Cappadelta (St. Louis: Herder, 1911), I, 118; 193–94.

[28] Perkins, *loc. cit.*, pp. 80–81.

built directly above the place where the martyr was buried. These chapels were usually so small that only the celebrant and the ministers could enter, while the rest of the faithful remained in the corridor.[29]

THE LATIN BASILICA

With Constantine's victory over Maxentius in 312 and the consequent triumph of the Church over paganism, the number of Christians rapidly increased, thus necessitating larger buildings for worship.[30] The architectural style of these churches is regularly called the Latin basilica. For the early Romans, the term basilica signified a large hall or a grand public or private edifice, but by the fourth and fifth centuries writers were accustomed to reserve the term for churches.[31]

The characteristics of the Latin basilica can easily be outlined from a study of the churches constructed especially during the fourth and fifth centuries. Shortly after he had issued the edict of Milan, Constantine had an impressive basilica erected over what had once been a military en-

[29] Ludwig Hertling and Engelbert Kirschbaum, *The Roman Catacombs and Their Martyrs*, trans. M. Joseph Costelloe (Milwaukee: Bruce Publishing Co., 1956), pp. 132–33; H. Leclercq, "Cella," *DACL* II, 2885.

[30] Eusebius, *Historia Ecclesiastica*, 10, 2—*GCS* IX(2), 861.

[31] For example, in a letter to Macarius of Jerusalem, Constantine spoke of a church as a basilica: Eusebius, *Vita Constantini* 3, 31—*GCS* I, 8, and the Pilgrim from Bordeaux called the church of the Holy Sepulchre at Jerusalem a basilica: "Ibidem modo jussu Constantini imperatoris basilica facta est, id est dominicum."—*Iterarium Burdigalense*, ed. P. Geyer, *Corpus Scriptorum Ecclesiasticorum Latinorum* (Lipsiae: G. Freytag, 1898), XXXIX, 23 (hereafter cited *CSEL*).

campment near the ancient palace of the Lateran family in Rome. The basilica, originally called the Basilica of the Savior but renamed the Basilica of St. John Lateran by Pope Lucius II in the twelfth century, was the first cathedral church of all Christendom. The structure was thoroughly modified by Innocent X, Pius IX, and Leo XIII.[32]

To show his devotion to St. Peter, Constantine had the first martyr's shrine built over the apostle's tomb in the Vatican cemetery, but in the sixteenth and seventeenth centuries the original structure was completely destroyed and replaced in another style.[33] By 345, the Basilica of the Savior and that of St. Peter, both erected under Constantine's direction, had set the architectural style for years to come. Although Constantine had constructed a small church in honor of St. Paul on the Ostian Way, an impressive structure was erected under Valentinianus II (386), which remained standing until 1823, when it was destroyed by fire. The present basilica is a generally faithful reproduction of the form and dimensions of the original.[34]

The Basilica of St. Mary on the Esquiline was originally constructed under Pope Liberius (357–366) and restored by Sixtus III (432–440). The present edifice more or less preserves the original form, except for the suppression of the atrium.[35] Other Roman churches which represent the basilica style are those of Santa Maria in Cosmedin, Santa Sabina, San Clemente, San Lorenzo in Campo Verano, Santa Cecilia, S. Pudentiana, S. Marco, S. Crisogono,

[32] Van der Meer and Mohrmann, *op. cit.*, pp. 60–62.
[33] *Ibid.*, p. 62.
[34] *Ibid.*, pp. 75–76.
[35] *Ibid.*, p. 85.

S. Anastasia, SS. Giovanni e Paolo, and SS. Nereo ed Achilleo.[36]

The basilica introduced no new architectural elements, since its form was determined by the functional synthesis of the five basic requirements of Christian worship: (1) a large assembly room destined to house the entire community, hierarchically arranged about an axis; (2) the cathedra of the presiding bishop; (3) the ambo for the reading of the Holy Scriptures; from here too the singing of the psalms was conducted; (4) the baptismal font which, in view of the baptismal ritual, stood outside the assembly room, and (5) the table for the Eucharist.

The assembly room and the ambo were taken over from the synagogue. The baptistry and the cathedra were also found in the synagogues; the latter rested beside the Torah shrine. The table for the Eucharist, however, distinguishes the Christian church from the synagogue and also from the pagan temples.

By the beginning of the fifth century, the plan of the basilica was uniform in all countries of the Roman Empire; this uniform type, however, came into existence not immediately after the edict of Milan, but rather after an experimental period. There are scarcely any archeological traces of the earliest plans after 313, but excavations in Syria and Africa have brought to light traces of early dispositions of the basilica. There are noticeable variations. For example, in Syria the altar is in the apse, whereas the cathedra and

[36] For a complete list of early Latin basilicas of various centuries, cf. H. Leclercq, *Manuel d'archéologie chrétienne* (Paris: Letouzey et Ané, 1907), I, 434–493; Carl Kaufmann, *Manuale di archeologia cristiana*, trans. Ettore Roccabruna (Roma: F. Pustet, 1908), pp. 63–93.

the ambo are often in the nave. In Africa, the altar seems to have regularly stood in the middle of the nave. In Rome, it was placed beneath the triumphal arch.[37]

The original, simple arrangement of the basilica was later modified as a result of the complications introduced by the increasing intricacy of the liturgy. The dispositions were modified first of all in those basilicas which contained a *memoria*. In the beginning, the *memoria* stood apart from the basilica itself, but by the time the Basilica of St. Peter was erected the *memoria* was incorporated into the church edifice itself. For centuries *memoriae* and *martyria* were erected along the side walls of the basilica or at the side of the apse, and these were surrounded in turn by the ordinary mausolea of rich and pious citizens. This custom prevailed in the West up until the Carolingian period. Another complication arose from the combination of the martyr's tomb and the altar. This was an obvious development in the cemetery *memoria*, but it became general when the relics of the martyrs were transferred from the cemeteries and lodged within the churches themselves. A third complication developed from the presence of permanent seats for the increasing number of *continentes* or monks who daily sang the psalms in the basilica.[38]

An analysis of the early basilicas indicates that in general they comprised three principal elements: the atrium, the nave, and the chancel. The *atrium* was a rectangular courtyard in front of the basilica. Open to the exterior through a single door, it was surrounded on all sides by a

[37] Pasquale Testini, *Archeologia Cristiana* (Roma: Desclée, 1958), pp. 603–20; Van der Meer and Mohrmann, *op. cit.*, p. 135.
[38] Van der Meer and Mohrmann, *loc. cit.*

colonnade, and in the center there was a fountain used for ritual ablutions. The section of the colonnade nearest the façade of the basilica was called the narthex, and corresponded to the vestibule in the modern church.

The *nave* constituted the basilica proper. It was a vast rectangular space, about twice as long as it was wide, usually divided into three sections by two rows of parallel columns. The middle section was normally raised above the other two and had windows opening to the outside. In the middle of the nave, immediately in front of the chancel, was a fenced-off area for the *schola cantorum*. An ambo stood outside the balustrade to hold the books for the reading of the Scripture and the singing of the Psalms.[39]

The *chancel*, located at the far end of the nave, opposite the atrium, was slightly elevated above the rest of the basilica floor. It terminated in a semi-circular apse, at the very back of which stood the bishop's throne, with simple stone benches for the clergy on either side. Since the bishop's throne stood against the back wall of the basilica, the altar, a simple stone table resting under a ciborium supported by four columns, was placed between the throne and the people. This was most probably the arrangement of the altar also in the house-churches. Ordinarily the faithful did not occupy the central part of the nave, but rather they assembled on the two sides of the *schola cantorum*, the men on the right and the women on the left. Gathered around the altar, they shared intimately in the action of the liturgy which the bishop celebrated facing his people.

The principal reason why the altar faced the people in the Latin basilica was the hierarchical arrangement of the

[39] *Ibid.*

church. Since the bishop's throne was the center of activity, it stood facing all the people. When the bishop approached the altar, he naturally stood at the side closest to his throne. Both at the altar and at the throne, he played his role as the mediator between God and the people of God.

Some scholars propose the veneration of the martyrs' relics placed within or beneath the altar and the principle of orientation as reasons for the altar facing the people.[40] It is an unconvincing argument that the altar was placed between the bishop's throne and the people in order that the people might more easily approach the altar to venerate the relics of the martyrs or because of the presence of a confession, or sunken pit, immediately in front of the altar. Confessions were not built in front of the altar until the sixteenth century.[41] Although there were confessions in existence before this time, they regularly took the form of crypts built behind the altar or beneath the sanctuary floor. Since the confessions of the latter type date only from the sixth century, the arrangement of the altar facing the people antedates their construction. Consequently the confession or the veneration of the martyrs' relics could not have been the determining factors in the celebration of Mass facing the people.[42]

Nor did the principle of orientation, that is, of facing

[40] Cf. Peter Anson, "Mass Facing the People," *Liturgical Arts*, XXIV (1955), 3; Joseph A. Jungmann, *The Mass of the Roman Rite*, trans. Francis A. Brunner (New York: Benziger Brothers, 1951), I, 255–56; Joseph Braun, *Der christliche Altar in seiner geschichtlichen Entwicklung* (München: Karl Widmann, 1924), I, 412–13.

[41] Felice Grossi Gondi, *I Monumenti Cristiani* (Roma: Università Gregoriana, 1923), II, 431.

[42] *Ibid.*, p. 429; John Miller, *Fundamentals of the Liturgy*, p. 84.

the east while at prayer, have any effect on the position of the altar in the Latin basilica. Although the orientation of churches was the rule in the East,[43] the practice seems to have had little or no effect on the Latin liturgy, at least in Rome. In fact, Leo I was strongly opposed to the practice of orientation as a remnant of paganism.[44] Only in the Oriental and Gallican rites did the principle of orientation find general acceptance, although the concept of orientation was strong in the West in later periods.[45] Certainly the practice had nothing to do with the altar facing the people in the Latin basilica. When the principle of orientation was rightly carried out, the apse was at the east end of the church and the façade at the west end.[46] Consequently, the normal position of the priest in oriented churches where the principle of facing the East for prayer was observed was with his back to the people.[47] The only plausible reason for the altar facing the people in the Latin basilica was the hierarchical arrangement of the church.

If one is to have even an elementary understanding of the development of the Christian church, one must understand something of the origins of the Latin basilica. There are few archeological problems that have been so much debated with so few definite conclusions as the origin of the Chris-

[43] Cf. *Didascalia,* II, 57; *Constitutiones Apostolorum,* II, canon 47.

[44] Cf. Franz J. Dölger, *Sol Salutis* (Münster in Westfalia: Verlag der Aschendorffschen Verlagsbuchhandlung, 1925), pp. 3–5.

[45] Johannes Quasten, *Monumenta eucharistica et liturgica vetustissima,* Florilegium Patristicum, VII (Bonn: Peter Hanstein, 1935), 35, note 1.

[46] *Didascalia,* II, 57, 2–5; Quasten, *op. cit.*

[47] Mario Righetti, *Manuale di Storia Liturgica* (Milan: Ancora, 1950), I, 355; Miller, *op. cit.,* p. 84.

tian basilica. Ever since the celebrated Florentine architect of the fifteenth century, Leon Battista Alberti (1404–1472), noted the similarity of architectural form and name between the early Christian basilicas and the forum basilicas of imperial Rome,[48] archeologists have attempted to determine the origins of the Christian basilica.

The proposed theories fall more or less into three classes. First, there are those who maintain that the Christian basilica was derived from the Roman forensic basilicas.[49] Secondly, there are those who have held that the Christian basilica had its origins in the classic Greco-Roman house.[50] A third theory, the most widespread among archeologists today, maintains that the Christian basilica was a combination of various elements derived from several sources.[51] Since the first two theories have been abandoned by the archeologists, the tenets of the third theory alone will be summarized here.

Before it was adopted by the Christians, the basilica had existed as an architectural form for five centuries. By the early second century, the basilica tradition had been estab-

[48] Leon Battista Alberti, *De re aedificatoria* (Florence, 1485).

[49] Cf. Adolfo Venturi, *Storia dell'arte italiana* (Milan, 1901), I, 126; Gondi, *op. cit.*, pp. 416–17; Perkins, *loc. cit.*, XXII (1954), 69.

[50] Cf. Victor Schultze, *Archeologie der altchristlichen Kunst* (München: C. H. Beck, 1895), p. 37; Grisar, *History of Rome and the Popes in the Middle Ages*, II, 88; Georg Gottfried Dehio, "Die Genesis der christlichen Basilika," *Sitzungsberichte der philosophisch-philologischen und historischen Classe der k. b. Akademie der Wissenschaften zu München* (München: Akademische Buchdruckerei von F. Straub, 1882), pp. 301–41.

[51] Testini, *Archeologia Cristiana*, pp. 603–605; Wilhelm Lübke Semran, *Die Kunst des Mittelalters, Grundriss der Kunstgeschichte* (Esslingen: P. Neff, 1904), II, 67; Louis Brehier, *Les basiliques chrétiennes* (Paris: Bloud et Cie, 1905), pp. 5, 9, 15; H. Leclercq, "Basilique," *DACL*, II, 536.

lished in Rome and central Italy through the construction of the great public halls. The term basilica had served to designate markets, court houses, covered promenades, and meeting halls, but little by little it was reserved to those buildings which had a more or less definite form.[52]

The problem that confronted the Christians after the conversion of Constantine was the creation of an architecture that would serve the requirements of a cult which had suddenly become officially recognized by the state. Although the Church was ready to adopt and adapt the elements of pagan art and ritual which it found serviceable, the traditional pagan temple was unsuited to the needs of the Christian community.[53]

Although the early Christian basilica regularly consisted of a "more or less monumental hall with two (occasionally four) longitudinal colonnades, clerestory lighting, and an apse at the far end of the central nave,"[54] this norm admitted of many variations. For example, there were basilicas with no apses or with two apses; there were basilicas without clerestories; and there were small churches which were often known as basilicas, even though they consisted only of a simple hall without any internal subdivisions. The pious woman who went on pilgrimage to the Holy Land referred to the circular structure over the Holy Sepulchre as *basilica Anastasis.*[55] Constantine himself, in a letter written to Bishop Macarius of Jerusalem, referred to the church

[52] For an ancient Roman architect's conception of a basilica, cf. Vitruvius, *De architectura,* I, 1–4; VI, 3–9.

[53] Perkins, *loc. cit.,* p. 77.

[54] *Loc. cit.*

[55] *Peregrinatio Aetheriae,* ed. P. Geyer, *CSEL,* XXXIX, 48, 1.

just east of the site of the Holy Sepulchre as a basilica,[56] and the Pilgrim from Bordeaux a few years later also called the same church a basilica.[57]

The development of the Church during Constantine's reign was rooted in already existing Christian practices. Nevertheless, at the present stage of archeological investigation, there is nothing to show that the Christian Church before the time of Constantine had evolved a monumental architecture that might have served as a model for the Constantinian or post-Constantinian basilica. The Church of St. John Lateran, almost certainly the first church to be built under the emperor's patronage, most probably was built as a basilica of standard early Christian style. Three of Constantine's later foundations—the churches of the Holy Sepulchre in Jerusalem, the Nativity in Jerusalem, and St. Peter in Rome—were also built to a common pattern, developed about a large central basilica hall.[58]

Although it is possible that the basic design of the basilica was an artificial, eclectic creation, this is improbable. Throughout all his reforms, Constantine wove a thread of conservatism. Whenever possible, he sought to breathe new life into old forms rather than create new ones; consequently, it would have been more in keeping with his basic attitude, particularly in the early years of his reign, had he taken over an already-existing architectural style for use in his churches. Both for its ceremonial and for the furnishings required for the liturgy, the early Christians borrowed heavily from contemporary imperial practice. Thus it would

[56] Eusebius, *Vita Const.*, III, 29–32—GCS I, 91–93.
[57] *Iterarium Burdigalense—CSEL*, XXXIX, 23.
[58] Perkins, *loc. cit.*, p. 85.

have been quite natural that the architectural style embodied in the Constantinian churches should have been derived from the ceremonial halls of the contemporary courts. One must remember that the secular audience halls themselves played an important role in the life of the early Church. In 325, the ordinary sessions of the Council of Nicaea were held in the largest church in Nicaea, but the final session was held in the grand central hall of the palace.[59]

The audience halls of the contemporary courts may have been the immediate models for Constantine's great basilicas and those which were built after him, although this assumption does not preclude the possibility that other types of pagan basilicas may have had an influence in the development of the early Christian church.[60]

Whatever may have been their origin, it is certain that, when the Christian basilicas appeared in the fourth century, they appeared as well-planned, functional churches. Whether they were intended as meeting places for the Christian communities or as memorial chapels in honor of the places in Christ's life, as was the case in the Holy Land, the Christian basilicas were always great forums representing the City of God laid out in its hierarchical structure. In these churches, the Christian community assembled in orderly fashion under the leadership of the bishop and his priests, all divinely commissioned mediators between God and men. The bishop presided together with his priests, and through them the whole community worshipped God and functioned as a holy people.[61]

[59] Eusebius, *Vita Constantini* 3, 10—*GCS* I, 8.
[60] Perkins, *loc. cit.*, pp. 87–88.
[61] Wagner, "Liturgical Art and the Care of Souls," *op. cit.*, pp. 87–88.

THE ROMANESQUE PERIOD

The Romanesque style of architecture developed in Italy and western Europe between the decline of early Christian art and the development of Gothic. It was in vogue from the eighth until the thirteenth centuries, although the most important edifices in the style were constructed in the eleventh and twelfth centuries. By the end of the eighth century, the western world was ready for a renewal of many of the things which antiquity had cherished. Although civil strife was still rampant at this time, great men like Charlemagne stood as poles around which the forces of order rallied. Through his strong ecclesiastical and political links with Rome, Charlemagne synthesized Germanic and Roman culture, but it was a synthesis which was also affected by persistent Byzantine and Oriental influences which found their way into the West through the trade centers of Marseilles, Ravenna, and Venice.[62] These various elements are reflected in the architecture which is called Romanesque.

The churches which were built during the Carolingian period were intended to serve relatively small groups of people, since the towns were few and the countryside was sparsely populated. Societal conditions were such that the solutions posed for architectural problems in barbarian times were applicable to the building of Carolingian churches. The impulse for a novel architecture came mostly from the monasteries, some of which served the needs of a thousand people or more. Monasticism itself had come into the Carolingian period with the strong Roman imprint of

[62] Kenneth J. Conant, *Carolingian and Romanesque Architecture* (Baltimore: Penguin Books, 1959), pp. 1–2.

St. Benedict. As the great religious houses developed into imposing financial, territorial and educational institutions, new architectural problems developed. The solutions which the monks offered in building their churches laid the foundations for the church architecture of the whole period.[63]

In its basic plan, the Romanesque church was T-shaped. To enlarge the capacity of the building, the chancel was lengthened and transepts, generally of the same breadth as the nave, were added. In later Romanesque churches, these transepts were of structural necessity, for they carried the strain of the great arches east and west of the crossing. The barbarian invasions which razed towns and churches induced architects to construct fire-proof churches. Consequently the timber roofs which appeared in the basilicas were replaced by vaulted stone ceilings which were supported by thick walls often reinforced by internal flying buttresses. The chancel was usually elevated above the level of the nave and rested on piers above a vaulted crypt. This marked division between the chancel and the nave had been foreshadowed by the fourth canon of the II Council of Tours in 567 which forbade laymen to stand among the clergy during the liturgy, and which reserved the chancel for the clergy.[64]

In some of the later Romanesque churches, an aisle, connecting the aisles of the nave, extended completely around the sanctuary, thus forming an ambulatory. With this plan, the layman could visit the votive shrines which were often

[63] *Ibid.*, pp. 3–4; Ernst Short, *A History of Religious Architecture* (3rd ed. rev.; New York: W. W. Norton and Company, Inc., n.d.), p. 145.

[64] Mansi, IX, 793.

built behind the chancel. Towers were frequently erected at the east and west ends of the church and above the meeting place of the nave and transept. Their introduction marked the beginning of the vertical characteristic so prominent in later Romanesque and Gothic churches. Since the church was the largest and most substantial building in the community, the people regularly fled there in time of invasion. The towers were erected mainly for fortification purposes. They also served to house the church bells and, when pierced with windows, they admitted light into the otherwise dark church interiors. Because of the thick walls, there were few windows in the Romanesque churches, and these were regularly quite small.[65]

It is important to realize that many of the characteristics of Romanesque were affected by the shape which the liturgy took from the eighth to the thirteenth centuries. About the middle of the eighth century, Pepin decreed the general acceptance of the Roman liturgy throughout his empire. Transported to Franco-German soil, the Roman liturgy acquired a new home which influenced its growth and development for the next few centuries.[66]

When the Roman liturgy was introduced into Franco-German territory, it entered an area where only a small fraction of the population understood the language of the liturgy, and these were predominantly clerics. Consequently, in the Carolingian empire the liturgy was a clerical

[65] Conant, *op. cit.*, pp. 9–10.

[66] Jungmann, *The Mass of the Roman Rite*, I, 74–75; Theodor Klauser, "Die liturgischen Austauschbeziehungen zwischen der römischen und der fränkischdeutschen Kirche vom achten bis zum elften Jahrhundert," *Historisches Jahrbuch im Auftrage der Görres-Gesellschaft*, LIII (1933), 170.

reserve. A *disciplina arcana* or discipline of the secret developed in which holy things were concealed, not from the heathens, for there were none, but from the Christians themselves.[67]

Furthermore the Church was no longer conceived of as the communion of the redeemed people of God united with the glorious Christ in the one Mystical Body. In France and Spain the fight against Arianism had accentuated Christ's divinity and overshadowed his role as mediator and high priest. As a result, there was greater awareness of the external organization of the Church as a hierarchical structure of clerics and laymen. Within this structure the social position and prestige of the clergy, who constituted the governing class in society and who were almost alone in possessing a higher education, estranged them and lifted them above the laymen.

During the Romanesque period, a great change also took place in the concept of the Eucharist. In the earlier period the emphasis had been placed on the Mass as a prayer of thanks offered by the people of God. Later, strongly influenced by the teaching of St. Isidore of Seville,[68] the Church emphasized the significance of the Eucharist as the great gift which God grants His creatures and which descends upon them at the consecration of the Mass. The canon of the Mass became veiled in mystery since the priest recited it in a low quiet voice. The priest alone was deemed worthy to enter the holy of holies, while the people prayed outside, as they did when Zachary burned incense in the temple. The line of separation between clerics and lay-

[67] Jungmann, *op. cit.*, I, 81.
[68] Isidore of Seville, *Etymologiae* 10, 38—*PL*, LXXXII, 255b.

men, between altar and people, a separation which was always considered essential to the Church's constitution, was now made into a line of demarcation and a wall of division.[69]

As a result of these theological attitudes, the altar was moved to the rear wall of the apse, seemingly as far away from the people as possible. In the cathedral churches, this necessitated transferring the bishop's throne from the rear wall to a place at the side of the altar.[70] The choir-stalls of the assistant clerics, which formed a half-circle around the altar in the Christian basilica, were set in rows facing one another in front of the altar. This opened the way for the development of the rood-gallery or choir, which became in the late Romanesque period the rood screen. In almost all cathedral, collegiate, and monastic churches, the rood screen consisted of a massive wall located between the chancel and the nave and surmounted by a cross (rood) or the figures from Calvary. Although historians are not agreed on the origin of the screen, it is certain that it did not help to bring the liturgy close to the people.[71] The narrow doors in the wall permitted only a small part of the faithful to peer into the sanctuary. Although the people were not excluded from the so-called "private" Masses, which were offered silently and without ceremony on many side altars close to the congregation, they were excluded from the solemn celebration of the liturgy in the principal churches.

[69] Jungmann, *op. cit.*, I, 83; *Pastoral Liturgy* (New York: Herder and Herder, 1961), pp. 70–71.

[70] This arrangement is clearly demonstrated by a comparison of *Ordo Romanus*, II, n. 1, 5 (*PL*, LXXVIII, 969a, 970c) and *Primus Ordo Romanus*, n. 4, 8 (*PL*, LXXVIII, 939b, 942a). The later edition reads: "pergit ad dexteram altaris ad sedem suam."

[71] Jungmann, *The Mass of the Roman Rite*, I, 88.

They could no longer see, but only hear what was going on at the altar.[72]

Since the faithful could not see what was going on at the altar, they were entertained by elaborate music. In the royal cathedrals of France, polyphonic song accompanied with a variety of musical instruments was admitted into the Church's worship for the first time. This led eventually to the development of a splendid court art within the church itself.[73]

In many areas, the simple faithful became accustomed to leave the church after the elevation of the Mass. This rite was usually so arranged that the people could view the host despite the rood screen. To some extent, such an abuse is understandable if one recalls that, apart from the entrance procession and the recession of the clergy, the only ceremony in the Mass visible to the people was the elevation.[74]

A final modification during the Romanesque period, the introduction of the communion rail, was effected eventually by the change from the use of leavened to the use of unleavened bread. The increased reverence for the Blessed Sacrament brought about the use of small wafers, which could be easily distributed without crumbs. The particles were no longer handed to the communicants, but were placed directly upon the tongue. Late in the Romanesque period, the faithful began to receive holy Communion while kneeling. Thus a low communion rail, distinct from the traditional barrier between the nave and the chancel, was introduced. It was a feature totally unknown to the ancient Church.[75]

[72] Wagner, *loc. cit.*, p. 64.
[73] *Ibid.*
[74] *Ibid.*
[75] Jungmann, *op. cit.*, I, 85.

As examples of early Romanesque architecture, one might cite Charlemagne's Chapel at Aachen (796–804), the Church of Germigny-les-Prés (806) in France, the remains at Lorsch (774) in Germany, and the complex monastery of St. Gall (ninth century) in Switzerland. Examples taken from the eleventh and twelfth centuries include St. Sernin in Toulouse, Notre Dame la Grande in Poitiers, St. Ambrose in Milan, the Cathedral of Modena, the Cathedral of Parma, San Miniata in Florence, the Cathedral and Baptistry at Pisa, the Abbey Church of Maria Laach, the Cathedral of Speyer, and the Cathedral of Mainz.

THE GOTHIC PERIOD

The evolution of Romanesque architecture into Gothic occurred almost insensibly. The skeletal lines of the churches gradually shed the weight of their heavy walls, so that the stresses became more and more apparent. The strong thrust of the pointed arches was carried away by flying buttresses, thus relieving the weight of the walls which then could be pierced with larger windows. Born in the north of France in the twelfth century, Gothic architecture reached its apogee in the thirteenth and fourteenth centuries, and began its decline in the fifteenth century when it was scorned by the Renaissance.[76]

There is no doubt that the Gothic church was a tremendous engineering feat; in fact, for its age, it seems almost miraculous. The essential characteristics of Gothic churches are the use of flying buttresses, pointed arches,

[76] Righetti, *Storia Liturgica*, I, 368; Miller, *Fundamentals of the Liturgy*, p. 87.

and ribs. The thrust of the vaulted ceiling of these churches was both downward by reason of gravity, and outward, by reason of the action of the wedge-shaped stones in the arches. The resulting pressure was counteracted and transmitted to the ground by flying buttresses, which were weighted down by the pinnacles. The pointed arch directed the thrust downward rather than outward, so that the weight of the pinnacles prevented the buttresses from overturning. Actually the network of ribs supported the panels of the vaults. The arched ribs gathered the thrust from above, carried it along to the angles of the vaults, and from there passed it on to the flying buttresses.

With the stresses and strains so well disposed of, heavy walls were no longer necessary for support. They were replaced by thin stone panels, which were pierced with large delicately-designed windows. In many of the Gothic churches the walls were constructed mostly of glass, interrupted occasionally by ribs and buttresses. Furthermore, great height and slenderness were characteristics of Gothic structures.[77]

Although the architecture of the church was greatly refined during the Gothic period, the interior arrangement of the edifice was scarcely different from what it was in the Romanesque era. The bishop and his priests no longer presided over the assembled holy people. Seated at the side of the altar, the clergy demonstrated that they considered themselves only secondarily as heads of the community, but primarily as ministers of the altar. What they performed

[77] Righetti, *op. cit.*, I, 368–70; Miller, *op. cit.*, p. 87–88; L. Lefrançois-Pillion, *Abbayes et Cathédrales* (Paris: Librairie Arthème Fayard, 1956), pp. 57–67.

was a sacred office. In fact, the term *officium* was one of the principal names for the Mass.[78]

The old principle that there be but one altar in a church was forgotten during the Middle Ages. Additional altars were constructed to accommodate the priests who offered Mass privately; they were also built in honor of relics, which were often one of the most cherished possessions of medieval churches. With the erection of memorial chapels or chantries, altars were constructed so that Masses could be offered in fulfillment of pious foundations. Toward the end of the Middle Ages, special chapels, each with its own altar, were founded by various kinds of guilds and confraternities.[79]

The concept of the Gothic church might well be summed up in the idea of God's castle, where Christ reigned as a high and noble Lord. Although far away, God was still the object of man's inquisitiveness and contemplation. Bearing these things in mind, one comes to understand, then, why active participation in the liturgy by the faithful was practiced in an ever diminishing degree during the Middle Ages. It is clear, also, why popular devotions developed to such a degree apart from the official worship of the Church. Finally, it becomes evident why the clergy, who were in practice merely performers of the liturgy, simply shut themselves off from the people.[80]

[78] Wagner, *loc. cit.*, p. 63.

[79] C. Cornelius Bouman, "History of the Architectural Setting of the Interior of the Church," *Participation in the Mass: Twentieth North American Liturgical Week* (Washington, D.C.: The Liturgical Conference, 1960), p. 93.

[80] Henze, *Contemporary Church Art*, p. 38; Wagner, *loc. cit.*, p. 64.

The cathedrals in Paris, Chartres, Amiens, Rheims, Cologne, Ulm, Toledo, Burgos, Strasbourg, Lincoln, Ely, Salisbury, Bristol, and Gloucester are among the finest examples of structures built in the Gothic style.

THE RENAISSANCE AND BAROQUE PERIODS

The historical events and influences that led to the close of the Middle Ages and to the development of the Renaissance and Baroque periods are so well known that they need only be briefly outlined here.

In the fourteenth century, there were the first signs of the breakdown of the medieval order. It is not surprising that Italy was the birthplace of the Renaissance, for the Gothic spirit had never really been firmly rooted there. Motivated by new discoveries in science and by the exploration of America, the spirit of inquiry, criticism, and humanism rapidly developed. The theocentric view of the universe and the awe of the transcendent were replaced with a philosophy in which man rather than God became the focal point of the universe. The authority of the individual began to rival that of the Church. In art, there was an increasing mingling of Christian traditions and pagan myths. Asceticism more or less vanished, and the beauty and care of the human body became more important than the welfare of the soul. Even the papal court assumed the new spirit and became a center of humanism.[81]

Although the outward form and decoration of churches

[81] John Bourke, *Baroque Churches of Central Europe* (London: Faber and Faber, 1958), pp. 28–29.

in the Renaissance were classical, nevertheless, Gothic methods of construction were almost always used. Ancient Roman columns, cornices, and arches found their way into the framework of the church building, but the interior of the building was not too different from what it had been in the Gothic era.[82] With the spread of the Mendicant Orders throughout Europe in the late Middle Ages, the pulpit was erected in the nave of the church, for one of the principal missions of these Orders was the instruction of the masses. The friars sang the office and the conventual Mass just as the canons and monks had done, but they were opposed to the rood screen which obstructed the view of the main altar and of the liturgy which took place there. Consequently, toward the end of the Middle Ages the rood screens were torn down and removed.[83]

Most of the devotional additions which were made to the interior of the church in the form of shrines date from the fifteenth century. Especially in Germany, the churches were crowded with statues which conveyed the impression that Catholicism was predominantly a religion of tears and blood. The realistic representations of Christ on the cross, of the scourging, and the descent from Calvary, as well as the figures which would later become the stations of the cross, were all introduced at this time.[84]

The sixteenth century saw the culmination of the Renaissance, but it also saw the assertion of older traditions and allegiances. With the Protestant Reformation, the spirit of independent thought that had been alive in art and

[82] Miller, *op. cit.*, p. 89.
[83] Bouman, *loc. cit.*, p. 93; Wagner, *loc. cit.*, p. 65.
[84] Bouman, *loc. cit.*

letters was carried over to religion and theology. An attempt was made on the part of the Church to counteract the Reformation by a powerful assertion of its own authority in the second half of the sixteenth century. There were two principal forces behind the Counter Reformation. The first came from the personality of St. Ignatius Loyola, who founded the Jesuits in 1543, and the second was the decisive influence of the Council of Trent (1545–1563).

The primary aim of the Council of Trent was the re-establishment of all Christians under the pope. The post-Tridentine pastoral theology preoccupied itself especially with stressing the real presence of Christ in the Eucharist, and with preaching this truth by means of the architectural arrangement of the church interior.[85] In fact there seems to be little doubt that the Counter-Reformation was the most influential factor in the development of Baroque architecture.[86]

In expressing the spirit of the Counter-Reformation, Baroque was animated by man's vivid sense of his dependence on God, who revealed himself to man in Christ. Consequently, the church took the form of God's salon, where Christ as the heavenly king awaited the homage of his subjects. Public worship during this period was above all festival; in this regard worship simply reflected the culture of the period which aimed at placing all possible sensuous creation at the service of lofty ideals. However, if festivity was the main characteristic of the worship, it was a festivity in which the majority of the people did not take part; they merely gazed and listened. On the whole, worship was car-

[85] Wagner, *loc. cit.*, p. 65.
[86] Bourke, *op. cit.*, p. 31.

ried out according to the old prescribed liturgical books, but the festive character of the period was expressed not so much in the celebration of Mass as in the solemn processions which were held in conjunction with the feasts of Holy Thursday and Corpus Christi and in other Eucharistic devotions. On these occasions, however, the Eucharist was not whorshipped in its fulness as the sacrament and the sacrifice of thanksgiving but simply as the Body of Christ.[87]

In the late Middle Ages, the tabernacle was often placed on the main altar, but during the Baroque period much more emphasis was placed on it. It took a larger form and was surmounted by an elaborate exposition throne. As a result the altar itself was dwarfed beneath an elegantly sculptured or painted background. The monstrance, which regularly took the form of a sun with golden rays beaming forth on every side, became the principal item among the liturgical vessels, and the altar, no longer the altar of sacrifice or the table of the Eucharistic meal, became a pedestal to support the throne of the Real Presence.[88]

Because of the emphasis placed on Eucharistic devotion during the Baroque period, veneration of the saints lost the importance which it had in the religious lives of medieval Christians. To a great extent, the Blessed Sacrament and the monstrance replaced the reliquaries and statues.[89] Several other minor changes took place in the furniture of the church. For example, confessionals date from the sixteenth century, and in the same period pews began to fill the nave, especially in the churches of the northern countries, where

[87] Henze, *op. cit.*, p. 39.
[88] Bouman, *loc. cit.;* Jungmann, *Pastoral Liturgy*, pp. 81–86.
[89] *Ibid.*, p. 87.

Protestantism may have given the example. Although some late medieval paintings of church interiors show a few benches in front of the pulpit, pews, which were constructed in such a way that they served both for sitting down and for kneeling, were not introduced until the Baroque period.[90]

THE MODERN PERIOD

Although the spirit which produced Baroque had disappeared by the beginning of the nineteenth century, church art and architecture continued to echo the temper of former times. In fact the buildings of the nineteenth century were buildings of all styles—Romanesque and Gothic, Renaissance and Baroque. Confronted with the chaos of society, the age was unable to produce a genuine culture of its own, and so it borrowed from the past in an effort to supply for its own deficiences. The resulting art was marked by theatricalism, historical illusion, and alluring deception.[91]

The nineteenth-century church architects supposed that Gothic and Baroque were the styles of the day, but they were at variance with contemporary architects of profane buildings. Extensive urban developments had grown out of the industrial revolution, but buildings in the old styles could not satisfy the needs of the nineteenth-century communities. Fortunately, new technical discoveries facilitated the use of iron, steel, glass, and concrete in the creation of functional edifices where historicism found no entrance.

[90] Bouman, *loc. cit.*, p. 93.
[91] Henze, *Contemporary Church Art*, p. 15; Miller, *Fundamentals of the Liturgy*, p. 93.

In the course of the century, several attempts were made to rescue church art and architecture from the snare into which it had fallen. For example, the Nazarene movement tried to create a new style of religious art based on a sincere naturalism, but in the end the effort degenerated into historicism. The latter half of the century saw the development of the Beuronese school of ecclesiastical art, in which rigid conformity to a geometrical canon was intended to produce a truly liturgical art and a liturgical piety as well. Although the correct goal was intended, by deliberately copying early Egyptian and Byzantine art this school too fell into the trap of historicism.[92]

With the end of the nineteenth century, however, a genuine church art and architecture began to emerge. Just as the cause of all art and architectural forms is to be found in society itself, so also the modern church and its art emerged from the Christian people who had once again discovered the meaning of the liturgy. Although it is true that the origins of the liturgical renewal go back to Dom Prosper Guéranger (1805–1875) and the monks of Solesmes,[93] and that St. Pius X prepared the way for the movement by his reform program, the decisive moment in the history of the liturgical movement came in 1909 with an address by Dom Lambert Beauduin (1873–1960), a young Benedictine monk of Mont César in Belgium. With the support of Cardinal Mercier (1851–1926), Dom Beauduin was enabled to put forward at a Catholic conference at Malines the

[92] Henze, *op. cit.*, p. 17.

[93] For a critical appraisal of Dom Guéranger's liturgical efforts, cf. Olivier Rousseau, *The Progress of the Liturgy* (Westminster, Maryland: The Newman Press, 1951), pp. 3–21.

proposals which led to the creation of the Belgian liturgical movement.[94]

Dom Beauduin's program was preoccupied with pastoral rather than archeological problems. Consequently, the Belgian liturgical movement was from the start not the work of a group of specialists nor an esoteric activity in the Church. From the beginning it was understood to be a general renewal of Christian life and teaching, or a renewal of the Church itself through a renewal of its parishes.[95]

After World War I, the Belgian liturgical movement joined with two other reform movements. The first, which was predominantly intellectual and theological in character, was centered around the German abbey of Maria Laach, and especially around its two outstanding scholars, Abbot Ildefons Herwegen (1874–1946) and Dom Odo Casel (1886–1948). The second, more popular than scholarly, was concerned with the rediscovery of the Bible. It was an outgrowth of the work of Pius Parsch (1884–1954) and the Augustinian canons of Klosterneuberg in Austria. After World War I, the liturgical, theological, and scriptural movements began to coalesce. The liturgical renewal was strengthened by the rediscovery of the Bible; the theological appreciation of the Church's corporate worship intensified the liturgical apostolate; and the work of the theologians provided a basis for a critical appraisal of church art and architecture.[96]

In Switzerland, the *Societas S. Lucae* was organized to promote the building of churches planned in accordance

[94] *Ibid.*, pp. 161–170.
[95] *Ibid.*
[96] Hammond, *Liturgy and Architecture*, p. 51.

with the rediscovered concepts of the liturgy. Dominikus Böhm (1880–1955) and Rudolf Schwarz, whose churches at Cologne and Aachen are among the best examples of edifices which are functional instruments of the liturgy, were deeply involved in the program of liturgical renewal carried out in the Germany between the two world wars.[97] In the United States, the groundwork for the liturgical movement was laid by Dom Virgil Michel (1890–1938). In 1926 he established the Liturgical Press at St. John's Abbey in Collegeville, Minnesota, and shortly afterwards began the publication of *Orate Fratres* (now *Worship*), which has continued to be the principal organ of the liturgical movement in this country.

In Germany, the results of liturgical studies combined with pastoral efforts were evident in the remarkable document published in 1946 by the German Liturgical Commission, entitled "Directives for the Building of a Church."[98] A similar directive was issued by the French hierarchy in 1952, although the latter was more concerned with modern pictures and statues in church than it was with the church building itself.[99]

It has become clear both to theologians and to architects that churches destined to be the setting for the newly discovered concepts of the liturgy cannot be built according to Baroque or Gothic patterns, which were based on entirely different concepts of the liturgy and a totally different kind of social order. The evolution of the modern church

[97] Cf. Rudolf Schwarz, *Kirchenbau, Welt vor der Schwelle* (Heidelberg: Kerle, 1960).

[98] An English translation of the text may be found in *Orate Fratres*, XXIV (December, 1949), 9–18.

[99] *Nouvelle Revue Théologique*, LXXIV (1952), 958–59.

dates back to Notre Dame du Raincy built in 1923 by Auguste Perret in that area of Paris which later saw the beginnings of the priest-worker movement. Constructed of steel and concrete, the edifice is built on a floor-plan which is that of the ancient basilica; however, the choir has been eliminated and the altar has been brought closer to the people. The roof is supported by slender rods, rather than by heavy pillars, and the walls are formed by a honeycomb of cement, filled with patterns of colored glass. Although the hierarchical division of the church is obvious because of the elevation of the sanctuary, there is no structural division between the nave and the chancel. The church is an integrated space focused upon an altar.[100]

The next church of any real architectural importance was that of St. Antony at Basel in Switzerland which was built by Karl Moser in 1927. At first sight this church seems to be a repetition of Perret's church in Paris; however, the walls of Moser's church are solid surfaces once again. The flat wall behind the main altar seems to bring the altar down to ground level, so that it becomes part of the same spatial unit as the nave.[101]

In December, 1930, Rudolf Schwarz's church of the Blessed Sacrament was consecrated at Aachen. There, one undivided room embraces both the sanctuary and the nave, and yet the altar is somewhat removed from the congregation, as it should be. Although the church is brightly illuminated by natural light, one's attention is still concen-

[100] R. Gieselmann and W. Aebli, *Kirchenbau* (Zürich: Girsberger, 1960), p. 43; Hammond, *op. cit.*, pp. 53–54; Henze, *op. cit.*, pp. 21–22.

[101] Henze, *loc. cit.*

trated on the altar. Everything that is not directly concerned with the liturgy has been relegated to the porch at the front of the church or to a hall set at right angles to the nave.[102]

These three churches—Notre Dame du Raincy, St. Antony's at Basel, and Blessed Sacrament at Aachen—were all built on the plan of a long rectangle. In an attempt to bring the altar closer to the people, architects soon began to experiment with other plans based on the circle and the ellipse. In 1932, Dominikus Böhm built the circular church of St. Engelbert in Riehl (Cologne). The main altar is set in a shallow chancel opening off the nave with the result that it is somewhat withdrawn from the faithful and raised above them.[103] Subsequent experiments with the circular church have attempted to establish a closer relationship between altar and nave.

Architectural experiments in Germany virtually ended when the Nazis came into power. The initiative passed to Switzerland and bore fruit in a fine series of churches dating from the early nineteen-thirties. There is probobly no other country where modern churches take their place so naturally among the outstanding profane buildings of the day. As Régamey noted, "if one wants to see a mature religious architecture, one must go to the region which lies between St. Gallen, Lucerne, and Basel. . . . The qualities which are so striking when one first sees these churches—their logical construction, their adaptation to the demands of the liturgy, and the way in which they express a modern sensibility—

[102] Gieselmann and Aebli, *op. cit.*, pp. 50–53.
[103] Henze, *Contemporary Church Art*, p. 23.

become more and more apparent as one studies them."[104]

One of the earliest Swiss achievements was Fritz Metzger's church of St. Charles in Lucerne. Consecrated in 1933, the church is based on the plan of a horseshoe with the altar standing in the semi-circular chancel raised above the level of the nave. In this church, the pulpit is once again brought into close relationship with the altar. During the next few years, Metzger and two of Karl Moser's former pupils, Otto Dreyer and Hermann Baur, built a series of churches of splendid quality. However, these pre-war churches are comparatively conventional in that they are based on a simple rectangular plan. It was only after the II World War that Baur and Metzger began to explore the possibilities of more complex designs.[105]

In the time which has elapsed since the end of World War II, the influence of the liturgical movement has been extensive and has stimulated a ferment of architectural experiment. Important progress has been made in France and Germany, largely due to the work of the Center of Pastoral Liturgy in Paris and the Liturgical Institute in Trier. The Dominican Fathers Couturier (1897–1954) and Régamey played an important role in the quality of the new French work through their publication, *L'Art Sacré*. In the United States, fresh liturgical thinking is still confined to minority groups, but there has been progress. The Benedictine Abbey of St. John the Baptist in Collegeville, Minnesota, has become the focal point of the liturgical movement in this

[104] Pie Régamey, "L'example de la Suisse alémanique," *L'Art Sacré*, Nos. 1–2 (1947), as quoted by Hammond, *Liturgy and Architecture*, p. 62.

[105] Cf. *Kirchenbauten von Hermann Baur und Fritz Metzger* (Würzburg: Echter-Verlag, 1956).

country, and the new abbey church designed by Marcel Breuer is without doubt a landmark in church building. The edifice is a clear expression of that theology upon which all contemporary churches should be based.[106]

Italy has produced a number of interesting churches in the last few years, but the struggle between old styles and modern styles is still raging. The situation in Spain is quite readily told. There the development of the modern church lies in the future, but how far in the future nobody knows.[107]

In Switzerland and Germany, the work in liturgical art and architecture done before the II World War has provided the foundation for post-war experimentation. These two countries, together with France and especially the French diocese of Besançon, are the most profitable areas in which to study the influence which modern liturgical scholarship has had on church buildings. The post-war program of church construction in the British Isles, however, has been tragic. Although numerous churches were destroyed in the war, their replacements reveal a lack of insight into the relationship between the church and the life of the Christian people. The situation in Great Britain may be summed up in the words of Lewis Mumford in the introduction to his work on *The Culture of Cities:* "The ignorant were completely unprepared, but that did not prevent the building."[108] Within the last few years, however,

[106] Cf. W. S. Stoddard, *Adventures in Architecture: Building the New St. John's* (New York: Longmans, Green and Company, 1958).

[107] Cloud Meinberg, "The New Churches of Europe," *Worship,* XXXI (January, 1957), 68–77.

[108] Lewis Mumford, *The Culture of Cities* (New York: Harcourt, Brace and Company, 1938), p. 7.

the fresh insights of theologians and liturgists have begun to find expression in the plan of British churches.[109]

Although all over Christendom one can sense a deepened understanding of the liturgy and its expression in a dynamic architecture, it is necessary that one be discriminating. In itself, there is no virtue in an unconventional plan, and it would seem that the great diversity in the planning of post-war churches both in Europe and in America is not always due to a concern for liturgical function. The builder must begin with a clear understanding of the liturgy of the church and the nature of the liturgy which takes place there, and then he should design the church accordingly. He should not design a fascinating structure, and next attempt to adapt the liturgy to the structure he has already planned.

Frequently it seems that new structural forms are exploited for their own sake, and the outcome is often an exciting structure from a purely esthetic point of view; the success or failure of a church must be judged in the light of criteria other than esthetic. In pursuing a program of plastic research, architects have at times designed new churches which resemble elongated tunnels in which the altar stands as far removed from the people as possible. Since the war, many new churches, especially in France, have been based on an ellipse orientated on its long axis, despite the fact that such a building is ill-adapted to the requirements of the liturgy. The church of Notre Dame de Royan, Maurice

[109] Hammond, *Liturgy and Architecture*, p. 100. This author, an Anglican clergyman, discusses church building in England in two chapters of his book: "Church Planning in England: 1928–1940" (pp. 67–78) and "Liturgy and Architecture in the Church of England since 1945" (pp. 100–136).

Novarina's church at Villeparisis, and the church of St. Julian at Caen are based on this plan. One gets the impression that these churches were designed from the outside walls into the altar, without the primary concern for function which informed the designs of such architects as Fritz Metzger, Hermann Baur, and Marcel Breuer.

Closely linked with this exaggerated concern for structure rather than function is the design of churches whose plan is determined by symbolism which is legitimate in two-dimensional arts such as mosaic or stained glass, but is usually quite inappropriate in architecture. Barry Byrne's church of St. Francis Xavier in Kansas City, Missouri, which is based on the plan of a fish, is an example of this false approach to church design.[110]

CONCLUSION

In any age architecture is a medium which expresses man and his relationship with other men and with God. New architectural forms correspond to new developments in society itself. These ideas have been verified in the history

[110] For detailed descriptions and analyses of modern churches, cf. Anton Henze, *Neue kirchliche Kunst* (Recklinghausen: Paulus-Verlag, 1958); R. Biedrzynski, *Kirchen unserer Zeit* (München: Hirmer, 1958); Willi Weyres and O. Bartning, *Kirchen: Handbuch für den Kirchenbau* (München: Callwey, 1959); H. Schädel, *Katholische Kirchen, Kappellen und Gemeindezentren* (Stuttgart: Krämer, 1956); *Die neue Kirche: Bau und Ausstattung* (Cologne, 1956); G. Trebbi, *Über den neuen Kirchenbau in Italien* (München, 1960); P. Pinsard, *Über den neuen Kirchenbau in Frankreich* (München, 1960); J. M. De Aguilar, *Liturgia, Pastoral, Arte Sacra* (Madrid, 1958); D. Duret, *Le Zèle de la Maison de Dieu . . . , Restauration, Décoration, Aménagement Ameublement de nos Églises* (Paris: Lethielleux, 1957).

of church building. After Constantine's edict of Milan, the Christian basilica was the standard church structure. It corresponded to the dominant social group among men, for the leaders of the fourth century were the Roman soldiers and officials, with the emperor at their head. The Christian basilica was most probably an extension and a development of the hall of justice and commerce which was dominated by a statue of the divine emperor in the last empire. Certainly the representations of Christ in the mosaics of the Christian basilicas are reminiscent, both in spirit and in attitude, of the representations of the emperors. The early Christians looked upon Christ as the divine Imperator, the successor of the emperors.[111]

Although Roman basilicas were still being built throughout Europe in the year 800, the more characteristic building of the time was the fortress-like palace. This was the age when German warriors were turning into a warrior-like nobility. The typical churches of the period were also heavy fortress-like structures, where God was worshipped as the heavenly King and Christ as his Son. Ninth and tenth century images of Christ present him on the cross, but he is not the Man of Sorrows. Without wounds or suffering, he is presented as a strong stark symbol of royalty upon a cross.[112]

By the end of the twelfth century, the center of life was the castle where knights dedicated their lives to the service of the emperor. In the minds of the faithful, Christ too was a noble Lord. He was served in the monasteries which took the form of castles, and He was worshipped in the rich and

[111] Henze, *Contemporary Church Art*, p. 38.
[112] *Loc. cit.*

splendid Gothic cathedrals, the castles of God, which spread throughout Europe.[113]

By the middle of the fifteenth century society had changed. It was the age of the cultivated bourgeois who paid homage to the ideal of humanism. The characteristic building was the Renaissance palace. Consequently, the typical church was a palace or a great hall where one found Christ as the great Humanist, the Hero of Heaven.[114]

In the seventeenth and eighteenth centuries, the ideal of society was the enlightened bourgeoisie who gathered around the absolutist prince in his spacious baroque castle. Churches were modeled after the great state rooms where the prince met his people, and in the midst of elegant ceremonies Christ as the heavenly Sovereign received the worship of his subjects. In short, the church became God's salon.[115]

The dominant role in society today is played by the man who works in industry and technology. He is a man on the move, but one who longs for security and stability. Despite all the advances in science and technology, he foresees little security in the material world; consequently he is led to seek security in religion. The secular building which characterizes this modern man is the industrial building, the steel-frame structure. Likewise, to a great extent, modern churches are steel-frame buildings designed primarily for function rather than fashion. The better structures take the form of simple houses for God's people. Apart from the community which gathers in these churches, the buildings

[113] *Loc. cit.*
[114] *Ibid.*, p. 39.
[115] *Ibid.*

themselves have little meaning. Since the most characteristic image of God in the minds of men today is that of Christ as Redeemer and Brother, the congregation has been coming closer to the altar where Christ stands, fraternally and yet in detachment, in the midst of His people gathered for the Eucharistic Sacrifice.

The modern man is coming to realize more and more that it is not in a building that he will find security but rather in the Christian community of God's people. The modern churches, then, stand as symbols of man's passing to better things; they are expressions of the fact that Christians are a people on the march. In union with Christ their Head, they are on their way to the heavenly Jerusalem.[116]

[116] Miller, *op. cit.*, pp. 93–94; Henze, *op. cit.*, pp. 32–33, 41–43.

5

The Church as the Place for the Celebration of the Liturgy

In the legislation on sacred architecture, it is a basic principle that the ordinary may not give permission for the construction of a new church unless he has approved the architectural plan and has assurance that there are sufficient means for its construction and upkeep. One of the earliest laws on the matter is a decree which Gratian falsely attributed to one of the Councils of Orleans: "No one may build a church before the bishop of the city has come and has set up the cross and publicly outlined the place of the atrium; nor may he build until he has determined how much money will be sufficient for the lights, the up-keep, and the salary of the caretakers; when this has been determined and the amount already collected has been shown to the bishop, he may proceed to build."[1]

This prescription passed into the rubric of the older editions of the *Pontificale Romanum* under the title, "De benedictione et impositione primarii lapidis pro ecclesia aedificanda," but, while economic precautions are preserved in almost the same words, the architectural approval, which

[1] C. 9, D. I. *de cons.*

seemed to embrace the whole building in the original canon, is reduced to a mere designation of location and atrium.[2] The *Pontificale Romanum,* in turn, was the source for canon 1162, § 2, which mentions only the economic precautions to be taken before episcopal approbation is given to the building of a church. Mention of the investigation of the architectural plans is omitted, possibly because it pertains more to liturgical law than to disciplinary law in the stricter sense, or because it is implicitly contained in canon 1164, § 1.[3]

In spite of this prescription, errors in the matter of church building will be avoided only if the members of the diocesan commission on sacred art have a clear concept of what the church building is meant to be.[4] An understanding of the church building necessarily entails a profound appreciation of the liturgy. As the history of church architecture demonstrates, the connection between the concept of liturgy and the plan of the church building is so intimate that there is a reciprocal influence of the one on the other. For example, a liturgical assembly cannot pray together or

[2] *Pontificale Romanum, Summorum Pontificum iussu editum a Benedicto XIV et Leone XIII Pont. Max. recognitum et castigatum* (Mechliniae: Dessain, 1958): "Nemo Ecclesian aedificet, priusquam Pontificis iudicio locus et atrium designetur, et quid ad luminaria, quid ad rectoris, ministrorumque stipendia sufficiat, quidque ad Ecclesiae dotem pertineat, definiatur; et per eum, vel ejus auctoritate, per Sacerdotem crux in loco figatur, et lapis primarium in fundamento ponatur." This rubric has been omitted from the latest edition of part II of Roman Pontifical.

[3] Ignatius Gordon, "Quaestiones Recentiores de Locis Sacris et Legum Universalium Derogationes in Primo Synodo Romana," *Periodica de Re Morali, Canonica, Liturgica,* L (1961).

[4] Cf. O'Donohoe, "Administrative Aids to the Bishop," *The Jurist,* XX (1960), 25–27.

sing together with the same facility in a Romanesque church divided into various elongated naves as within a Roman basilica where the floor plan is free and open. Likewise a priest will preach in one manner if he speaks from an ambo where his words are an extension of the readings from the Mass, but his style will be vastly different if he speaks from a pulpit raised high above the level of the nave. Moreover, the role which music has played in the liturgy can be analyzed by tracing the location of the schola from one period to the next. Obviously, the liturgical action and the plan of the church exert a mutual influence on one another.[5]

Although it is the liturgical function which should determine the form of the church, form will also greatly affect the function. It is possible to celebrate the liturgy in any church open for worship, but it is not equally possible to make the celebration a dynamic function in which the faithful participate actively and intelligently. For that reason, church architects and their patrons must understand the principles which flow from the very nature of the liturgy, for errors which are perpetrated in the building and the restoration of churches are largely due to ignorance. These errors have not only a momentary effect, but they also influence the worship of generations of the faithful by inculcating in them a warped sense of the mysteries or by allowing them only an incomplete participation in the sacred rites.[6] Churches which are not properly designed and executed both corrupt the esthetic sensibilities of the faith-

[5] Joseph Gelineau, "L'Église, lieu de la célébration," *La Maison-Dieu*, No. 63 (1960), p. 42.
[6] *Loc. cit.*

ful and obscure the very nature of the Church and the gospel which it proclaims. They prevent the faithful from fully realizing what they do when they assemble for the liturgy, and consequently they frustrate the building up of the temple of living stones for the sake of which the houses of stone exist.[7]

If the church is not designed in accord with its primary function as a house for God's people gathered around the altar, or if it is informed by a distorted understanding of the corporate action of the community, the people will be prevented from attaining a full awareness of their Christian vocation. If the layman remains a passive spectator at the liturgy, he is likely to be passive also in regard to what the Church does outside the building. The lay apostolate is intimately linked with the liturgical movement. A clericalized liturgy results in a clericalized apostolate, but if the layman learns his role as a member of the priestly community and as an active participant in the Mass, he will better be able to reflect this awareness in his attitude toward the Church and its apostolic role in the world. One of the best ways to make plain to the people that they are the Church, and not mere passive recipients of spirituality at the hands of the clergy, is to make clear the full implications of the liturgy in the design of the church building.[8] "A serious responsibility, therefore, rests upon those who are entrusted with the task of church building. The result of their work will determine whether or not succeeding generations of the faithful will love this house of God with a true familiar feeling, and whether they will come joyfully or reluctantly to the sacred

[7] Hammond, *Liturgy and Architecture*, p. 167.
[8] *Ibid.*, pp. 168–69.

action of community worship. Therefore the planning of a new church edifice needs to be thought out with earnest conscience and with great care."[9]

THE LITURGICAL ASSEMBLY AND ITS PLACE OF WORSHIP

For the Christians of the New Law, the presence of God is no longer confined to the temple of Jerusalem. Since Christ's death and resurrection, the true temple is the risen Body of Christ and those who believe in him, all joined in the Mystical Body of the Lord. The mystery of man's encounter with God is expressed in visible signs in conformity with the nature of the Church, which is both visible and invisible. The principal sign of this encounter is the Christian assembly, but the assembly needs a place for meeting, so that it can manifest the sacred character of its encounter with God. Just as a market is built for buyers and sellers, so the church edifice is built for those who are united in the Mystical Body of Christ.[10]

The church building, then, is the house of the Church, the house of the people who are themselves the Church, the living temple of God. Apart from the community which it serves, the church edifice has no meaning, for it is first and foremost a building in which the Christians meet to carry out the liturgy. Above all the church is a room for the Eucharist.[11]

Besides its utilitarian function as a house for corporate

[9] "Directives for the Building of a Church," p. 18.
[10] Gelineau, *loc. cit.*, p. 43.
[11] Cf. canon 1161.

worship, the church building itself will take on a symbolic meaning, for if the church is properly designed, it will signify the people of God. Sacred buildings can grow only out of sacred reality, and it is the light of faith which begets such a reality.[12] A hall is not transformed into a church by the placing of a cross on the east wall or by the installing of stained-glass windows. A church will be truly symbolic only if it is informed by a theological understanding of its purpose. In other words, a church is not an autonomous, architectural expression of religious feeling.[13]

The church should be a symbolic structure in itself, apart from any decoration. It is much better to have a simple structure which derives its purpose from a worthy altar, set in the right place, than a pretentious structure, lavishly adorned within and without, which ignores its own *raison d'être* and that of the Church which it houses. Even if a church is built in the contemporary idiom, it will be anachronistic if it embodies an essentially medieval conception of the Church's liturgy.

If the church is properly designed, a religious atmosphere will most probably be created. In fact, it is desirable that the church should convey the tremendous mystery of the Church.[14] There is, however, nothing specifically Christian about the numinous. Since the faith of Christians is more than a vague theism, the church must express more than the

[12] Rudolf Schwarz, *The Church Incarnate*, trans. Cynthia Harry (Chicago: Henry Regnery Co., 1958), p. 10.

[13] H. A. Reinhold, "The Architecture of Rudolf Schwarz," *Architectural Forum*, VI (January, 1939), 26; Hammond, *op. cit.*, p. 155.

[14] Cf. the Introit for the feast of the Dedication of a Church: "Terribilis est locus iste: hic domus Dei est et porta caeli: et vocabitur aula Dei."

otherness of an unknown God. An exaggerated emphasis on the mysteriousness of God to the exclusion of any consideration of the presence of the risen Christ in the Mystical Body of the Church reflects a decay of informed faith into nebulous piety.[15] Since the Church of the New Law is the Mystical Body of Christ, the church building will take on the nature of a valid symbol only insofar as its plan and structure are informed by a true understanding of the nature of the Church and the worship which it renders to God.

Although the church edifice and the assembly of the faithful are both signs of the mystery of the Mystical Body, the first in importance and really the only essential sign is the Christian assembly. In the ontological order, the place of cult does not precede the assembly, but rather the Church creates a place for worship by reason of its visible members.[16]

In the same way as a human body exists in a space which

[15] It is interesting to note that the fourth-century emphasis on awe and dread in the liturgy and in church building coincided with the influx of recently converted pagans into the Church and the decline of both offering and communion among the faithful. For a discussion of this problem, cf. Johannes Quasten, "Mysterium tremendum: Eucharistische Frömmigkeitsauffassungen des vierten Jahrhunderts," *Vom Christlichen Mysterium* (Düsseldorf: Patmos-Verlag, 1951), pp. 66–75; also, Edmund Bishop, "Fear and Awe attaching to the Eucharist," *The Liturgical Homilies of Narsai*, trans. R. H. Connolly (Cambridge: University Press, 1909), pp. 92–97.

[16] There have been several recent attempts to summarize the theological significance of the church building. The doctrine is essentially based on the theology of Pius XII's two encyclicals, *Mystici Corporis* and *Mediator Dei*. Cf. also L. Cerfaux, *The Church in the Theology of St. Paul* (New York: Herder and Herder, 1959), pp. 95–117, 187–198; Aelred Tegels, "The Church: House of God's People," *Worship*, XXXV (August–September, 1961), 494–501; Robert Grosche, "Überlegungen zur Theologie des Kirchenbaues," *Das Muenster*, IX–X (1960), 344–49.

is its own proper place, so also the Body of the Church is organized and by its very nature occupies a place. The human body has a determined structure with a head at one end and feet at the other. Likewise, the Body of the Church, visibly represented by the liturgical assembly, has its own proper structure determined by its own nature. This structure should be visibly expressed as the Church assembles for its worship.

To analyze the church structure, one must first of all analyze the Christian assembly which functions as a personality, the personality of the Church, the Mystical Body of Christ. In determining the organic nature of an assembly, one asks first of all, "Why is there an assembly?" People assemble to listen to a lecture, to work, to take a meal, to make a friendly visit, and for each of these purposes they assemble in a different fashion. The Christians assemble to pray and sing, to listen to the Word of God, to take part in the Sacrifice of the Mass, to receive the sacraments, and to visit the Blessed Sacrament. The church building is normally designed to accommodate these various assemblies.[17]

Contemporary secular buildings are designed primarily from a functional point of view. Similarly the church edifice must be functional and it must also be the sign of a mystery, for the actions which are celebrated in the church are not simply utilitarian actions or purely human ceremonial, but they are mysteries. Because of the sacramental nature of worship, one must not only ask, "Why is there a liturgical assembly?" but also, "What does the liturgical assembly signify?" Material things become signs of faith when they are charged with the content of revelation. Both in its gen-

[17] Cf. "Directives for the Building of a Church," p. 9.

eral outline and in each of its elements, then, the church edifice should declare openly to the faithful the invisible mystery of the Church and it should symbolize the heavenly Jerusalem.[18]

ORGANIZATION OF THE PLACE FOR WORSHIP

In the human body, one can always distinguish the head from the other members. Likewise in the Mystical Body of Christ assembled for the liturgy, one can distinguish the head from the rest of the body. Although Christ is the true head of the Body, the celebrant takes the place of Christ; the faithful are the members of the Body.[19]

This distinction between clergy and faithful is expressed in various formulas from the canon of the Roman missal. For example, in the prayer, *Unde et memores,* following the consecration, the celebrant designates the assembly present for the sacrifice not by a single term but rather by two terms: *nos servi tui* (the clergy) and *plebs tua sancta* (the rest of the assembled faithful). In an analogous way, the *Hanc igitur* speaks of the "oblationem servitutis *nostrae,* sed et *cunctae familiae tuae.*" Obviously the supreme act of the liturgy includes the participation of two distinct groups, the clergy or the ministers on the one hand, and the Christian people or the faithful on the other.

This dual structure of the liturgical assembly proceeds from the hierarchical nature of the Church and especially

[18] Gelineau, *loc. cit.,* pp. 44–45.
[19] Cf. *Mediator Dei,* AAS, XXXIX (1947), 538–539.

from the structure of the priesthood of Christ. The spatial expression of this structure in a visible separation between the clergy and the faithful appears in Christian churches from the beginning. St. Ignatius of Antioch († ca. 115) suggested the two categories in his epistle to the people of Smyrna.[20] In the third-century *Didascalia Apostolorum*, the bishops were instructed concerning the arrangement which should prevail in the liturgical assemblies. The presbyters were to sit in the eastern part of the church with the bishop in their midst, and the laymen were to sit in another part of the church, the men in front and the women behind.[21] In the early Church, Christians realized the diversity of theological functions within the Body of Christ. The bishop, the presbyters, the deacons, and the baptized Christians all had their special functions. In short, the Church was considered an organic body, hierarchical in structure. By the Middle Ages, however, the categories of function were largely superseded by sociological categories of cleric and laymen, with the result that the people of God lost all sense of active participation in the priestly mission of the Church.[22]

Although the division in the Church between the clergy and the laity has not always been based on an adequate appreciation of the priesthood of the laity, nevertheless the history of church architecture demonstrates that the edifice has regularly been divided into two zones, the chancel reserved for the clergy, and the nave reserved for the faith-

[20] *Epistola ad Smyrnaeos*, VIII—*PG*, V, 713; cf. also his *Epistola ad Magnesios*, VI—*PG*, V, 668, and his *Epistola ad Philadelphienses*, IV—*PG*, V, 700.

[21] *Didascalia et Constitutiones Apostolorum*, II, 57, 3–4.

[22] Hammond, *op. cit.*, p. 20.

ful.[23] Frequently these two zones have been distinguished from one another by a material divider such as a jube or a communion rail, and usually there has been a difference in level between the sanctuary and the nave.

If these two areas, the zone for the clergy and the zone for the faithful, are clearly distinguished, what is the relationship which should exist between the two groups which occupy these zones in the course of the liturgy? In other words, what is their respective orientation? At a lecture, the speaker faces his audience; at a meal, the guests gather with the host around the table; to sing together, the performers assemble in a choir. The participants in the liturgy successively listen to the Word of God, sing His praises, and partake in the Lord's Supper. The question then arises: "What is the best arrangement of the liturgical assembly, so that it may function properly in the different aspects of the liturgy?"

In the early Church, the Christians could readily change their position in the course of the liturgy because the nave was not crowded with pews. The interior arrangement of contemporary churches, however, does not permit such flexibility. Nevertheless, the plan of the church must provide for an effective proclamation of the Word, for singing both by a schola and by the whole assembly, and for a common participation in the Eucharist. The church must be functional and at the same time it must express the mystery which is signified.

It sometimes happens that churches are constructed with

[23] A theology of the layman is just now in the process of being developed; it is not surprising, then, that the canonical legislation on the layman is limited to two canons, canon 682 and canon 683.

concern only for the altar, which is considered the moral center of the edifice. In the course of the liturgy, however, attention is not always focused on the altar. For the liturgy of the Word, the celebrant often presides from the *sedile*, and the attention of all, including the celebrant, is centered on the lectern or ambo.[24] One must remember that the liturgical assembly and its functions are much more important than liturgical places or things. Of course, liturgical places follow from the nature of the liturgical assembly and its functions, and these functions will determine the hierarchy of places. In evaluating church designs, however, one must approach the problem from the point of view of persons involved and functions performed rather than from the point of view of things.[25]

There are various possible conceptions of the liturgical assembly:

1. One can consider the liturgical assembly as "an advancing column, a procession headed by the priest who, as spokesman of the community, leads them in prayer and sacrifice before God."[26] Viewed in this light, the Christian people are a *people on the march* to meet their Lord; they are waiting for his return.[27] In this case, the clergy and the

[24] This arrangement is the norm for a pontifical Mass; during a solemn Mass the celebrant sits for the singing of the epistle, and he should also sit during a high Mass if the epistle is sung by a lector.

[25] Gelineau, *loc. cit.*, p. 49.

[26] Joseph Jungmann, *Public Worship* (London: Challoner Publications, 1957), p. 58.

[27] This theology is based on the first Paschal meal (Exod., 12:5–11) viewed as a type of the Christian Passover. There are also other Biblical narratives which prefigure the mystery of the Mass, the assembling of the Christian people, and its Passover; for example, the story of Elias as told in III Kings, 6, and the passages of Exodus to which St. Paul refers in I Cor. 10:1–4.

faithful are oriented in the same direction, just as in certain times and places all turned toward the east for prayer.[28] This concept may be diagramed as follows:

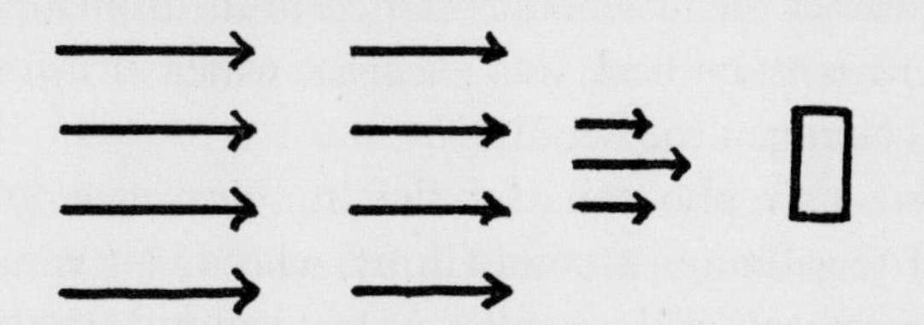

This disposition of the assembly corresponds to the arrangement found in most churches constructed since the Middle Ages. Unfortunately, it gives an incomplete expression to the mystery of the liturgical assembly. The first objection to be raised is that the faithful are no longer *circumstantes*,[29] Christians gathered around the celebrant for the sacrifice. It is true that the Christians are a people on the march, going back to the heavenly Father, and that they are waiting for the Lord's return at the *parousia*. The Lord's return, however, has already been inaugurated, for he truly comes to his people both in the Word and in the Eucharist.[30]

[28] Cf. Schwarz, *op. cit.*, pp. 114–53.

[29] In the *Memento* of the living, the faithful who are present are called *circumstantes*. During the first thousand years standing was the principal posture even during the canon. However, the *circum* should not be construed as though the faithful had ever completely surrounded the altar. The picture intended is that which is suggested by the floor plan of the Roman basilicas, where the altar stood between the chancel and the nave, so that the faithful could form a semi-circle around the altar.—Cf. Jungmann, *The Mass of the Roman Rite*, II, 166.

[30] The theology of God's presence through his Word in the liturgy is developed by Louis Bouyer in his essay, "The Word of God Lives in the Liturgy," *The Liturgy and the Word of God* (Collegeville, Minnesota: The Liturgical Press, 1959), pp. 53–66.

Christ is already present among his people, and the liturgical assembly is already a symbol, an anticipation of the heavenly Jerusalem. If the symbolism of the foregoing conception of the assembly is carried to its ultimate conclusions, one is taken back into Judaism, which is still waiting for the coming of the Messias.[31]

2. One may also consider the liturgical assembly as a concentric gathering around Christ, who said, "Where two or three are gathered together in my name, I am there in the midst of them."[32] This is the arrangement which one usually finds in a monastic choir where the divine office is chanted. It may be represented thus:

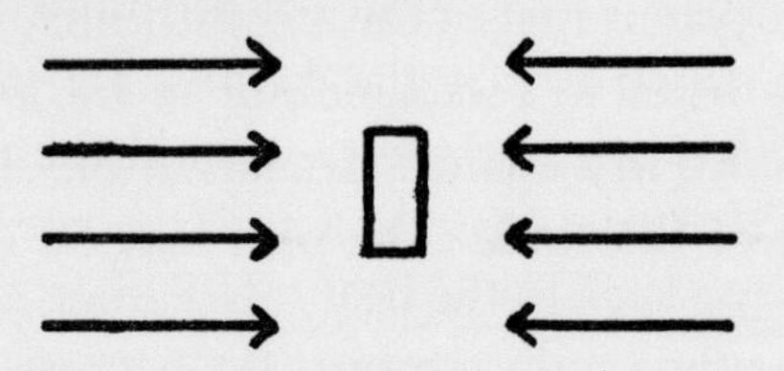

Applied to a more general liturgical assembly, the conception may be represented in this fashion:

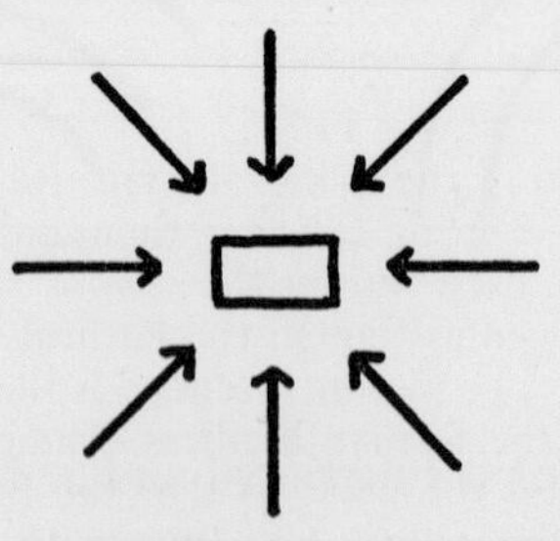

Although this is the arrangement which one finds in a number of modern churches, it is not at all satisfactory.[33]

[31] Gelineau, *loc. cit.*
[32] Matt. 18:20.
[33] Cf. "Directives for the Building of a Church," p. 12.

Applied to the Mass, this arrangement does not take into account the fact that the lector or subdeacon, the deacon, and the celebrant address the people in the epistle, the gospel, and the homily respectively. No matter where the ambo or lectern may be placed in a church based on this pattern, it is impossible for the celebrant, deacon, or lector to face all the people at one time. Psychologically, the people may find themselves at a disadvantage in that they are constantly facing one another. Furthermore, this arrangement does not take into account the hierarchical nature of the Church, since the area for the sacred ministers is absorbed in an indiscriminate circle.

3. Another plan is that of the amphitheater, in which the faithful are gathered in a semicricle or an arc, and the clergy too are assembled in a defined area facing the altar, which is in the center of the circle. The plan may be diagramed as follows:

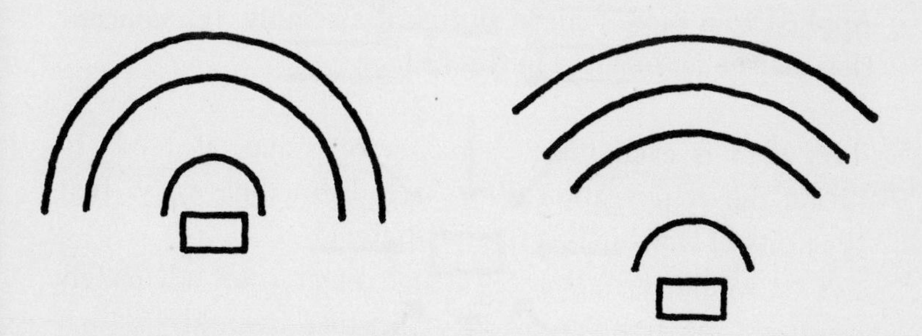

This arrangement is functional and at the same time the two hierarchical zones are preserved. The clergy and the faithful are oriented in the same direction, but the ministers can easily turn toward the faithful for the sacred readings. Furthermore none of the faithful are at a great distance from the altar or the ambo. It is more satisfactory if the faithful are arranged in an arc rather than in a semicircle, for then the ministers may more easily face the entire congregation at one time.

At its best, however, this arrangement does not symbolize the total mystery of the liturgical celebration. The liturgy is not a spectacle performed by actors on a stage before a number of spectators. The liturgy is the sacred action of the whole community. In that action the altar is not a terminus, behind which there is a wall or an empty space. It is rather the center of the sacrifice and should stand between the priest, representing Christ, and the faithful.

The above indicated arrangement is often modified in such a way that the faithful are gathered on three sides of the chancel, in this fashion:

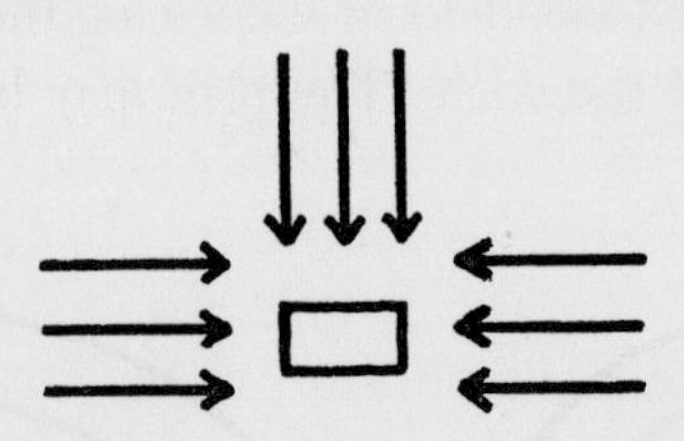

This plan is even more unsatisfactory, since it tends to divide the congregation into three distinct naves, so that the unity of worship is certainly hindered.

4. It would seem that the image which most adequately expresses the mystery of the Christian assembly is that which is based on the floor plan which prevailed in the ancient basilicas.

This arrangement is functional and, at the same time, it symbolizes the Church on the march, waiting for the return of the Lord, and the Church which has already received the Savior. Between the two personal zones of the chancel and the nave, there is rapport and circulation. The Word is readily proclaimed by the ministers and received and con-

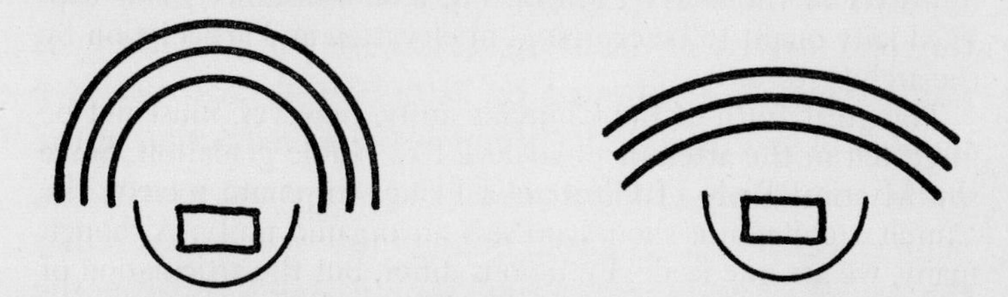

fessed by the faithful. Throughout the whole liturgy there is a concentration of the assembly, both ministers and faithful, on the sacrifice which is accomplished at the altar. All the members of the assembly can hear and see and act. Above all, the arrangement facilitates a genuine dialogue between the faithful and the celebrating priest.

SUMMARY

The design of a church involves the creation of a space in which the Christian assembly gathers for the liturgy. In considering the character of the spatial setting, the architect must keep in mind two fundamental truths concerning the nature of the worshipping Church. First, the liturgy is always a *communal* action; it is the united action of the whole Church, which is the Body of Christ. Secondly, within the Christian community, there is a diversity of function based on a hierarchy of persons.

In the Diocesan Church Building Directives for the diocese of Superior in Wisconsin, the architectural implications of these two principles are quite clearly stated:

Since the Church is a hierarchical or graded society, not all of her members share the same function, but each participates in her worship of the Father according to his God-given capacity. This hierarchical differentiation of function of priest, ordained ministers of the altar (e.g. deacons, altar assistants), and baptized laity ought to be expressed in elevation and articulation by the architecture.

The great truth of the Church's unity, however, must not be forgotten in the attempt to achieve this visible gradation. Since the Mystical Body of Christ is a living, corporate society, the church architecture should possess an organic unity. Although many, we are one Body. Functions differ, but the articulation of graded membership ought not to destroy the organic relationship of member to member.

Although distinct in treatment, the sanctuary containing the altar and the nave housing the community of the baptized ought to be visually and psychologically one. Visual or architectural separation should be avoided. The arrangement of space relations should lend itself to the active participation of the laity in the sacred action of the liturgy. Architects should achieve unobstructed vision of the sanctuary permitting easy dialogue between priest and people. Long, narrow churches which remove the laity from close contact with the altar are undesirable.[34]

In an attempt to create an area which would promote communal worship, architects have at times designed circular churches with the altar in the center of the building. The directives of the German Liturgical Commission explicitly condemn this plan with cogent reasons:

It is a mistaken, although a widespread, notion that the altar should be placed in the midst of the congregation, and that therefore the circular form of edifice is the only satisfactory one.

The Christian church building is intended primarily for the celebration of the eucharistic Sacrifice. This holy Sacrifice is, according to the mind of the Roman liturgy, an action: above all the action of Christ, our High-priest, and of his representative in

[34] "Diocesan Building Directives," compiled by William Wenninger, *Liturgical Arts,* XXVI (November, 1957), 7.

the priestly office; but it is also the action of the entire Christian community. Climactic moments in the action of the congregation are the acclamations before the preface, the *Amen* at the end of the Canon, as well as the offertory and communion processions, of which the former now rarely appears in our day. The concurrence and concord of these actions suppose a spatial arrangement directed toward the altar, so that there is exchange of address and response between sanctuary and nave, between priest and people, and between processional movements to and from the altar. The ideal therefore is a church building arranged with regard to these wishes of the Roman liturgy: direction toward the altar, opposite positions of priest and people, provision for orderly processions to and fro; while at the same time the altar must not be too far removed from the farther end of the nave.[35]

It would seem that the spatial arrangement found in the early Christian basilicas is the most satisfactory plan for the church building, because this floor plan gives the most functional accommodations to a hierarchically ordered community of Christian worshippers. Of course, contemporary architects should seek to express in a modern idiom those same truths which were embodied in the liturgy of the early Church.[36]

[35] "Directives for Building a Church," *loc. cit.*

[36] Giacomo Lercaro, "The Christian Church," *The Furrow*, VI (June, 1957), 341–49; also Hammond, *loc. cit.*, p. 27.

6

The Sanctuary—
The Place for the Clergy

In the *Apostolic Constitution*, there is a description not only of the liturgy of the fourth and fifth centuries but also of the church setting. The work is addressed to the bishop as the head of the Christian assembly, and in part it is as follows:

> When thou callest an assembly of the Church as one that is commander of a great ship, appoint the assemblies to be made with all possible skill, charging the deacons as mariners to prepare places for the brethren as for passengers, with all due care and decency. And first let the building be of oblong shape, with its head to the east, with its vestries on both sides at the east end, and so it will be like a ship. In the middle, let the bishop's throne be placed, and on each side of him let the presbytery sit down; and let the deacons stand near at hand, in close and small girt garments, for they are like the mariners of the ship. With regard to these, let the laity sit on the other side, with all quietness and good order. And let the women sit by themselves, also keeping silence. In the middle, let the reader stand upon some high place.[1]

Three distinct areas for the sacred ministers are designated in this text. At the east end of the church is the place

[1] *Constitutio Apostolorum*, II, 57, 2–4.

for the bishop, with his presbyters on either side of him. There is a place for the deacons who direct the assembly, and there is also an elevated place where the lectors proclaim the Word.

An analysis of the early Christian basilicas confirms the tradition that there were four principal locations in the area reserved for the clergy: the seat for the head of the assembly, the altar, the place for proclaiming the Word, and a place for the deacons. Likewise, an analysis of the contemporary liturgy demonstrates that there is a need for the same four areas within the chancel or presbytery. In the present chapter, an attempt will be made to clarify the concepts of these four areas.

THE PLACE FOR THE CELEBRANT

It is customary to consider the main altar as the place of prime importance in the presbytery. In the ontological order, however, it would seem that the place for the celebrant, who represents Christ in the midst of his people, is of first importance.[2]

The Lord is present in the liturgy in various ways. He is in the liturgical assembly as the head of the Mystical Body; he is present in the proclamation of the Word and in the grace conferred by the sacraments; and above all, he is substantially present in the Eucharist. But as Pius XII pointed our in *Mediator Dei*, Christ is present in a special way in the celebrant of the liturgy,[3] and his presence there confers on the sacred minister a dignity and a place apart.

[2] Joseph Gelineau, "Le sanctuaire et sa complexité," *La Maison-Dieu*, No. 63 (1960), pp. 56–57.
[3] *AAS*, XXXIX (1947), 528.

It is the bishop, or the priest functioning in his place, who convokes the Christian assembly, and it is by his authority that the liturgy is organized. In short, he is the living head of the assembly.

In the early days of the Church, Christians were more sensitive to the personal aspect of the liturgical assembly than to the material aspect. For example, there was no permanent altar, but at the desired moment the table of sacrifice was carried into place by deacons.[4] Consequently, during the liturgy the bishop was the center of the assembly. As the head of the community, he presided at his throne where he was the image of Christ enthroned in heaven. Today, the celebrant of the liturgy fufills the same role. In the words of the Instruction of the Sacred Congregation of Rites on Sacred Music and Liturgy, "the celebrating priest presides over the entire liturgical function."[5] It is a logical sequence of these words that the first place of honor, both spatially and visually, should be accorded to the celebrant.[6]

In order to appreciate the full significance of the place for the celebrant, one must understand the history and the symbolism of the episcopal throne, for the bench which is used by the celebrating priest finds both its origin and its meaning in the *cathedra*.

The history of the pontifical throne begins with apostolic times. From the earliest days of the Church, the bishop's throne or *cathedra* has been the symbol of his authority. In antiquity, teachers regularly taught while sitting down; consequently, the *cathedra* came to signify the *magisterium*.

[4] Cf. *Quaestiones veteris et novi testamenti*, 101—*PL*, XXXV, 2301.

[5] September 19–22, 1958, No. 93: *AAS*, L (1958), 656.

[6] Gelineau, *loc. cit.*, p. 58.

The thrones used by the apostles and their successors were jealously preserved and were symbolic of the teaching power and authority of the priesthood as an extension of the teaching power and authority of Christ.[7] An example of such a *cathedra*, dating from the middle of the third century, is represented in the celebrated statue of St. Hippolytus of Rome, preserved now in the Lateran Museum at Rome.[8]

In the early Church, not only did the bishop preside at his throne, but it was also from his throne that he preached to his people.[9] Seated on the *cathedra*, he could survey the whole community, like a true bishop, an overseer, watching over the people. As St. Augustine explained, it was necessary that the bishop should sit in the place of honor, so that he could be distinguished by the place that he took and so that his office would be apparent to all.[10]

The connection between the episcopal dignity and the

[7] It would seem that Tertullian's words should be taken literally: "Percurrenti enim ecclesias apostolicas, apud quas abhuc ipsae cathedrae apostolorum suis locis praesidentur."—*Liber de praescriptionibus*, XXXVI: *PL*, II, 48.

[8] Polycarpus Radó, *Enchiridion Liturgicum* (Romae: Herder, 1961), II, 1412. It is interesting to note that from the end of the second century Christ is frequently represented in art seated on a throne teaching his apostles. He is pictured in this way in the fresco in the Roman cemetery of St. Hermes, in the mosaic of the Roman church of St. Pudentiana, and on the fourth-century ivory pyx in the Kaiser-Friedrich Museum in Berlin. Later the *cathedra* itself, empty or surmounted by a cross, became the symbol of Christ. It is called the ἑτοιμασία τοῦ θρόνου (the preparation of the throne) and is an allusion to the throne in which Christ will sit in general judgment. The latter representation may be seen in the triumphal arch of St. Mary Major at Rome.—Righetti, *Storia Liturgica*, I, 384.

[9] Van der Meer and Mohrmann, *Atlas of the Early Christian Church*, p. 136.

[10] *Sermo XCI*, 5: "Oportet ut in congregatione christianorum praepositi plebis eminentius sedeant, ut ipsa sede distinguatur et eorum officium satis appareat." *PL*, XXXVIII, 569.

cathedra is effectively placed in relief in the ceremony of enthronization during a bishop's consecration. The present edition of the *Pontificale Romanum* prescribes that, if possible, the new bishop should be consecrated in his own church and enthroned in his *cathedra.*[11] The latter ceremony symbolizes that the bishop is taking possession of his diocese, and also explicitly demonstrates to the faithful that he is their pastor, teacher, and high priest.[12]

In the ancient basilicas and in most of the cathedral churches constructed until the twelfth century, the *cathedra* was generally made of marble or stone and richly ornamented with mosaic or sculpture.[13] Standing in the middle of the back wall of the semi-circular apse, the *cathedra* was approached by three or more steps so that it was raised above the priests' benches on either side.[14] If the priests were numerous, the benches for the presbyters were placed in two or three rows, as in the basilica of Torcello, where there are three rows arranged like an amphitheatre.[15]

The above indicated arrangement is still contemplated as one of the alternatives in the *Caeremoniale Episcoporum:* "The bishop's throne may be placed in various manners according to the location of the altar, close to which it should

[11] *Pontificale Rom.*, tit. *De consecratione Electi in Episcopum.*

[12] Righetti, *op. cit.*

[13] Very few *cathedrae* dating from the first centuries of Christianity have been preserved. Plates and descriptions of a number of early *cathedrae* may be found in Van der Meer and Mohrmann, *op. cit.*, p. 136. Cf. also St. Augustine, *Epistola XXIII*, 3: *CSEL*, XXXIV, I, 66.

[14] This is the arrangement in the Church of S. Clemente in Rome. Although the church is eleventh century, the disposition of the *cathedra* and the seats for the presbyters is fifth century.—Van der Meer and Mohrmann, *op. cit.*, p. 136.

[15] Righetti, *op. cit.*, I, 385.

be placed. If the altar is in the middle of the chancel, distinct from the wall, in such a way that a choir is formed, then the bishop's throne is placed against the back wall, at a distance from the altar, in such a way that the bishop, sitting in his throne, rightly appears to be the bishop of the diocese, presiding over all the canons."[16] This seems to have been the traditional place for the bishop until the late Middle Ages. From the end of the fourteenth century, however, he ceased to take this place, but instead he presided on a throne erected on the gospel side of the altar. This is the alternative arrangement in the *Caeremoniale Episcoporum:* "If the choir is in the middle of the church, and the altar rests against the back wall, or is separated from the back wall by a small space, the episcopal throne should be placed on the gospel side."[17] This latter arrangement prevails in most cathedral churches today, and in noncathedral churches the bench for the celebrant is regularly placed not in the apse but on the epistle side of the altar.

Contrary to the more prevalent arrangement, the location of the throne or the bench at the back of the apse most clearly signifies the presence of Christ in the celebrant and his role as head of the assembly. It is also the arrangement

[16] "Sedes Episcopi vario modo collocatur pro diversitate altarium, apud quae statui debet. Nam aut altare est in medio sub tribuna, pariete disjunctum, ita ut in spatio illo constitutum sit chorus, et tunc sedes episcopalis e regione altaris parieti applicabitur, ita ut Episcopus, in ea sedens, respiciat recta Episcopum Diocesanum super omnes Canonicos." *Caeremoniale Episcopor.*, lib. I, c. XIII, n. 1.

[17] Si vero chorus sit in medio ecclesiae, et altare adhaereat parieti, vel ab eo modico sit intervallo separatum, ipsa sedes episcopalis erit collocanda a latere Evangelii.—*Caeremoniale Episcopor.*, lib. I, c. XIII, n. 2.

which best corresponds to the hierarchical concept of the Christian community. In the liturgical assembly which is the sign of faith proclaimed and received, and which symbolizes God coming to his people and remaining among them, the celebrant is best situated facing the people. This arrangement maintains the two zones of the church, it facilitates dialogue between sanctuary and nave, and it expresses the mystery of Christ who has come, who comes now, and who is yet to come.[18]

The question may arise whether or not it is proper for a priest who is celebrating the liturgy to occupy the place at the back of the apse which is traditionally reserved for the bishop. It is true that in the early basilicas the only person who occupied the throne at the back of the apse was the bishop, but almost all the important churches were presided over by a bishop. In modern times, the bishop regularly pontificates in his cathedral church; the liturgy is celebrated in the parish churches by the pastor and his assistants. Although the New Code of Rubrics states that the celebrant at a solemn Mass may sit between the deacon and subdeacon, at the epistle side of the altar, while the *Kyrie*, *Gloria*, Sequence, and Creed are being sung,[19] this permissive rubric would not preclude his sitting at the back of the apse if the bench were placed there. Since the celebrating priest is the bishop's own representative, it would seem that he may occupy the place

[18] Gelineau, *loc. cit.*, p. 58; Whitney S. Stoddard, *Adventures in Architecture*, p. 91; Lercaro, "The Christian Church," *loc. cit.*, 436; J. D. Crichton, "The Church—The House of God's People," *Liturgy*, XXVIII (October, 1959), 43, 47.

[19] No. 523, July 26, 1960: *AAS*, LII (1960), 684.

which is reserved solely for the bishop in cathedral churches.[20]

In extant churches where the altar stands against the back wall of the apse, or where the Blessed Sacrament is reserved at the main altar in a large tabernacle, or where there is only one altar in the church,[21] the arrangement described above is impossible. As provided by the New Code of Rubrics, a place on the epistle side of the altar is the logical alternative. In building a new church or in restoring an old one, however, both patrons and architects must keep in mind the basic liturgical principle concerning the celebrant: he is the head of the assembly and should appear to be what he actually is. The most fitting location for the celebrant's bench seems to be a place at the vertex of the apse.[22]

Most of the legislation concerning the construction of the bench is of a negative character. The seat should be

[20] If the bishop is present for the liturgy but not celebrating, as the true head of the assembly, he should preside from the back of the apse, and the bench for the priest who is taking his place may easily be set up to the right of the bishop. It would seem that this is the place the celebrating priest should take in cathedral or collegiate churches, even when the bishop is not present. Cf. *Caeremoniale Episcop.* I, c. 12, 22: "In Ecclesiis Collegiatis, ubi Episcopus nec celebrans nec praesens . . . satis erit scamnum oblongum coopertum aliquo tapete aut panno aptari a latere epistolae, in quo sedeat Sacerdos celebrans cum Diacono et Subdiacono."

[21] Cf. the decree of the Sacred Congregation of Rites of June 1, 1957: "In ecclesiis ubi unicum extat altare, hoc nequit ita aedificari, ut sacerdos celebret populum versus; sed super ipsum altare, in medio, poni debet tabernaculum ad asservandam Sanctissimam Eucharistiam." *AAS*, XIL (1957), 426.

[22] Gelineau, *loc. cit.*, pp. 58–59; Aimé-Georges Martimort, "Place du siège du celebrant," *La Maison-Dieu*, No. 63 (1960), pp. 135–37.

long enough to hold three people comfortably; there should be no divisions making a distinction between the three occupants; and the bench should be without arms and without a canopy.[23] The bench must be placed on the floor, not on a platform, so that one ascends it by steps.[24] By a series of decrees, the Congregation of Sacred Rites has forbidden the use of armchairs or chairs of domestic pattern, since the former are reserved for prelates and the latter are not suitable for liturgical places.[25] The bench may be covered with a cloth, either green or corresponding to the office of the day.[26] For tenebrae, Good Friday, and for requiem functions, the bench is uncovered.[27]

The rubrics make no mention of fixed benches attached to the wall of the apse or chancel, but tradition allows their use.[28]

[23] *Caeremoniale Episcop.*, lib. I, c. VIII, n. 4; lib. II, c. II, n. 6; lib. II, c. III, n. 4; lib. II, c. VIII, n. 36; lib. II, c. XVIII, n. 3; lib. II, c. XXVII, n. 13.

[24] S.R.C., *Turritana,* April 26, 1704, ad 2: *Decr. Auth.*, n. 3135; cf. S.R.C., *Burgi S. Sepulchri,* April 4, 1699, ad. 2: *Decr. Auth.*, n. 2027.

[25] S.R.C., *Turritana,* May 19, 1614: *Decr. Auth.*, n. 320; *Anconitana,* March 23, 1641: *Decr. Auth.*, n. 743; *Dubiorum,* Sept. 17, 1822, ad 6: *Decr. Auth.*, n. 2621; *Sancti Iacobi de Cile,* March 14, 1861, ad 4: *Decr. Auth.*, n. 3104; *Goana,* June 16, 1893: *Decr. Auth.*, n. 3804; *Nicosien.*, March 14, 1908: *Decr. Auth.*, n. 4214; *Dubiorum,* Nov. 7, 1905, ad 1: *Decr. Auth.*, n. 4172.

[26] *Caeremoniale Episcop.*, lib. I, c. XII, n. 22; lib. II, c. III, n. 4; lib. II, c. XVIII, n. 3.

[27] *Caeremoniale Episcop.*, lib. II, c. XXV, n. 1. Cf. lib. II, c. XI, n. 1. For requiem functions, it may be covered in black or violet: S. R. C., *Dubiorum,* Nov. 7, 1905, ad. 1: *Decr. Auth.*, n. 4172.

[28] O'Connell, *Church Building and Furnishing,* p. 68. For details concerning the erection and appointment of pontifical and abbatial thrones, cf. Joachim Nabuca, *Jus Pontificalium* (Tournai: Desclée & Cie., 1956), pp. 270–79; Léon Gromier, *Commentaire du Caeremoniale Episcoporum* (Paris: La Combe, 1958), pp. 128–46.

THE ALTAR

Whereas the celebrant has the most important role in the Church which is the Christian assembly, the altar is the most important place in the church building. Its eminent position, however, is derived not from law, but rather from theology, which gives meaning to the various prescriptions concerning the construction, the location, and the ornamentation of the Christian altar.

Theology of the Christian Altar

An altar may be briefly defined as a table for sacrifice. In the Old Testament, the altar was not something accidental to the sacrifice, but it was rather an essential element. In fact, one may say that there was no sacrifice without an altar. An object offered became a victim not merely by destruction, but the material action took on the nature of a sacrifice through the cult of a priest who placed the sacrifice on the altar. The altar, then, was less a utilitarian object than a sacred symbol, for it was the place of man's encounter with God. In a sense, the altar was the place where man was assured of meeting God, for once an offering was religiously placed on the altar, there was a guarantee that it would be kindly received.[29]

However, it does not seem that the concept of an altar which was valid for the ancient pagans and Jews is still ap-

[29] Martimort, "L'autel," *La Maison-Dieu*, No. 63 (1960), pp. 96–97; cf. Lev. I–VIII; Roland de Vaux, *Les institutions de l'Ancien Testament*, II (Paris: Les Editions du Cerf, 1960), 279–90, 291–384; Albert Gelin, "L'autel dans l'Ancien Testament," *La Maison-Dieu*, no. 29 (1952), 9–17.

plicable to the Christian altar. The early Christian apologists maintained that God "does not demand an offering of victim or drink or of any visible thing."[30] For this reason, so the apologists explained, the Christians had neither temple nor altar. The first Christians were strongly conscious that the Church is essentially a heavenly institution: the Christian altar, so they said to themselves, is in heaven, and so is the one true priest, Christ, and in heaven he offers up the gifts of the Church.[31] Just as the Christians have no temple where God is localized, so also they have no altar where contact suffices to sanctify the victim, for the Christians have no sacrifice in which sanctification depends wholly on the accomplishment of a rite. The Christians have an altar, but it is the unique, incomparable altar which is Christ.[32]

The Christian altar is "the table of the Lord,"[33] or it is the "holy table," as it is still called in the Eastern rites.[34] It is the table upon which Christ, through the ministry of his priest, prepares the royal wedding feast at which he feeds

[30] Aristides, *Apology*, I: *The Ante-Nicene Fathers*, IX, 263; cf. Justinus, *Apologia I pro Christianis*, XIII: *PG*, VI, 345; Minucius Felix, *Octavius*, XXXI: *CSEL*, II, 45; Tertullianus, *De spectaculis*, XIII: *CSEL*, XX, 15.

[31] Cf. Yves Congar, *Lay People in the Church*, trans. Donald Attwater (Westminster, Maryland: Newman Press, 1956), p. 140; Jungmann, *The Mass of the Roman Rite*, I, 25.

[32] Cf. *Pontificale Rom.*, tit., *De ordinatione subdiacono:* "Altare quidem sanctae Ecclesiae ipse est Christus, teste Johanne, qui in Apocalypsi sua altare aureum se vidisse perhibet, stans ante thronum, in quo, et per quem, oblationes fidelium Deo Patri consecrantur." Also Pseudo-Dionysius, *De Ecclesiast. Hierarch.*, IV, 12: *PG*, III: 484–85; Paschasius Radbertus, *Expositiones in Lamentationes Jeremiae*, II: *PL*, CXX: 1118; Honorius Augustodunensis, *Gemma animae*, I, c. 106: *PL*, CLXXII: 579; Sicardus Cremonensis, *Mitrale*, III, c. 6: *PL*, CCXIII: 132.

[33] I Cor. 10:21.

[34] Hammond, *Liturgy and Architecture*, p. 105.

his guests with the bread of life and the drink of salvation. The altar is the table which bears the Lamb, for upon it the Pasch of the people of God takes place; the altar, then, is the stone of sacrifice upon which the sacrifice of the Lamb of God is reenacted for the deliverance and reconciliation of the faithful. It is to the altar that the Lord constantly returns to effect the meeting of God and his people; it is at the altar that the *admirabile commercium*, the wonderful exchange, takes place between God and men.[35]

Besides its primary function of being the place of sacrifice and the sacramental meal, the altar also has a profound symbolic meaning. Its interpretation, dating from the fourth century, is expressed by the bishop in the conferring of the subdiaconate: "Holy Church's altar is Christ Himself, as St. John testifies in his Apocalypse, when he says that he saw a golden altar standing before the Throne upon which and by which the offerings of the faithful are brought to the Father."[36] The symbolism expressed here is very complex, and for that reason is difficult to analyze. For example, the altar represents Christ as the eternal high priest. Since man's gifts and prayers ascend to God by means of the altar, and God's gifts come down to men upon the altar, it is an image of Christ, who is the divine mediator between God and men.[37] In another interpretation, the altar, which is anointed with chrism at its consecration, represents

[35] Maurice de la Taille, *Mysterium Fidei* (Paris: Gabriel Beauchesne, 1924), pp. 153–165; Jean Leclercq, "Le mystère de l'autel," *La Maison-Dieu*, No. 29 (1952), 60–70; Henze, *Contemporary Church Art*, p. 53.

[36] *Pontificale Rom.*, tit. *De ordinatione subdiaconi.*

[37] Cf. Johannes Möllerfeld, "Der Altar ist Christus," *Geist und Leben*, XXXIV (1961), 261–71; Joseph Schmitt, "Petra autem erat Christus," *La Maison-Dieu*, No. 29 (1952), 18–31.

Christ who is the Anointed of the Holy Spirit.[38] Although there are various interpretations of the altar, they all see the symbolism in the altar itself, without any addition or appurtenances. However, the altar itself derives its true meaning from the sacred actions which are performed upon it. In short, it is the sacred liturgy which underlies the unsurpassable dignity and holiness of the Christian altar.

Development of the Christian Altar

The first Christians offered the sacrifice of the Mass at a common supper table. In fact, it was in the context of the Passover meal that Christ instituted the Mass. Since there were no church buildings in the apostolic era, the early Christians offered the Sacrifice of the Mass in private homes, and to the celebration of the Eucharist they added the *agape*, a meal of fellowship.[39] It is not suprising, then, that the early Christians called the altar *mensa dominica*, the table of the Lord.[40]

Most probably the first altars were simple wooden tables which did not rest permanently in the church buildings. In one of his letters, St. Cyprian († 258) spoke of a portable altar,[41] and the author of the *Quaestiones veteris et novi testamenti* mentioned that the deacons carried the altar

[38] Cf. Olivier Rousseau, "Le Christ et l'autel: note sur la tradition patristique," *La Maison-Dieu*, No. 29 (1952), 32–39; Noële-Maurice Boulet, "L'autel dans l'antiquité chrétienne," *La Maison-Dieu*, No. 29 (1952), 40–59; Friedrich Wulf, "Gedanken zu einer Theologie des Altars," *Geist und Leben*, XXXIV (1961), 337–47.

[39] Cf. Acts 2:46; 20:18; Oscar Cullmann, *Le culte dans l'Église primitive* (Paris: Delachaux & Niestlé S. A., 1948), pp. 8–10; Jungmann, *The Mass of the Roman Rite*, I, 7–22; Righetti, *Storia Liturgica*, III, 1–15.

[40] Cf. Acts 10:21.

[41] Cyprian, *Epistola* XXXXV, 2: *CSEL*, III(2), 600–601.

into place at the beginning of the sacrificial part of the Mass.[42] Optatus of Mileve noted about 370 that the Donatists made a fire with the wood of an altar.[43]

In the East, stone altars appeared during the fourth century, but not in the West until two centuries later.[44] It was St. John Chrysostom (ca. 344–407) who first mentioned stone as the material for an altar.[45] In 517 stone altars were prescribed by the French Synod of Epao,[46] and eventually this particular legislation was incorporated into the *Decree* of Gratian, which determined the practice of the universal Church.[47]

As early as the time of Constantine, the altar was surmounted by a baldachin or ciborium, a canopy-like structure resting on four columns.[48] Authors differ in interpreting the origin of the baldachin. Edmund Bishop (1846–1917) saw here an example of the ancient tendency to veil sacred objects,[49] and Boulet agrees with this opinion.[50] Eisenhofer (1871–1941) and Lechner suggest that the custom may have been derived from the Byzantine court, where the throne of the emperor was sheltered by a covering called the κιρωριον.[51] They refer to the opinion of Heisenberg (1869–1930), who explained the canopy as an element derived from Phoenician religious thought and Syro-

[42] 101. *PL*, XXXV, 2301.
[43] *De schismate Donatistarum*, VI, 1: *PL*, XI, 1065.
[44] Van der Meer and Mohrmann, *op. cit.*, pp. 138–39.
[45] *Homilia in Epist. II ad Corinthios*, XX, 3: *PL*, LXI, 539.
[46] Canon 26: Mansi, VIII, 562.
[47] C. 31, D. I, *de cons.*
[48] Cf. Boulet, "L'autel dans l'antiquité chrétienne," *La Maison-Dieu*, No. 29 (1952), p. 45.
[49] *Liturgica Historica* (Oxford, 1918), p. 22.
[50] *Ibid.*, pp. 22–23.
[51] *Liturgy of the Roman Rite* (New York: Herder and Herder, 1961), p. 123.

Hellenic art, which influenced the construction of the edifice over the tomb of Christ in the Church of the Resurrection at Jerusalem.[52] It is true that the latter canopy was copied throughout Christendom. In fact, the term *ciborium* is derived from the Semitic word for grave.[53] Peter Anson prefers the opinion that the ciborium comes from the Byzantine court arrangement, since it resembles so closely the *tegurium* which stood over the chief magistrate's seat in the civil basilicas and also over the statue of Roman deities.[54] However, since the word *tegurium* is simply a corrupted form of *ciborium*, there seems to be little difference in these views.[55]

Up until the sixth century the altar was arranged so that the celebrant faced the people during Mass. This explains the position of the altar in the principal Roman basilicas and also the rubrics of the suppressed *Ritus celebrandi Missam*, which designated the *cornu Evangelii* on the right or more honorable side of the sanctuary (but now on the left) and the *cornu Epistolae* on the left (but now on the right).[56]

[52] A. Heisenberg, *Brabeskirche und Apostelkirche*, I (Leipzig, 1908), 215–16, cited by Lechner-Eisenhofer, *op. cit.*, pp. 123–24.

[53] Syriac: kᵉbôrâ, Hebrew: kebar, Greek, κιβούριν. Cf. Joseph Braun, *Der christliche Altar in seiner geschichtlichen Entwicklung*, II, 190.

[54] *Churches: Their Plan and Furnishing* (Milwaukee: Bruce, 1948), p. 100. Cf. Ildephonse Schuster, *The Sacramentary*, I, (New York, 1924), 162.

[55] Miller, *Fundamentals of the Liturgy*, p. 100.

[56] IV, 2; VI. The latest changes in the rubrics of the Roman Missal direct that wherever the word *cornu* occurs, *latus* should be substituted.—Carolus Braga, "Ordinationes ad Librum Liturgicorum Editores circa Novas Missalis Romani Editiones" (Roma: Edizioni Liturgiche, 1961), n. 666.

In his *Der christliche Altar in seiner geschichtlichen Entwicklung,* Joseph Braun (1857–1947) indicated that in the early Church the altar faced the people for three reasons:

> First, in episcopal churches, where the cathedra of the bishop stood in the vertex of the apse behind the altar, it would have been too bothersome for the bishop and his ministers to go from the throne at the far end of the apse to the front side of the altar, as often as the sacred action would have demanded this. Second, when the altar was attached to a *confessio* (tomb of a saint), the celebrant assumed his place opposite the faithful to allow the latter to get as close as possible to the altar in order to venerate the relics buried beneath it and to lay pieces of cloth or other objects in the forechamber or confession of the tomb. Third, when the axis of the church was directed toward the west (northwest or southwest), the altar faced the nave so that the priest standing behind it could assume the customary meaningful direction toward the east.[57]

These three assertions should be examined. First, a cursory study of the early Roman basilicas and titular churches demonstrates that the principle of orientation had little effect in Rome.[58] Facing the east while at prayer was an oriental practice. The *Didascalia Apostolorum,* probably a North Syrian text, indicates that the church itself should point to the east and all should face in that direction while at prayer.[59] A similar directive is found in the *Apostolic Constitution,* also of Syrian provenance.[60] Franz Dölger (1879–1941) maintained that except for Augustine and the Pseudo-Augustine no western writer before 1000 indicated

[57] (München: Karl Widmann, 1924) I, 412–13.
[58] Cf. Henri Leclercq, "Orientation," *DACL,* XII, 2665.
[59] II, 57, 2–5.
[60] II, 57, 14.

that this oriental practice had any influence in the West.[61] Paulinus of Nola (d. 431), however, affirmed that there were oriented churches in the West.[62]

The only Roman document which speaks of orientation at Mass is the *Ordo Romanus Primus*. In part it is as follows:

> And rising the pontiff kisses the book of the gospels and the altar and goes to his seat and stands facing the East. . . .
>
> When they have finished, the pontiff turns toward the people and begins the *Gloria in excelsis Deo*. And immediately he turns to the East until it is finished. After this he turns again to the people and says: *Pax vobis*, and turning to the East he says: *Oremus*, and the oration follows.[63]

In commenting on the *Ordo Romanus Primus*, Andrieu (1886–1956) asserted that this rubric is certainly a Gallic addition to the original Roman *Ordo*.[64]

In this connection it is interesting to note that the practice of celebrating Mass with one's back to the faithful seems to have originated also in Gaul. This was necessitated by the construction of oriented churches which were built with the apse at the east end and the façade to the west. In such churches the priest's normal position was on the side of the altar closer to the nave.[65]

From the history of the practice of orientation, one must conclude then that the principle had nothing to do with the

[61] Franz Dölger, *Sol Salutis* (Münster, 1925), p. 255.

[62] *Epistola* XXXII, 13: *PL*, LXI, 337.

[63] Nos. 51, 53. Michel Andrieu, *Les Ordines Romani du Haut Moyen Age*, II (Louvain: Spicilegium Sacrum Lovanense, 1948), 83–84.

[64] *Op. cit.*, II, 55; cf. Andrieu, "Note sur une ancienne redaction de l'Ordo Romanus Primus," *Revue des Sciences Religieuses*, I (1921), 394–95. The rubric is taken from a ninth-century manuscript from the monastery of St. Gall.

[65] Leclercq, *loc. cit.*, 2666.

custom of facing the people when offering Mass; instead, orientation caused the discontinuance of the practice of offering Mass *versus populum*.[66]

The second reason offered by Braun for the altar facing the people is the veneration of relics beneath the altar and the presence of a *confessio* or sunken pit in front of the altar. Obviously such a situation would have prevented the priest's standing on the side of the altar nearer the people. However, the altar *versus populum* antedates the construction of confessions. According to Grossi-Gondi, the confession in St. Paul's Basilica in Rome was the first example, dating only from the sixteenth century.[67] Before this period, confessions did exist, but they took the form of crypts behind or beneath the altar, rather than sunken pits in front of the altar. But even in its earlier form, the confession dates only from the sixth century, that is, from the period of the transfer of martyrs' relics from the catacombs to the Roman churches.[68] The altar *versus populum* existed at least two centuries before this in the Roman basilicas constructed during the reign of Constantine.[69] Veneration of the martyrs, then, does not seem to have been the motivating factor in constructing the altar *versus populum*.

It is the first assertion made by Braun, namely the loca-

[66] Miller, "Altar Facing the People: Fact or Fable?" *Worship*, XXXIII (January, 1959), 85–86.

[67] F. Grossi Gondi, *I Monumenti cristiana* (Roma, 1923), p. 431, note 2.

[68] *Ibid.*, p. 429; cf. Ludwig Hertling and Engelbert Kirschbaum, *The Roman Catacombs and their Martyrs*, trans. M. Joseph Costelloe (Milwaukee: The Bruce Publishing Company, 1956), pp. 10, 48, 82.

[69] Cf. J. Kirsch, *Die römischen Titelkirchen im Altertum*, pp. 118–37.

tion of the bishop's throne, which was the most significant factor in the practice of offering Mass *versus populum.* The bishop's throne occupied the central position in the church, at the apex of the apse.[70] Braun maintained that, in going to the altar, the bishop naturally went to the side nearer him out of mere convenience.[71] Convenience was undoubtedly one cause, but it would seem that other factors may have entered into the development of this practice. At the present stage of research, however, there is no evidence to support the theory that there was a theological motive for offering Mass *versus populum.*[72]

Today, however, theological foundations support the position of those who advocate the location of the altar facing the people. The priest at the altar is not a mere man among men, but rather he is the minister of Christ, his representative, his instrument. As Pius XII pointed out in *Mediator Dei,* the priest does not act in virtue of an office committed to him by the community, but he acts for the people simply because he represents Jesus Christ. He goes to the altar as the minister of Christ, inferior to Christ, but superior to the people.[73]

Although the primary reality of the Mass is its sacrificial aspect, nevertheless the sacrifice takes place within the framework of a meal. Christ himself willed this format, for he instituted the Eucharist under the sign of food and related this institution to the Passover meal. The sybolism of a meal is more clearly evident if the Christians gather around the table of the altar at which the priest presides

[70] Cf. *supra,* p. 161.
[71] *Der christliche* Altar, I, 412.
[72] Miller, *loc. cit.,* p. 89.
[73] *AAS,* XXXIX (1947), 538–39.

in the place of Christ. Naturally, he must preside facing his people.

A further reason for placing the altar *versus populum* is the psychological advantage which the visibility of the sacrifice affords the people. It would seem that where the faithful can follow closely the actions of the priest, they are prompted to greater concentration and participation in the sacrifice.[74] The altar *versus populum* is not a plea for antiquarianism; instead, it is motivated by pastoral theology, whose aim is to bring the Mass to the people.

Mass facing the people is specifically recognized and permitted as one of the alternative rites in the rubrics of the Roman Missal. The *Ritus servandus in celebratione Missae* notes: "If the altar is facing the East, *versus populum*, and the celebrant is facing the people, he does not turn his back to the altar when he is to say *Dominus vobiscum. . . .*"[75] And in another place: "If the celebrant standing at the altar is facing the people, he does not turn, but stands as he is, and blesses the people . . . from the middle of the altar."[76] Strictly taken, if an altar is consecrated, one may offer Mass on any of its four sides. Mass facing the people is certainly an authentic way of offering the Sacrifice, and it is approved by the liturgical books.[77]

The Mass *versus populum*, however, presents various technical difficulties. In his allocution to the participants

[74] Roguet, "L'autel," *La Maison-Dieu*, No. 63 (1960), 107.

[75] V, 3. This rubric has not been changed in the new edition of the rubrics for the Roman Missal. Cf. Braga, "art. cit.," *Ephemerides Liturgicae*, LXXV (1961), 429.

[76] XII, 2. Cf. Braga, *ibid.*, p. 437.

[77] Cf. S.R.C. Instruction on Sacred Music and Sacred Liturgy—*AAS*, L (1958), 632, n. 1; 634, n. 12.

in the international congress of pastoral liturgy at Assisi on September 22, 1956, Pope Pius XII recalled the traditional doctrine and legislation of the Church concerning the reservation of the Blessed Sacrament. The basic principles are contained in two canons of the Code:

Canon 1268, § 2: The Blessed Sacrament should be reserved in the most fitting and distinguished place in the church, and therefore regularly at the main altar.

Canon 1268, § 1: The Blessed Sacrament must be kept in an immovable tabernacle, placed in the middle of the altar.

Recognizing the increased desire for the practice of offering the Mass *versus populum*, Pope Pius XII noted: "The question of how the tabernacle could be placed on the altar with celebration facing the people admits of several different solutions. On these the experts will give their opinions."[78] On June 1, 1957, the Congregation of Sacred Rites issued a detailed decree on the form and use of the tabernacle. In part the decree reads as follows:

> The tabernacle must be attached to the altar so firmly as to be immovable. As a rule it should be at the main altar, unless some other be considered more convenient and suitable for the veneration and worship of so great a Sacrament, as is ordinarily the case in cathedral, collegiate, or conventual churches, where choral functions are usually performed, or sometimes at the great shrines, lest the peculiar devotion of the faithful toward the object of their veneration overshadow the supreme worship of adoration which is due to the Most Blessed Sacrament.
>
> In churches where there is only one altar, this may not be so constructed that the priest celebrates facing the people; but on the altar itself, in the middle, should be placed the tabernacle for keeping the Most Blessed Eucharist, built according to liturgical

[78] *AAS*, XXXXVIII (1956), 722; *The Assisi Papers*, p. 234.

laws, in a form and dimension altogether worthy of so great a Sacrament.[79]

In no way did the foregoing decree prohibit the celebration of Mass facing the people, nor did any commentator suggest that the decree contained any such prohibition. Josef Loew, the vice-relator of the historical section of the Congregation of Sacred Rites stated quite clearly. "This obviously does not forbid celebration of Mass *versus populum.*"[80]

In dealing with the rare case of a church with only one altar, the Congregation decreed that this altar at which the Blessed Sacrament is reserved may not be used for Mass *versus populum*. There is no explanation given for the terms of this prohibition. However, the decree does not state that Mass may not be offered facing the people at an altar where the Blessed Sacrament is reserved. The prohibition holds only in churches where there is only one altar.

[79] "Tabernaculum adeo firmiter cum altari coniungatur, ut inamovibile fiat. Regulariter in altari maiore collocetur, nisi aliud venerationi et cultui tanti Sacramenti commodius et decentius videatur, id quod ordinarie contingit in ecclesiis cathedralibus, collegiatis aut conventualibus, in quibus functiones chorales peragi solent; vel aliquando in maioribus sanctuariis, ne propter peculiarem fidelium devotionem erga obiectum veneratum, summus latriae cultus Sanctissimo Sacramento debitus obnubileter. . . .

"In ecclesiis, ubi unicum exstat altare, hoc nequit ita aedificari, ut sacerdos celebret populum versus; sed super ipsum altare, in medio, poni debet tabernaculum ad asservandum Sanctissimam Eucharistiam, tanto Sacramento omnino dignum."—*AAS*, XLIX (1957), 425–26.

[80] "Tabernacle and Altar," *Worship*, XXXI (Nov., 1957), 576. Cf. A. Bugnini, *Ephemerides Liturgicae*, LXXI (1957), 442–45; D. Baibini, *Monitor Ecclesiasticus*, LXXXIII (1958), 34–35; J. O'Connell, *The Clergy Review*, XLIII (January, 1958), 15; B. Avery, *The Homiletic and Pastoral Review*, LVIII (May, 1958), 768–69; F. McManus, *Worship*, XXXIII (1958–59), 122–25.

The decree states that the tabernacle should regularly be placed on the main altar. Two exceptions are listed: cathedral, collegiate, and conventual churches, and sanctuaries in which an image or relic is exposed for veneration on the main altar. In cathedral, collegiate, and conventual churches the Blessed Sacrament should be transferred to another altar, lest the rite and order of the liturgical ceremonies be disturbed.[81] In churches where an image or relic is exposed for special veneration on the main altar, the Blessed Sacrament should be reserved at another altar, lest the faithful give greater reverence to the image or relic than they do to the Blessed Sacrament.[82]

The two exceptions listed in the decree, however, are not exclusive in character, for the desire to offer Mass facing the people is also a valid reason for reserving the Blessed Sacrament at an altar other than the main altar. It is more convenient and more fitting (*commodius et decentius*) that this arrangement should be made. As has been indicated, the primary reasons for offering the Mass facing the people are pastoral reasons. One of the principal objectives of the liturgical movement is to effect a renewed understanding of and a participation in the Sacrifice of the Mass on the part of the faithful. The history of the liturgy demonstrates that the Mass has frequently been obscured by the sacramental presence of Christ on the altar. Many Catholics still seem unaware that the Mass is the Church's sacrifice, the act of public worship rendered to God in the name of Christ and of the Church. In stressing the Mass one does not detract from the sacrament, for the sacrifice and the

[81] Cf. *Caeremoniale Episcop.*, lib. I, c. XII, n. 8.
[82] Bugnini, *ibid.*, p. 441.

sacrament are simply two ways of approaching the one reality of Christ among men. In order to bring the Mass into clearer focus, it seems advisable to remove the Blessed Sacrament from the altar of sacrifice to a special altar of reservation.[83] This arrangement facilitates the offering of Mass *versus populum* from an altar which is unobstructed by a tabernacle. It is for these various pastoral reasons that the altar facing the people is recommended today.

Construction and Location of the Altar

Since the altar is the place of sacrifice, it is not a mere accessory to the church or a simple piece of furniture. If Mass is offered facing the people, there should be two altars in the church, an altar of sacrifice and an altar of reservation. In this case, if it is possible, a special Blessed Sacrament chapel should be constructed, which will serve not only for the private adoration of the Eucharist but also for liturgical functions in which only a small number of the faithful take part, such as weekday Masses, funerals, and weddings. If the tabernacle is of a reasonable size, the altar in the Blessed Sacrament chapel may also be constructed in such a manner that the priest faces the people when he celebrates Mass.

In addition to the altar of sacrifice and the altar of reservation, there should not be a needless multiplication of

[83] This arrangement is in keeping with the directive of the *Caeremoniale Episcoporum*, lib. I, c. XII, n. 8, which prescribes that the Blessed Sacrament should be removed from the main altar for pontifical Mass. The *Ordo Hebdomadae Sanctae* (Typis Polyglottis Vaticanis, 1956), directs that the tabernacle, if it is on the main altar, should be empty for the evening Mass on Holy Thursday, which commemorates the institution of the Mass.

altars in a church. Where additional altars are necessary for the celebration of Mass by a number of priests, these altars should be relegated to a crypt or to distinct chapels. These altars should be located in such a way that they do not detract from the main altar in the church.[84] In the East, if it is necessary to have secondary altars, they are always placed in a separate structure, a *parekklesion* or side chapel.[85]

The main altar's autonomy should be maintained by way of a position of centrality and independence. It should stand in close proximity to the people. Above all, it should not be placed against the back wall of the sanctuary where it stands like a side-board just as far removed from the faithful as possible. The altar should be free-standing. Although the bishop must encircle the altar while incensing it during the rite of consecration,[86] this rubric is certainly not the reason why the atlar should be free-standing. The free-standing altar gives rise to the rubric, not vice versa. The altar should be so placed because it is an independent entity, whose dignity demands that it should stand autonomously.

Moreover the altar should not be excessively elevated. In most churches the altar stands at the head of a tread of stairs, elevated above the level of the sanctuary. Certainly this is a means of placing emphasis on the altar and of enabling the faithful to follow the actions which go on there,

[84] R. Grosche, *Überlegungen zur Theologie des Kirchenbaues* (München, 1960), pp. 344–49.

[85] Hammond, *Liturgy and Architecture*, p. 36.

[86] *Pontificale Rom.*, tit. *Ordo ad altare consecrandum sine ecclesiae dedicatione*. A new diagram to be inserted in the Roman missal also indicates that the priest should encircle the altar while incensing it at liturgical functions. Cf. Braga, *loc. cit.*, *Ephemerides Liturgicae*, LXXV (1960), 433.

but the faithful should be able to follow everything that takes place in the entire sanctuary, not only what is enacted at the altar. If the altar is excessively elevated and the celebrant presides from the vertex of the apse, he cannot be seen from the nave. Although it is the general teaching of commentators that the high altar should have at least three steps,[87] there is no reasonable explanation for this assertion. It is better to elevate the whole sanctuary somewhat above the level of the nave than to elevate the altar excessively. The church, however, must not be transformed into a theater in which the sanctuary is a stage. It would seem that a difference of one step between the level of the sanctuary and the level of the altar is sufficient.[88]

The altar itself should take the form of a table. As a matter of fact, the Code of Canon Law regularly speaks of the top of the altar simply as a *mensa*, a table.[89] In the Middle ages the altar often resembled a tomb, and in the Baroque period it generally took the form of a throne, but these designs were motivated by secondary aspects of the altar.[90] To consider the altar as a tomb is to attribute to the Mass a funereal aspect which is foreign to it; likewise, to consider the altar as a throne is to neglect the Mass as a sacrificial action. The altar should take the form of a table, because the Mass is essentially a sacrifice in the framework

[87] Cf. Adrian Fortesque and J. B. O'Connell, *The Ceremonies of the Roman Rite Described* (Westminster, Maryland: The Newman Press, 1958), p. 27; Anson, *op. cit.*, p. 78; Laurence J. O'Connell and Walter J. Schmitz, *The Book of Ceremonies* (Milwaukee: The Bruce Publishing Company, 1956), p. 4; Geoffrey Webb, *The Liturgical Altar* (New York: Benziger Brothers, 1939), p. 84.

[88] S.R.C., *Granaten.*, June 16, 1663: *Decr. Auth.*, n. 1265, ad 4.

[89] Cf. canons 1197, § 1; 1198, §§ 1, 2; 1200, § 1.

[90] Anson, *op. cit.*, pp. 64–65; Webb, *op. cit.*, pp. 25–34; O'Connell, *Church Building and Furnishing*, pp. 134–38.

of a meal. Although the Holy See allows a retable, a reredos, gradines, and other superstructures,[91] they should be excluded from the altar, because they tend to obscure the table of sacrifice. Certainly the holiness of the altar precludes its use as a pedestal or a stand for various accessories.[92]

One may object that Pius XII in his encyclical *Mediator Dei* reproached those who would restore the altar to its primitive table form.[93] The reference, however, was to those who would prefer to use an ordinary dinner table for an altar. Although the altar is fundamentally a table, it is a very special table and should not take on the appearance of a table for an ordinary meal. From its material, its form, and its dimensions, the altar should appear as a table for a sacred meal and for a sacrifice.[94]

The Code of Canon Law contains legislation on the altar in Part II, Section I, Title XI, of the Third Book. First of all the Code distinguishes between an immovable or fixed altar and a portable or movable altar. An immovable altar consists of a table (*mensa*) with its supports (*stipites*). It is consecrated as a whole.[95] It is fixed in relation to its supports, so that if the table is separated, the altar loses its consecration.[96] The term movable or portable altar means a stone, usually small, which is consecrated by itself, that is, without a base or supports, or it may consist of the same stone with a base, in which case the base is not conse-

[91] O'Connell, *op. cit.*, p. 182.

[92] A. M. Roguet, "L'autel," *La Maison-Dieu*, No. 63 (1960), 108.

[93] *AAS*, XXXIX (1947), 545.

[94] Roguet, *loc. cit.*; Gelineau, "Le sanctuaire et sa complexité," *La Maison-Dieu*, No. 63 (1960), 59–63.

[95] Canon 1197, § 1.

[96] Canon 1200.

crated.[97] In many churches, one finds a fixed altar in a wide sense. This is an immovable structure, made of wood or stone, in which a small altar stone has been installed. Strictly taken, such a structure is a portable altar in spite of the fact that it may be in fact permanent or immovable. The Congregation of Sacred Rites has referred to such an altar as *ad modum fixi*.[98] The new edition of Part II of the Roman Pontifical provides for the consecration of such a portable altar.[99] In a consecrated church at least one altar, preferably the main altar, should be consecrated; in other churches, the altars may all be movable.[100] The present legislation allows great freedom in the design of an altar provided that its essential features of a table and supports are preserved. The table must consist of a single natural stone, which is of one piece and not easily broken.[101] Any hard stone such as granite, marble, or sand stone is permitted, but cement, pumice, or plaster are obviously excluded.[102] In an immovable altar the stone table must extend the entire length of the altar and must be suitably joined to its supports. The lower part of the altar, or at least the sides or columns which support the table, must also be stone.[103] To mark the places where the table is signed with blessed water and anointed at its consecration, it is customary, though not prescribed, to incise a cross at

[97] Canon 1197, § 1.

[98] S.R.C., *Sancti Hippoliti*, Aug. 31, 1867, ad 1—*Decr. Auth.*, n. 3162.

[99] Tit. *Ordo ad altare portatile consecrandum.*

[100] Canon 1197, § 2.

[101] Canon 1198, § 1.

[102] S.R.C., *Fanen.*, June 17, 1843: *Decr. Auth.*, n. 2862; *Lamacen.*, April 29, 1887, ad 2: *Decr. Auth.*, n. 3674; *Americae*, June 13, 1899, ad 2: *Decr. Auth.*, n. 4032; *Aesina*, Nov. 25, 1904, ad 1: *Decr. Auth.*, n. 4145.

[103] Canon 1198, § 2.

each of the four corners and one in the center of the table.[104]

The supports for the table may consist either of a stone slab or of a number of stone columns. The table must rest immediately on the supports; stone resting on stone is sufficient, but a firm junction with cement is safer.[105]

Besides the *mensa* and the supports, the third essential part of a fixed altar is the sepulcher, a small, square or oblong cavity cut into the table or into the stone supports. This cavity contains a sealed vessel with authenticated and primary relics of two canonized martyrs,[106] and also three grains of incense and a document attesting to the consecration.[107]

In general, the same rules which govern the construction of a fixed altar apply also to a portable altar, except that there are no *stipites*. The sepulcher must be cut into the upper surface of the stone slab, the relics are put directly into the cavity, and the lid is cemented on with blessed cement.[108]

As in the case of a church, every altar, or at least every fixed altar, must have a proper titular.[109] The titular of the main altar must be the same as the titular of the church itself.[110]

No exact rules can be given concerning the dimensions of

[104] S.R.C., *Maurianen.*, May 2, 1892: *Decr. Auth.*, n. 3771.

[105] Cf. canon 1200, § 1.

[106] S.R.C., *Bituricen.*, Dec. 5, 1851, ad 3: *Decr. Auth.*, n. 2991; *Vicen.*, Aug. 30, 1901, ad 1: *Decr. Auth.*, n. 4082.

[107] *Pontificale Rom.*, tit. *Ordo ad altare consecrandum sine ecclesiae dedicatione.*

[108] S.R.C., *Sancti Joannis in America*, Dec. 15, 1882, ad 2: *Decr. Auth.*, n. 3567; *Feltren.*, May 10, 1890: *Decr. Auth.*, n. 3726.

[109] Canon 1201, § 1; cf. *Pontificale Rom.*, tit. *Ordo ad altare consecrandum sine ecclesiae dedicatione, De titulo altaris.*

[110] Canon 1201, § 2.

an altar. There is no reason, however, why an altar should be excessively large, for its significance is achieved not so much by size as by the strength of its lines and its placement. The earliest Christian altars were rather small.[111] The significance of the celebrant walking from the center to the side of the altar is practically negligible; furthermore, excessive length of the altar is both inconvenient and awkward for the sacred ministers. When scales and proportions are properly drawn, altars ranging from six to eight feet in length are adequate.[112]

Since the altar itself is the symbol of Christ and his sacrifice, symbolic ornamentation of the altar is not necessary, but, if it is applied, it should be simple and comprehensible to the faithful. The symbols used should be immediately related to the meaning of the altar or to the Eucharist.[113]

Although the *Caeremoniale Episcoporum* prescribes that a canopy of cloth should be suspended over the high altar of a cathedral,[114] and the Congregation of Sacred Rites has prescribed that there be a canopy over every altar at which the Blessed Sacrament is reserved,[115] there is no rubric requiring it for all altars.[116] This canopy may take the form of a civory or a baldachin. The civory is an edifice consisting of four columns and a roof built over the altar. The most familiar example would be Bernini's civory over the main altar of St. Peter's Basilica in Rome. The baldachin or tester

[111] Van der Meer and Mohrmann, *op. cit.*, pp. 138–39.
[112] Roguet, "L'autel," *La Maison-Dieu*, No. 63 (1960), 108–109; Anson, *op. cit.*, p. 77; Gelineau, *loc. cit.*, 62–63.
[113] "Diocesan Church Building Directives," Superior, Wisconsin.
[114] Lib. I, c. XII, n. 13; c. XIII, n. 3; c. XIV, n. 1.
[115] S. R. C., *Catronen.*, Apr. 27, 1697: *Decr. Auth.*, n. 1966; *Cremen.*, May 4, 1709: *Decr. Auth.*, n. 2192.
[116] Anson, *op. cit.*, p. 101; Webb, *The Liturgical Altar*, p. 77; O'Connell, *Church Building and Furnishing*, p. 191.

is a lighter structure which is either suspended from the roof or attached to the back wall, so that it hangs over the altar like a canopy over a throne. If a civory is used, it should not be cumbersome and should not block the view of the altar. It would seem that a free-standing altar would preclude the use of a baldachin attached to the back wall. If the baldachin is suspended from the ceiling, it should not be too high above the altar. Since its purpose is to enrich and enhance the altar, it should form a visual unit with the altar and should not attract attention to itself.[117]

Altar Appointments

The final chapter of the New Code of Rubrics is entitled "On the Preparation of the Altar for Mass." It made no attempt to cover the legislation on sacred furnishings in its entirety, for it sought only to bring up to date the norms which have existed in the Roman Missal. Likewise, no attempt will be made here to analyze the legislation in detail; only the more essential furnishings will be discussed.

Both the *Missale Romanum*[18] and the *Caeremoniale Episcoporum*[119] make it quite clear that a cross must be placed upon the altar for Mass. The New Code of Rubrics specifically refers to a "cross sufficiently large with the

[117] "Diocesan Church Building Directives."

[118] *Rubricae Generales Missae*, XX; *Ritus Servandus in Celebratione Missae*, VIII, n. 6; *De Defectibus in Celebratione Missarum Occurrentibus*, X. These rubrics have not been affected by the latest changes in the Roman Missal. Cf. Braga, "ordinationes ad Librorum Liturgicorum Editores circa Novas Missalis Romani Editiones," *Ephemerides Liturgicae*, LXXV (1961), 404, 427–439, 442–447.

[119] Lib. I, c. XII, nn. 11, 12, 16, 24; c. XXIX, n. 4; lib. II, c. XI, n. 1.

crucified."[120] In other words, the altar cross must be a true crucifix with the image of Christ upon it. In conformity with *Mediator Dei*,[121] the image of Christ should not be exclusively glorified but should also show traces of His sufferings. Nevertheless the image should not be excessively realistic. An image of the latter type accords an exaggerated emphasis to the Mass considered as the memorial of the bloody passion of Christ, and it suggests that Christ is the *terminus* of the sacrifice rather than the mediator.[122] Furthermore, one should keep in mind that the cross on the altar originates from the processional cross.[123]

The expression *satis magna* in the New Code of Rubrics is directed against the practice of using small crucifixes on the altar, as often happens when a large statue is erected behind the altar. The cross, however, should not be excessively large, in the sense that it dominates the whole church. The cross should be proportionate to the altar and candlesticks.[124] It should not dwarf the altar nor should it draw attention away from the altar. It should be visible to both the celebrant and the faithful, and it should be large enough that the figure of Christ stands above the candlesticks.[125]

Although the rubrics indicate that the cross must be *super altare*, it is often more convenient to hang the crucifix from the canopy or to affix it to the floor, as is often done when the processional cross is used for the Mass. If the

[120] N. 527.

[121] "One would be straying from the straight path were he to order the crucifix so designed that the divine Redeemer's Body shows no trace of His cruel sufferings."—*AAS*, XXXIX (1947), 545.

[122] Roguet, *loc. cit.*, p. 109.

[123] Martimort, *L'Église en Prière* (Paris: Desclée & Cie, 1961), p. 168.

[124] *Caeremoniale Episcop.* lib. I, c. XII, n. 11.

[125] *Loc. cit.*

tabernacle is resting on the altar, it is often impossible to place the cross on the altar.[126] There is an advantage in using the processional cross, for it can easily be removed, for example, during the funeral of a child[127] and when the Blessed Sacrament is exposed upon the altar.[128] If the priest when offering the Mass faces the people, the image of Christ should face the priest, and not the faithful. There is no need to have an image on both sides; it is sufficient for the people to see the cross itself.[129]

Like the altar cross, the candles are to be placed on the altar, in a line on either side of the cross.[130] However, the candles are the important things, not the candlesticks; consequently, there is no reason why the latter need be elaborate in size or ornamentation. They should take the form of simple holders for substantial candles in proportion to the altar. When Mass is offered *versus populum*, circumstances might dictate placing the candlesticks at the sides of the altar rather than on its surface, or they may rest on the far ends of the altar in lines perpendicular to the altar cross, but ordinarily this is not necessary. If the candlesticks are small, the visibility of the Mass is not obstructed.[131]

The kind of Mass should determine the number of

[126] O'Connell, *op. cit.*, p. 207; Webb, *op. cit.*, p. 55.
[127] Fortesque and O'Connell, *op. cit.*, p. 409.
[128] S.R.C., *Carthaginien.*, Nov. 29, 1738, ad 4: *Decr. Auth.*, n. 2340; *Aquen.*, Sept. 2, 1741, ad 1: *Decr. Auth.*, n. 2365.
[129] Roguet, *loc. cit.*, p. 110.
[130] *Caeremoniale Episcop.*, lib. I, c. 12, n. 11; New Code of Rubrics, n. 527.
[131] Anson, *op. cit.*, pp. 104–113; O'Connell, *op. cit.*, pp. 208–213. Since the Holy See permits the candlesticks to be placed on the gradines, which are not part of the altar, it is reasonable to maintain that the candlesticks may be placed at the sides of the altar if circumstances seem to require this.

candlesticks which are placed on the altar. Unlighted candles on the altar do not add dignity to the sacrifice; consequently, if an altar is regularly used for low Mass, there should be two candles on the altar, and no more. Although there is no absolute rule or prohibition in this regard, generally the altar should hold only the candles to be lighted for Mass. This recommends the practice of carrying the lighted candles at either side of the processional cross during the entrance procession and then placing the candles on the altar at the same time as the cross is placed in position. Since the altar is not a sideboard or stand for ornaments, its dignity demands that only what is essential for the sacrifice should be placed upon it, and after the Mass is over the appurtenances should be removed.[132]

It is for the reason indicated above that the New Code of Rubrics specifies that the altar cards should be placed on the altar only during Mass.[133] The prayers printed on the altar cards should be memorized, but for the avoidance of a memory lapse the printed text is permitted on the altar.[134] The cards should be clearly and simply printed; there is no need for elaborate frames or ornamentation. The cards are necessary during Mass, but should be removed afterwards. The same is true of the missal stand. The missal may rest on either a cushion or a stand.[135] Although a stand is more common, in many cases a cushion would be less cumber-

[132] Cf. New Code of Rubrics, n. 529.

[133] N. 527.

[134] Fortesque and O'Connell, *op. cit.*, p. 39; Anson, *op. cit.*, p. 128; O'Connell and Schmitz, *op. cit.*, p. 17; *Caeremoniale Episcop.*, lib. I, c. XII, n. 15.

[135] *Caeremoniale Episcop.*, lib. I, c. XII, n. 15; New Code of Rubrics, n. 527.

some.[136] Like the altar cards, some sort of missal support is a practical necessity, but once the Mass is over, it should be removed from the altar.

The basic principle concerning the adornment of the altar is contained in rule 529 of the New Code of Rubrics: "Nothing whatsoever is to be put on the altar which does not pertain to the sacrifice of the Mass or to the adornment of the altar itself."[137] Although it is true that the rubrics do permit flowers,[138] the altar should certainly not be made into a greenhouse. In fact, it would seem more fitting that, if flowers are used, they should be placed in vases on the floor, possibly at the edges of the sanctuary.[139] Although artificial flowers made of silk or other precious materials are permitted by law,[140] they are normally outlawed by good taste.

Likewise, the rubrics permit the exposition of the relics of canonized saints on the main altar.[141] Here again, however, there is the danger that the altar will become a pedestal. The proper place for the relics is in the *sepulchrum* of the altar. If relics are to be displayed, they should be exposed at a special shrine set aside for that purpose, rather than on an altar.

Although the New Code of Rubrics mentions the altar cloths with the insistence that the sides of the altar should

[136] Anson, *op. cit.*, p. 129.
[137] AAS, LII (1960), 685.
[138] *Caeremoniale Episcop.*, lib. I, c. XII, n. 12; *Ordo Hebdomadae Sanctae*, Sabbato Sancto, n. 29: "Altare paratur pro missa solemni, luminaribus accensis et floribus."
[139] Fortesque and O'Connell, *op. cit.*, p. 29; Anson, *op. cit.*, p. 125.
[140] *Caeremoniale Episcop.*, lib. I, c. XII, nn. 12, 14.
[141] *Caeremoniale Episcop.*, lib. I, c. XII, n. 12.

be covered with a cloth reaching to the floor, the rubric from the Roman Missal prescribing the use of a frontal has been omitted.[142] In many churches the use of an antependium or frontal at all altars where Mass is offered has fallen into desuetude. The omission of this rubric from the New Code would seem to be a tacit approval of this fact. Nevertheless, the antependium, as a worthy vestment for the altar which is Christ, is still appropriate. If the color of the frontal is changed according to the feast or Mass, it can take away the monotonous, cold appearance of a simple block of stone, and at the same time it will serve as an effective means of directing the eye toward the altar.[143]

Tabernacle

Although the tabernacle is not an essential part of the altar, it must always be joined to an altar.[144] Consequently, it will be convenient to treat the tabernacle in conjunction with the altar.

The history of the Catholic doctrine concerning the reservation of the Blessed Sacrament can be summed up in Dom Lambert Beauduin's concise formulary: "It is not reserved to be adored, but because it is reserved, therefore it is adored."[145] As the Sacred Congregation of the Sacraments noted in its Instruction on the Eucharist, October 1,

[142] *Rubricae Generales*, XX; *Caeremoniale Episcop.*, lib. I, c. XII, nn. 11, 16.

[143] Roguet, *loc. cit.*, p. 111; O'Connell, *op. cit.*, pp. 192–95; McManus, *Handbook for the New Rubrics* (Baltimore: Helicon Press, 1960), p. 203.

[144] Canon 1269, § 1; S.R.C., decr. "De forma et usu tabernaculi," June 1, 1957.—*AAS*, XXXIX (1957), 425.

[145] Cited by Roguet, "Le lieu de la réserve," *La Maison-Dieu*, No. 63 (1960), 114.

1949,[146] the primary reason why the Blessed Sacrament is reserved is that it may be carried as Viaticum to the dying; the distribution of Communion outside of Mass and the adoration of the Blessed Sacrament are secondary reasons for its reservation and developed only by degrees.[147]

The custom of reserving the Blessed Sacrament dates from the first centuries of the Church. It was reserved to provide a means of communion for those who could not be present at the liturgy and also for the *fermentum*, the custom of sending a portion of the Bread consecrated at the bishop's Mass to all the other Masses celebrated elsewhere by those priests who acknowledge him to be their bishop.[148]

In the pre-Nicene period, the place of reservation was in the homes and on the persons of the Christians. Later it became customary to reserve the Sacrament in a cupboard in the sacrarium, a room adjoining the sanctuary of the church. In some places this custom continued until the twelfth or thirteenth century, and seems to have been rather

[146] *AAS*, XXXXI (1949), 509–10.

[147] The history of the reservation of the Blessed Sacrament is extensively studied by the following authors: W. H. Freestone, *The Sacrament Reserved* (Alcuin Club Collection, 1917); J. Braun, *Der christliche Altar in seiner geschichtlichen Entwicklung*, II; E. Dumoutet, *Le desir de voir l'hostie et les origines de la devotion au Saint Sacrament* (Paris, 1928); F. Raible, *Der Tabernakel einst und jetzt* (Freiburg, 1908); Edmund Bishop, *Liturgica Historica* (Oxford, 1918); Gregory Dix, *A Detection of Aumbries* (Westminster: Dacre Press, 1942); S. J. P. van Dijk and J. Hazelden Walker, *The Myth of the Aumbry* (London: Burns & Oates, 1957); Daniel R. Cahill, *The Custody of the Holy Eucharist* (Washington: The Catholic University of America Press, 1950). A number of Dix's conclusions have been challenged by van Dijk and Walker, but the matter will not be treated in detail in this work.

[148] Dix, *op. cit.*, p. 16; Jungmann, *The Mass of the Roman Rite*, II, 312. Dix is of the opinion that the practice of reservation in all its later adaptations originated in the *fermentum*.

common in northern Italy as late as the sixteenth century. There is no certain case of an altar being used as the place of permanent reservation before the year 800.[149] Reservation in an ambry was customary in Italy, Germany, and Spain until the sixteenth century. From about the eleventh century in the West, it was also common to reserve the consecrated particles in a dove, tower, pyx, or basket made of precious material and suspended from the civory of the high altar or from a crozier-like pole. In England this was the usual form of reservation until the Reformation;[150] in France, the custom prevailed until the Revolution.[151] The practice, however, was not common in Italy, Germany, or the Low Countries, and seems to have been almost unknown in Spain.[152]

In 1215, the IV General Council of the Lateran decreed that the Blessed Sacrament should be kept under lock and key, within the church itself.[153] Although the council made no specific mention of the tabernacle, nevertheless the demands of the law paved the way for the tabernacle as the best means of fulfilling the law. In Italy, Spain, and Portugal the decree was generally enforced. The custom of the ambry came into general use in these countries and continued to be the standard receptacle throughout the Middle Ages.[154] North of the Alps and the Pyrenees, various methods of reserving the Blessed Sacrament prevailed, but the custom of reserving the particles in a tabernacle on the altar

[149] Braun, *op. cit.*, II, 682; Dix, *op. cit.*, p. 25.
[150] Dix, *op. cit.*, pp. 37–42.
[151] *Ibid.*, pp. 35–36.
[152] *Ibid.*, pp. 34, 36–37.
[153] Canon 20: Mansi, XXII, 1107.
[154] Dix, *op. cit.*, p. 34.

seems to have originated in France.[155] By the fifteenth century, the tabernacle on the altar was common on the continent of Europe.[156] In 1614 the *Rituale Romanum* required the use of a tabernacle to be set on the main altar or some other altar.[157] There is no doubt that from that time onward the tabernacle was to be connected with the altar. Various decrees of the Congregation of Sacred Rites mentioned this fact with relation to the tabernacle.[158]

In spite of the decrees that the tabernacle rest upon the middle of the altar and be inseparable from it, the older methods of reserving the Blessed Sacrament did not cease. Certainly in those places where through immemorial custom other methods had never been discontinued, they could be tolerated and actually were tolerated by church authorities.[159] However, under no circumstances was the reintroduction of the *armarium* or ambry or suspended Eucharistic vessel to be permitted. The Congregation of Sacred Rites reprobated any such practice in a letter which

[155] *Ibid.*, p. 35.

[156] Cahill, *The Custody of the Holy Eucharist*, p. 22.

[157] "Curare porro debet parochus, ut perpetuo aliquot particulae consecratae eo numero, qui usui infirmorum et aliorum fidelium communioni satis esse possit, conserventur in pyxide ex solida decentique materia, eaque munda, et suo operculo bene clausa, albo velo cooperta, et quantum res feret, ornato in tabernaculo clave obserato. Hoc tabernaculum . . . in altari maiori vel in alio, quod venerationi et cultui tanti Sacramenti commodius ac decentius videatur, sit collocatum. . . ." *Rituale Rom.*, tit. IV, c. 1, *de sanctissimo Eucharistiae sacramento*, nn. 5–6.

[158] S.R.C., *Sarnen.*, July 17, 1688: *Decr. Auth.*, n. 1796; *Augustae Praetoriae*, July 21, 1696, ad 3: *Decr. Auth.*, n. 1946; *Sancti Iacobi de Cile*, March 14, 1861, ad 13: *Decr. Auth.*, n. 3104; *Urgellen.*, Dec. 5, 1868, ad 2: *Decr. Auth.*, n. 3192; Gandaven., May 18, 1878, ad 1, 2: *Decr. Auth.*, n. 3449; Cuneen., June 2, 1883, ad 6: *Decr. Auth.*, n. 3567.

[159] Vermeersch-Creusen, *Epitome Iuris Canonici*, II, 418.

it sent to the bishops of Belgium in the name of the Holy Father on August 21, 1863.[160]

As a place for reserving the Blessed Sacrament, the tabernacle seems to have been a compromise between the Italian and Spanish ambry, which preserved the Sacrament securely, and the hanging pyx or the open pyx on the altar, common in the northern countries where the people wanted to see the Blessed Sacrament. Dix (1901–1952) was of the opinion that Rome accepted the compromise of the tabernacle and discarded the traditional Italian ambry as a response to the more frequent communion of the laity which accompanied the Counter-Reformation. Suspension of the Blessed Sacrament in a pyx presupposed that the Eucharist would only be required for an occasional sick-call. The tabernacle was not only in conformity with the rule of the IV General Council of the Lateran, but it was also convenient for the administration of the Eucharist both in and outside of Mass.[161]

In his discourse to the participants in the First International Congress of Pastoral Liturgy at Assisi in 1956, Pope Pius XII discussed the relationship between the tabernacle and the altar:

In the same way that We were just saying: "Christ is in some respects greater than the altar and the sacrifice," We could now ask: "Is the tabernacle where our Lord, come down among His people, dwells, superior to the altar and to the sacrifice?" The altar surpasses the tabernacle because on it is offered the sacrifice of the Lord. The tabernacle, doubtless, possesses the *sacramentum permanens;* but it is not an *altare permanens,* because it is

[160] Van der Stappen, *Sacra Liturgia* (Vol. IV, 3. ed., Mechliniae, 1912), IV, 112. This decree is not contained in the official collections of decrees of the Congregation of Sacred Rites.

[161] Dix, *op. cit.*, pp. 71–72.

> only during the celebration of the holy Mass that Christ offers Himself in sacrifice on the altar—not after, nor outside of, Mass. In the tabernacle, on the other hand, He is present as long as the consecrated species remain, without, however, offering Himself perpetually. One is fully justified in distinguishing between the offering of the sacrifice of the Mass and the *cultus latreuticus*, the supreme form of worship offered to the God-man hidden in the Eucharist. A decision of the Sacred Congregation of Rites, dated July 27, 1927, limits as much as possible the exposition of the Blessed Sacrament during Mass: but this is easily explained by the desire of keeping habitually separate the act of sacrifice and the worship of simple adoration in order that the faithful would clearly understand their proper character.
>
> Nevertheless, it is more important to recognize the unity than this diversity: it is one and the same Lord who is immolated on the altar and honored in the tabernacle and who pours out from there His blessings . . .[162]

From this statement, it seems clear that although there is a theological unity between the Lord sacrificed on the altar and the Lord present in the tabernacle, there is no theological reason why the tabernacle must be *spatially* united with the altar; in fact sound liturgical principles seem to indicate that the tabernacle should not be on the altar during Mass. The *Caeremoniale Episcoporum* prescribes that the Blessed Sacrament should be removed from the main altar for pontifical Mass, and the *Ordo Hebdomadae Sanctae* directs that the tabernacle, if it is on the main altar, should be empty for the evening Mass on Holy Thursday, which commemorates the institution of the Mass. The altar is the table of sacrifice, not the throne of exposition. Furthermore, the communion particles should be consecrated at each Mass when this is possible, as is clearly indicated in *Mediator Dei.*[163] However, the present discipline concerning the reservation of the Blessed Sacrament clearly states that the

[162] *The Assisi Papers*, p. 233.
[163] AAS, XXXIX (1947), 565.

Eucharist must be reserved in a tabernacle which is firmly joined to an altar at which Mass is celebrated at least once a week.[164]

Practically considered, the tabernacle may be considered as a safe with tight-fitting doors which exclude dust, humidity, and insects.[165] No material is prescribed for the tabernacle, but at least the interior, including the door, must be lined with gold or white silk.[166] If the celebrant follows the recommendation of *Mediator Dei* and consecrates the particles required for Communion at each Mass whenever this is possible, there will be no need for an excessively large tabernacle.[167] It would seem, then, that the tabernacle need only be large enough to hold one or two ciboriums and, if needed for Benediction with the Blessed Sacrament, a vessel containing a large host. Certainly there is never any need for the tabernacle to be excessively high. With a design dictated by its purpose, the tabernacle should stand in simple dignity.

Since the tabernacle should be covered with a veil,[168] which may be white or of the appropriate liturgical color,[169] it is sometimes recommended that the upper part of the tabernacle should take the form of a dome or a pyramid.

[164] Canons 1269, § 1, and 1265, § 1; S.R.C. decr. June 1, 1957, nn. 2, 3.—*AAS*, XXXXIX (1957), 425.

[165] S. C. de Sacr. Instruction of May 26, 1938: *AAS*, XXX (1938), 199.

[166] S.R.C., *Urgellen.*, Aug. 7, 1871, ad 5–8: *Decr. Auth.*, n. 3254; *Calven. et Theanen.*, June 5, 1889: *Decr. Auth.*, n. 3709; *Romana*, June 20, 1889, ad 4: *Decr. Auth.*, n. 4035.

[167] *AAS*, XXXIX (1947), 565.

[168] *Rituale Rom.*, tit. IV, c. 1, *de sanctissimo Eucharistiae sacramento*, n. 6; S.R.C., *Ianuen.*, July 11, 1857, ad 10: *Decr. Auth.*, n. 3035; *Auxitana.*, Aug. 7, 1880: *Decr. Auth.*, n. 3520; *Dubium*, July 1, 1904: *Decr. Auth.*, n. 4137.

[169] S.R.C., *Briocen.*, July 21, 1855, ad 10: *Decr. Auth.*, n. 3035; New Code of Rubrics, n. 117.

This prevents placing statues on top of the tabernacle, while making it possible to veil the tabernacle with dignity.[170]

Although the function of the tabernacle is utilitarian, it is also a symbol. The word tabernacle means tent. It evokes the tent of the Old Testament, which covered the ark of the covenant, thus signifying the presence of God in the midst of his people. That tent prefigured the mystery of the Incarnation, in which the "Word was made flesh and pitched his tent among us."[171] It is unlikely that the tabernacle will resemble a tent if it is not covered by the veil prescribed by law.[172] This veil is the one true sign which should identify the place of the Blessed Sacrament in the church. Although the law prescribes that a lamp should be kept burning before the Blessed Sacrament,[173] it is also customary to burn lamps before relics and statues. The tabernacle veil thus is the one sure sign of the reservation of the Blessed Sacrament.

At least one lamp must be kept burning constantly night and day before the tabernacle in which the Blessed Sacrament is reserved.[174] The glass of the lamp should be white, but colored glass is tolerated.[175] The *Caeremoniale Episcoporum* requires many lamps in greater churches, three in front of the main altar and at least five before the Blessed Sacrament, at least on greater days.[176] The lamp may be

[170] Roguet, "Le lieu de la réserve," *La Maison-Dieu*, No. 63 (1960), 118.

[171] John 1:14.

[172] Roguet, *loc. cit.*

[173] Canon 1271.

[174] Canon 1271; *Rituale Rom.*, tit. IV, c. 1, *de sanctissimo Eucharistiae sacramento*, n. 5.

[175] S.R.C., *Cuneen.*, June 2, 1883: *Decr. Auth.*, n. 3576, ad 5.

[176] Lib. I, c. XII, n. 17.

placed anywhere near the tabernacle, but it should not be placed on the altar itself or on top of the tabernacle.[177] The substance to be burned may be either olive oil, beeswax, or vegetable oil.[178] In short, a crystal container in which a clear flame burns brightly is the best symbol of sacrifice as the substance is consumed in the presence of the Eucharist.

THE PLACE FOR THE PROCLAMATION OF THE WORD

The liturgy of the Word is frequently thought of as distinct from the Eucharistic liturgy. Various factors are responsible for this unfortunate dichotomy. For example, the term *Foremass* designating the first part of the Mass suggests that it is not an essential part of the Mass. The same idea seems to be implicit in the terms *Mass of the Catechumens and Mass of the Faithful.*[179] Although in ancient times the celebration of the Eucharist was occasionally not preceded by the liturgy of the Word, as in the Mass of Holy Thursday at Rome,[180] it is only by archeologizing that this fact can be projected into the present Mass. Since apostolic times, the liturgy of the Word and the Eucharistic liturgy have constituted a single celebration.[181]

It may be said that there would be no liturgy without

[177] Cahill, *op. cit.*, pp. 80–81; S.R.C., *Romana,* June 20, 1899, ad 6: *Decr. Auth.*, n. 4035; *Ordinis Capuccinorum*, Aug. 20, 1699: *Decr. Auth.*, n. 2033.

[178] Canon 1271; S.R.C., *Plurium Diocesium,* July 9, 1864: *Decr. Auth.*, n. 3121.

[179] Roguet, "The Whole Mass Proclaims the Word of God," *The Liturgy and the Word of God* (Collegeville, Minnesota: The Liturgical Press, 1959), pp. 67–68.

[180] Innocent I, *Epist. ad Decentium*, VII: *PL*, XX, 559.

[181] Jungmann, *The Mass of the Roman Rite*, I, 391–93.

the Word, without the Bible. Not only are the readings drawn from the Bible, but the whole liturgy resounds with echoes from the Bible, from the Word of God. The liturgical assembly is the privileged place for the proclamation of this Word. The first part of the Mass is neither a Foremass nor a mere catechesis, but it is a liturgy of the Word of God, which is a proclamation in the Church of the mystery of salvation realized in the Eucharist.[182]

With this in mind, one can appreciate the importance which the early documents of the Church and the writings of the Fathers gave to the Word of God and the place for its proclamation.[183] From a functional point of view, it is easy to understand that the place was above all an elevated structure, from which the Word carried to all parts of the church. The early names for the place seem to indicate this fact: *bema* signifies a tribune or platform; *ambo* seems to come from the verb ἀναβαίνειν which means to mount; and *suggestum* likewise means an elevated place.[184] The admonition which the bishop addresses to candidates for the lectorate also alludes to the fact that the Word should be proclaimed from a high place, so that it may be heard by all.[185] Aside from acoustical reasons, the important position which tradition has given to the place for the proclamation of the Word emphasizes the dignity of the sacred minister, who

[182] Conclusions formulated by the Third National Congress of the Centre de Pastorale Liturgique at Strasbourg, France, in 1958, *The Liturgy and the Word of God*, pp. v-vi.

[183] Cf. Jungmann, *op. cit.*, I, 391–419.

[184] Gelineau, "Le sanctuaire et sa complexité," *La Maison-Dieu*, No. 63 (1960), 63.

[185] "Ideoque, dum legitis, in alto loco Ecclesiae stetis, ut ab omnibus audiamini." Pontificale Rom., tit. *De ordinatione lectorum*.

spreads the message of salvation and also the sacred character of the Word itself.[186]

The location of the elevated place from which the Word was read has not been determined with any regularity in the course of the Church's history. Very early in the development of the liturgy, a special reader was appointed to perform the readings; it was someone distinct from the leader of the liturgical service, as is clear from Justin's *First Apology*, written in Rome about 150.[187] In the basilicas built after 313, the ambo was a lofty and sometimes grand structure with steps and a marble stand on which to rest the codices. The singing of the psalms and the long alleluias was also conducted from the ambo. There was as a rule only one ambo. In fact, Amalarius of Metz (780–850) is the first to mention an *excellentior locus* for the reading of the gospel.[188] The *Ordo Romanus II*, which originated in northern Europe in the tenth century, directs the subdeacon who reads the epistle to mount the ambo, but he is not to stand on the highest step, for it is reserved for the singing of the

[186] English-speaking people regularly refer to the place of proclamation as the *pulpit*, a word which comes from the Latin *pulpitum*, meaning a tribune or platform. The French and German words, however, are more significant. The Germans use the word *Kanzel*, which is derived from the *cancelli*, the choir enclosure in the early Roman basilicas, at the edge of which was constructed the ambo for the reading of the epistle and gospel. In French, the word for the place of proclamation is *chaire*, seat, a usage that goes back to the time when the bishop preached to the faithful from his throne at the back of the apse. Note that the homily must be associated with the *cathedra* and the readings of the scriptural lessons with the ambo.—Van der Meer and Mohrmann, *Atlas of the Early Christian World*, p. 137.

[187] LXVII: *PG*, VI, 430.

[188] *De ecclesiasticis officiis*, III, 18: *PL*, CV, 1126 C.

gospel.[189] It was Durandus (1237–1296) who first spoke of a specially built ambo for the gospel.[190] In churches where there were two ambos, both were built in the middle of the nave within the ambit of the area reserved for the *schola cantorum*. The ambo on the right was more elevated and was reserved for the bishop when he could not speak from his throne, and for the deacon when he sang the gospel. The ambo on the left had two levels: the *cantor* stood on the lower level to sing the gradual,[191] and the lector stood on the higher level to read the epistle.[192]

The clergy in the Middle Ages left their place at the back of the apse and assembled in the enclosed area directly in front of the altar. The enclosure gradually developed into a monumental structure, so designed that the choir could take its place on top of the structure. It was also from this elevated place that the epistle and gospel were read, and from here the celebrant preached to the people. The structure became known as the *lectorium* or *jube*, the latter term being derived from the request for a blessing, "Jube, domne, benedicere," which the lector made before reading a lesson.[193]

Preaching proved rather ineffective in the large medieval churches, at least when the speaker addressed the community from a place raised high above the level of the nave. Consequently, with the advent of the mendicant orders in the thirteenth century, portable pulpits were set up

[189] *Ordo Rom. II*, n. 7: *PL*, LXXVIII, 971.
[190] *Rationale Divinorum Officiorum* (Venetiis, 1568), IV, 24, 20.
[191] The term *gradual* is derived from the Latin *gradus*, the reference being to the step on which the *cantor* stood while singing the responsory after the epistle.
[192] Righetti, *Storia Liturgica*, I, 389–90.
[193] *Ibid.*, p. 390.

out in the nave of the church in the midst of the people. Occasionally, the pulpit was even set up out in the church yard. It should be noted that in the early centuries the sermon was regularly a homily or a commentary on the scripture readings from the liturgy, but in the late Middle Ages a dichotomy was not uncommon between the theme of the sermon and the theme of the Mass.[194]

About the fifteenth century, the pulpit took up a fixed position in the church. With a shell-shaped canopy erected above and to the rear of the preacher to favor the acoustics, the pulpit was placed against a pillar in the nave. In the Renaissance and baroque periods, it was customary to attach the pulpit to the church wall or to one of the pillars, without any architectural support beneath it. During these periods the pulpit was a very large structure with elaborate ornamentation. It was the place from which a preacher would deliver an oration rather than proclaim the living Word of God.[195]

There is no existing law governing the design or the location of the lectern or ambo. The present liturgical renewal with its movement back to meaningful essentials has restored the homily to its proper place,[196] and the lectern has once again taken its normal place in the sanctuary. There is no need for a pulpit distinct from the ambo or lectern.

The Roman liturgy provides for two distinct places for the reading of the epistle and the gospel. Consequently, two ambos may be erected, one on the epistle side, and the other, the more important, on the gospel side. But in

[194] *Loc. cit.*
[195] Eisenhofer-Lechner, *The Liturgy of the Roman Rite*, p. 134; Miller, *Fundamentals of the Liturgy*, p. 111.
[196] Cf. New Code of Rubrics, n. 474.

the normal parish church where the space is often somewhat restricted, it is usually neither possible nor opportune to construct two ambos. One suffices. It should be erected on the side of the church where the gospel is usually read.[197]

It is better to speak of the place from which the Word is spoken as a lectern or an ambo than as a pulpit, for the readings from sacred scripture are always more important than the word of the preacher, whose mission is not so much that of an orator as that of a minister of God's Word. It is this idea which should bring the lectern into close proximity to the altar. Both Word and sacrament come from the same God within the framework of the same liturgical sacrifice. Like the altar itself, the lectern should stand in simple dignity worthy of the function it fulfills. It should not be unduly massive, nor should it be a merely portable stand for notes. If it is elevated by a step, the lectern better depicts the apostolic office of announcing the good tidings. Finally, it has been recently recommended that the lectern should be so designed that the book of the gospels may be kept there in a place of honor outside of the time of Mass.[198]

TRANSITION BETWEEN PRESBYTERY AND NAVE—THE PRE-SANCTUARY

There is another area within the ambit of the presbytery which the contemporary liturgical renewal has brought into focus once again. In the *Apostolic Constitution* and *Didas-*

[197] Gelineau, *loc. cit.*, 64.

[198] Th.-G. Chifflot, "Les leçons d'un concours," *La Maison-Dieu*, No. 67 (1961), n. p.; "La Bible et l'ambon," (insert), *L'Art Sacré* (January–February, 1960).

calia Apostolorum, it was designated as the place for the deacons;[199] in the present church it is that undefined transition area which often exists between the sanctuary and the nave.

In the churches of the Oriental rites, in front of the chancel or the iconostasis which encloses the sanctuary and above the level of the nave, there is an area which the Greeks call *solea* or threshhold.[200] It is the area proper to the deacons and to those who direct the liturgical assembly. There they address their proclamations to the people and sing the prayers of the litanies; there they call the attention of the people to the readings and to the anaphora. The ancient Syrian documents indicated above assert that the deacons in their proper place should watch over the community so that good order reigns and all proceeds in the assembly with dignity. There seems to be a similarity between the *solea* and the area for the choir in the medieval Roman basilicas.

In the present Roman liturgy, the deacon does not frequently address the assembly during the Mass. He proclaims the gospel, dismisses the assembly with his "*Ite missa est,*" and if the liturgy requires it, he sings the "*Procedamus in pace,*" the "*Flectamus genua,*" "*Levate,*" and "*Humiliate capita vestra Deo.*" The primary function of the deacon is to assist the celebrant in the presbytery and at the altar. With the liturgical renewal and the active, intelligent participation of the faithful in the liturgy, there is a need for someone to direct the assembly. Taking cognizance of this fact, the Congregation of Sacred Rites has entrusted the function

[199] *Constitutio Apostolorum,* II, 57, 4; *Didascalia Apostolorum,* II, 57, 6–7.

[200] Stephen G. Xydid, "The Chancel Barrier, Solea, and Ambo of Hagia Sophia," *The Art Bulletin,* XXIX (March, 1947), 11–13.

of directing the participation of the assembly to a commentator.[201] A detailed discussion of the role of the commentator does not have a place here, but some attention should be given to his proper place within the church.

According to the Instruction, if the commentator is a priest or a cleric, he may take his place in the sanctuary, or at the altar-rail, or at an ambo or lectern; but if he is a layman, he takes his place in front of the assembly, but outside of the presbytery.[202] Although the cleric functioning as a commentator may legitimately take his place within the presbytery, even at the ambo or lectern, it would seem that his proper place is not within the presbytery, for he does not function as a minister, but his role is rather that of an intermediary between the presbytery and the nave. Nor is his place at the ambo or the lectern, for the latter is reserved for the proclamation of God's Word and for the homily which is an extension of that Word.

The commentator should be seen by the people, but he should not detract from the action of the liturgy. As the Instruction indicates, his explanations and directions should be brief, restrained, and delivered in a moderate voice. He should accompany the liturgical function so that the action proceeds with dignity and piety.[203] The commentator fills informally the function which the deacon only rarely and formally fills. A good part of his office is an expedient, made necessary by the lack of liturgical formation on the part of the faithful. If it is possible, then, a place should be provided for the commentator a step or so below the level of

[201] S.R.C., instr., De musica sacre et sacre liturgia, September 3, 1958, n. 96.: *AAS*, L (1958), 657.
[202] *Ibid.*, n. 96b.
[203] *Ibid.*, n. 96f.

the presbytery and a step or so above the level of the nave.

The area of transition between the nave and the presbytery is also the place where the faithful come to receive Holy Communion. The fact that they approach the altar to receive the Eucharist is a sign of their participation in the holy action of the Mass. The faithful really should communicate at the altar itself, but in most churches of the Roman rite there is a communion or altar rail where the people kneel to receive the Eucharist. The origin of this railing is nebulous. Some maintain that it is a compromise between the medieval rood screen and the high wall which enclosed the choir in the Roman basilica.[204] This opinion, however, is improbable. The rood screen was a late medieval development, whereas the altar railing was already in existence by the time of Constantine.[205] Rather it seems likely that the communion rail was revived from the enclosure for the choir or the low balustrade, the *pergula*, which separated the presbytery from the nave in the Roman basilica when a special choir enclosure was lacking.[206]

Besides marking off the sanctuary from the nave, the communion rail may also serve a nobler purpose. Communion should be given to all at the altar;[207] in a symbolic sense, then, the railing should be considered an extension of the altar itself. To emphasize the link between the altar and rail, the latter is sometimes broadened so that it resembles a narrow table. The white cloth which sometimes covers the

[204] Cf. Peter Anson, *op. cit.*, p. 136.

[205] Cf. Eusebius, *Historia Ecclesiastica*, X, 4: GCS, II(2), 863.

[206] Miller, *Fundamentals of the Liturgy*, pp. 110–11; O'Connell, *op. cit.*, p. 13.

[207] Cf. the prayer *Supplices* of the canon of the Mass: "ut quotquot, ex hac altaris participatione sacrosanctum Filii tui, Corpus et Sanguinem sumpserimus . . ."

rail at communion time further stresses this symbolism.[208]

Since the communion rail is nowhere prescribed, and since it often serves as a psychological barrier between the presbytery and the nave, the substitution of communion tables for the long rail extending across the sanctuary is a practice which recommends itself.

SUMMARY

In the present chapter, an attempt has been made to determine the role of the principal elements encompassed by the area of the sanctuary: the *sedile* or the place for the celebrant, the altar, the lectern for the proclamation of the Word, and the area of transition between the sanctuary and the nave. The sanctuary is an ordered complex of these elements, each with its own function and dignity.

Since the sanctuary is the focal point of the church, in area it should be adequate, but not excessively large. If the sanctuary is too deep, the rapport between the presbytery and the nave is hindered, as is the case in Gothic churches and in churches where a large choir intervenes between the altar and the nave. If the sanctuary is too wide, the unity of the liturgical action is hindered in the sense that attention is not concentrated on a specific area. One often finds this fault in square churches where the sanctuary is the same width as the nave.

The preeminence of the sanctuary in the church likewise

[208] Such a cloth is prescribed both by the *Rituale Romanum*, tit. V, c. II, *Ordo administrandi sacram Communionem*, ad 1, and the *Caeremoniale Episcoporum*, I. II, c. XXIX, n. 3. The omission of any specific mention of the communion cloth in the New Code of Rubrics would seem to indicate that it is no longer prescribed.

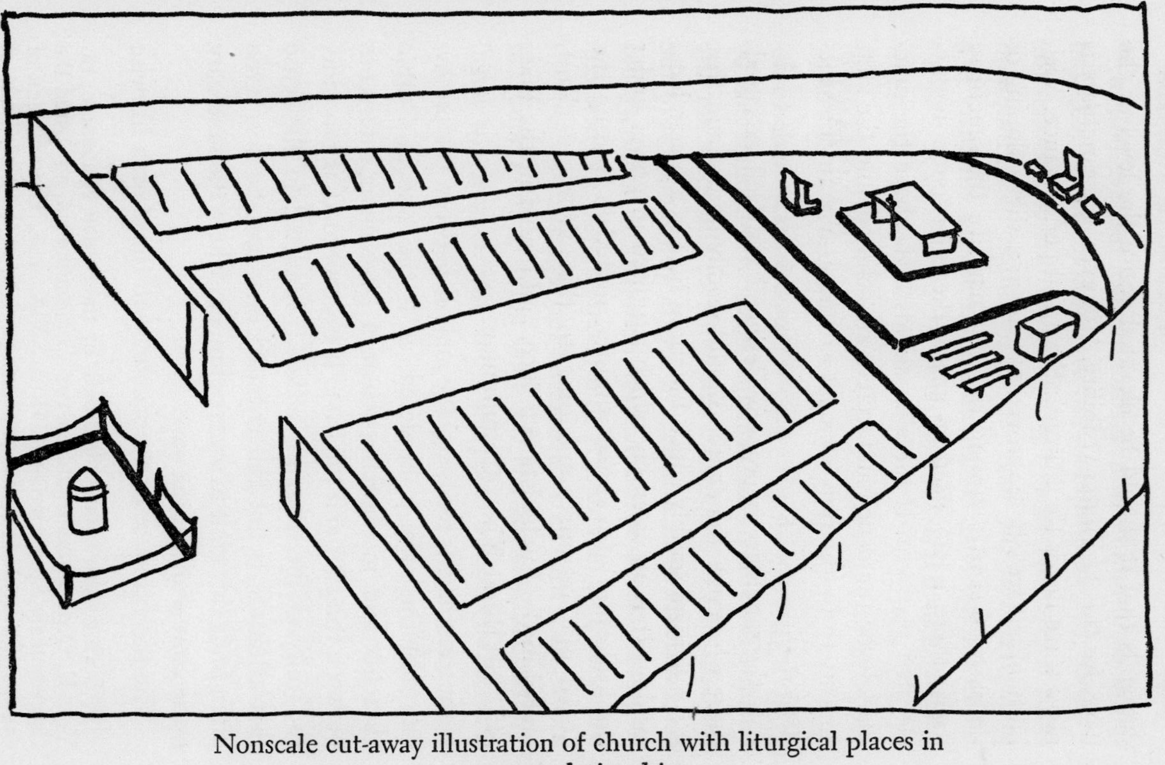

Nonscale cut-away illustration of church with liturgical places in proper relationships.

demands that it should be elevated above the level of the nave, for this facilitates visibility. However, the sanctuary is not a stage nor is the liturgy a theatrical performance. Visibility might well be improved by way of a slight sloping of the nave to slant it toward the sanctuary. In the sanctuary itself, there is no need to place the altar on a highly-elevated platform. If the altar stands high above the sanctuary level, the bench and lectern are eclipsed, and the altar appears to be the only element of importance in the sanctuary.

If the sanctuary is properly designed and well executed, those who enter the church should readily understand that it is a living assembly which functions here in a hierarchical fashion. It is an assembly which is united in prayer under the leadership of a sacred minister, united in hearing the Word of God and responding to that Word in chant, united in the Eucharistic Sacrifice, and united in the Body of Christ through holy Communion.

7

The Nave

In the preceding chapter, the writer attempted to demonstrate that the sanctuary is not a desert in which the altar stands as an oasis. Rather it is a complex area, where various elements and various participants find their proper place and function. In an analogous manner, the nave is not an anonymous area filled with chairs or benches where indifferent observers look at a spectacle. Although the function and organization of the nave will vary with the community which it serves, its essential nature is determined by the liturgy itself. Naturally the nave of a monastic chapel will be different from the nave of a city parish church, both by reason of its size and by reason of the needs of the people who assemble there. The present chapter, however, will be placed in the perspective of an ordinary Sunday assembly in an average parish church.

THE NAVE AS THE AREA FOR THE PEOPLE OF GOD

The nave of a church serves four principal liturgical functions. It is the area (1) for assembling the people of God; (2) for listening to God's Word; (3) for praying and singing to God, and (4) for offering the Eucharist and for receiving holy Communion. Each of these functions places special spatial demands on the edifice, and if the demands are properly met, the various aspects of the mystery of the liturgy will be symbolized.

The Assembly of the People of God

Above all, the nave is the area destined to house the parochial assembly. Since this is the function which regulates its dimensions, the first question to be asked is: How many people should the church hold? However, the functional aspect of the building is not the only one which the architect should consider. A purely quantitative or administrative approach to the problem of designing the nave may in the end produce a plan which is quite incompatible with the *raison d'être* of the liturgy. The liturgical assembly gathered in the nave should also be a sign of God's people united in prayer and action.

There is no doubt that the participation of the people in the liturgy is greatly affected by the dimensions of the nave. Very large edifices involve almost insoluble problems from a pastoral point of view. The celebration of the liturgy is complicated in these churches for the reason that there is scarcely any authentic dialogue between the sanctuary and the nave.[1] Without artificial amplification, the words of the sacred ministers scarcely reach the ears of the assembly. In small churches, it is much easier for the community to pray together, to sing together, to listen to the Word of

[1] Obvious examples of this dialogue in the Roman rite occur in the acclamations before the gospel and the preface.

God, and to go in orderly procession to receive the Bread of Life. There is no doubt, then, that the depth and fervor of the liturgical life of a community are affected by the dimensions of the nave.

Another factor whch should be taken into consideration by the architect is the diversity of assemblies which gather in the church. For example, the community is usually large on Sunday, but small during the week; likewise, the congregation is much larger at a parish mission than at a funeral or wedding. Regardless of its size, the community should form an organized unit focused on the sanctuary. These problems may be solved in various ways. One solution is a small chapel which may be used for weekday Masses and for the celebration of weddings and small funerals. This chapel might also serve for the reservation of the Blessed Sacrament, for various devotions, and for private prayer and meditation. The essential point is that the various needs of the community should be met in a practical yet intelligent manner.[2]

Hearing the Word of God

Assembled in the nave of the church, the Christian community receives and responds to the Word of God. All the faithful should be able to see the lector as he proclaims the Word of God, and they should be able to hear the Word both clearly and easily. The best electric reproduction of sound is never so effective as the living word; however, one should not hesitate to use these acoustical devices if the

[2] Filthaut, *Contemporary Church Art*, p. 51; Gelineau, "La nef et son organization," *La Maison-Dieu*, No. 63 (1960), 69–70.

word of the minister does not carry to all parts of the church.[3] It is also essential that the sacred minister or the lector should face the entire congregation while he is speaking. If the people are gathered on all sides of the altar or on three sides, the contact of the minister with the people is definitely hindered, for at best some of the people see only the priest's profile or back while he is speaking.

In the medieval and renaissance churches, where the pulpit often stood far from the altar, there seemed to be two distinct celebrations, that of the Eucharist and that of the Word. The liturgical renewal has emphasized the essenstial relationship between the lectern and the altar, and the practice of giving homilies based on the liturgy is increasing. No matter how much the liturgical rites are simplified and clarified, they still remain mysteries which the people can penetrate only by faith. Faith in turn must be clarified and formed by the preaching of God's Word.[4] If preaching is to be effective, it must be vital not only in its presentation but also in its reception.

To Pray and to Sing Together

The faithful respond to the Word through their own acclamations which are either spoken or chanted. All community prayer presupposes a coherent assembly. In general, modern architecture has facilitated the concentration of the assembled people in a determined area, but one still finds churches in which the nave is very long and narrow, or cut up into isolated nooks and corners. The unfortunate

[3] S.R.C., instr., *De Sacra Musica et Sacra Liturgia*, Sept. 3, 1958, n. 72, *AAS*, L (1958), 652.

[4] Roguet, "Liturgical Renewal and the Renewal of Preaching," *The Assisi Papers*, p. 92.

practice of building churches with several transepts, so that there are really several naves, is not at all uncommon. Churches of this type tend to divide the faithful into distinct communities.

The plan of the nave should favor exchange and dialogue not only between the faithful and the sacred minister but also among the faithful themselves. The people should be able to pray together and sing together as an organized unit under the leadership of one commentator or director. In short, the plan of the nave should symbolize that community of faith and charity which the liturgy inculcates in the members of the Body of Christ.[5]

Offering and Communicating

The liturgical action culminates in the actual offering of the Eucharist during which the entire assembly is centered on the altar where Christ is sacramentally immolated by the priest. There is an obvious need for visibility on the part of the faithful. Structural steel and concrete have facilitated the design of church edifices without pillars; there is no reason, then, why a clear view of the sanctuary should not be accessible from all parts of the nave. However, in designing the plan of the nave, one must also take into account the various ceremonies that take place within the Eucharistic action.

First of all, there should be a wide center aisle for the procession and recession of the sacred ministers and servers on the more important feast days. Although the offertory procession of the faithful no longer exists as it did in the early Church, the offertory collection which partially replaces

[5] Gelineau, *loc. cit.*, pp. 74–75.

the former offertory procession can be carried out under conditions which give better expression to its mystery. In smaller churches and communities, it is often customary for the faithful to place their own altar bread in the ciborium which rests on a table either at the head or the back of the nave. At the offertory, the ciborium is carried to the altar in a dignified procession.[6] This custom is certainly praiseworthy, since it facilitates the reception of Communion particles consecrated at the same Mass.

The reception of Communion and the procession to and from the altar also present problems for the church architect. With the increase in frequent Communions several hundred people often receive the sacrament at the same Mass. In order that the Eucharist may be administered with dignity and efficiency, the displacement of the people at the railing should be free and easy. If the faithful go in procession to Communion tables or areas where they receive the sacrament while standing, the displacement is greatly facilitated. The *Rituale Romanum,* however, prescribes that the communicant should kneel.[7] There should be more than one aisle of access to the Communion area, and there should be sufficient room between the pews so that the people may move in and out with as little disturbance as possible.

[6] Martimort, *L'Église en Frière,* p. 371.

[7] *Rituale Rom.,* tit. V, c. I, *Ordo administrandi sacram Communionem,* n. 1. Until the thirteenth century, it was customary for the faithful to receive holy Communion while standing. It became customary in certain places to spread a cloth for the communicants kneeling at the altar. In the sixteenth century, this cloth was laid over a table or bench which was placed before the communicants between the nave and the presbyterium. In place of tables or benches, solid rails of stone or wood came into use, but they were designed for communicants who received the Eucharist while kneeling. Jungmann, *The Mass of the Roman Rite,* II, 375.

The nave should also be designed to accommodate processions of the clergy and laity through the church. The restored Holy Week Order provides for a number of such processions. For example, on the Second Sunday of Passiontide the faithful should join with the clergy in the procession of the palms.[8] On Holy Thursday, the sacred ministers and servers go in procession to the altar to repose.[9] The faithful come in procession to adore the cross on Good Friday,[10] and on Holy Saturday the clergy and laity all take part in the solemn procession with the paschal candle.[11] Other processions take place within the church on Candlemass Day and during the Forty Hours' Devotion. The design of the nave and the placement of pews and kneeling benches should not immobilize the faithful, but should facilitate their movement throughout the church.

THE PLACE FOR THE CHOIR AND THE ORGAN

Depending on the role taken by music in the liturgy, the location of the choir has varied within the church edifice from century to century. In the fourth, fifth, and sixth centuries, it was sufficient to have a special place for the soloist who executed the versicles to which all the faithful responded with a refrain or a *responsum*.[12] By the seventh

[8] *Ordo Hebdomadae Sanctae Instauratus,* Dominica II Passionis seu in Palmis, tit. *De processione cum ramis benedictis,* n. 16.

[9] Feria V in Cena Domini, tit. *De Solemni translatione ac repositione Sacramenti,* n. 3.

[10] Feria VI in Passione et Morte Domini, tit. *De solemni sanctae Crucis Adoratione,* n. 18.

[11] Sabbato Sancto, tit. *De solemni processione et de praecomio paschali,* n. 10a.

[12] Jungmann, *The Mass of the Roman Rite,* I, 421–30.

century complex melodic chants had developed. Since these were reserved for specialists, the participation of the faithful was diminished, and the soloists took their places together in a choir. In the Carolingian period, the *schola* of trained singers stood opposite the celebrant when he took his place to the right of the altar. During the Middle Ages, the choir mounted the jube, and in the Renaissance, they were located in the lateral tribunes dominating the sanctuary. Finally, with the construction of the grand organs in the baroque period, the choir took its place near the console in a gallery at the rear of the church.[13] It is this latter position which the choir takes in most churches today.

The Choir and Its Position

There are various kinds of choirs. First, there is the *schola cantorum* properly so called. If the *schola* is composed entirely of clerics, they take their place within the sanctuary. They should wear choir dress, and since they exercise a proper and direct ministerial service, they function as liturgical ministers.[14]

Men and boys who are not clerics may also be appointed to perform the sacred music of the liturgy. In such a case, they exercise a direct liturgical ministry, although a delegated one.[15] They may take their place within the sanctuary and should be attired in choir dress.

The actual position of the *schola cantorum* within the

[13] Gelineau, *loc. cit.*, p. 77.

[14] S.R.C., instr., *De musica et sacra liturgia*, Sept. 3, 1958, n. 93a., *AAS*, L (1958), 656.

[15] *Ibid.*, n. 93c.

sanctuary is not determined, but since the choir should function as an intermediary between the faithful in the nave and the major ministers in the sanctuary, it would seem that the best position for the singers is between the altar and the nave. Such a position, however, necessitates great discipline on the part of the *schola*, lest the singers attract attention to themselves and away from the liturgy. Furthermore, if the choir is relatively large, as is the normal case in monastic or collegiate churches, the location of the singers between the altar and the nave removes the altar from its proximity to the people. In such a case, it is better for the choir to assemble at the back of the apse on either side of the bench or throne. The choir in such churches might well take the form of a semi-circle surrounding the altar.

Certainly a male choir whose members take their places somewhere in the sanctuary is the ideal to be striven for in every parish church. Experience with congregational participation demonstrates that the location of the choir in the sanctuary has many advantages. For example, the presence of the choir in the sanctuary helps to define the hierarchical roles in the liturgy: the celebrant presiding over the assembly, the clerics and choir gathered around the celebrant as his principal ministers, and the people facing the ministers, but all in the same line of psychological and visual focus. Furthermore, from his position in the sanctuary, the choir director can control the singing of the entire assembly by leading the responses, by directing their standing and sitting, and by conducting those sung texts in which the people alternate with the choir. Finally, by taking their position in the sanctuary, the choir members enter directly into the action of the liturgy in keeping with their role as sacred ministers.[16]

In churches where a male choir cannot be organized, the choir may be "mixed," or entirely of women or of girls only. Such a choir should take its position outside of the sanctuary or communion rail.[17] The precise location of this type of choir is best determined by the position of the organ. The Instruction of the Congregation of Sacred Rites on "Sacred Music and the Sacred Liturgy" prescribes that "the organ should be placed near the high altar, in the most convenient place, but always so situated that the singers or musicians in their tribune cannot be seen by the faithful assembled in the body of the church."[18] This norm does not imply that the singers must necessarily take their places in the tribune of the organ, but wherever the singers take their place they should not be a distraction to the faithful. If the choir is in an elevated tribune, it should have a grill. Certainly the choir should be in close proximity to the organ, and if the organ should be close to the main altar, there is greater reason why the choir should be near the altar.[19]

Since the choir is meant to be the main support for the singing of the faithful, it should take its place somewhere within close proximity to the nave, ideally at the head of the nave in the first rows of the assembly. This arrangement is both possible and practical, especially in small churches

[16] Theodore Marier, "Choir and Congregational Participation," *Bible, Life and Worship* (Washington, D.C.: The Liturgical Conference, 1961), p. 144.

[17] *De musica et sacra liturgia, AAS*, L (1958), 658.

[18] *Ibid.*, n. 67, 651.

[19] Gelineau, *loc. cit.*, p. 80.

where there is no acoustical problem, and in churches where the whole assembly participates in the singing. One of the most important roles of the choir in the matter of congregational participation is that of a teacher. No exhortation or demonstration is quite so effective as that of musical example on the part of the choir. By singing the responses with the congregation and by supporting the congregation as it sings its own parts, the choir can educate the people how they should take an active, intelligent role in the liturgical rites. To fulfill this role well, the choir should take up its place, if not in the sanctuary, then at the head of the nave.

Certainly, the ideal arrangement is for the entire assembly to sing as many of the chants as they can sing well, although there will be occasions on which the choir may wish to sing polyphony. If the choir takes up its place at the head of the nave on such occasions, there are often acoustical difficulties, and the movements of the director and the handling of musical scores are often a source of distraction for the faithful. From a musical point of view the solution of a gallery at the rear of the church may be excellent, but it is not a satisfactory solution from the point of view of pastoral liturgy. The choir loft at the back of the church is the symbol of the divorce between the liturgy and music, and presents various impediments to the execution of the liturgy.[20]

If there is a great distance between sanctuary and gallery, the choir is psychologically cut off from contact with the liturgy. At times this is made evident by the delay with which the choir sings its musical responses. Furthermore, if

[20] Marier, *loc. cit.*

the choir sings from a choir loft, there is sometimes a temptation for the singers to lose touch with the ritual functions and to execute a repertoire of musical selections as though it were a sacred concert. It seems desirable, then, that the location of the choir at the back of the church should be abandoned.[21]

Above all, the choir should be located where the sound will fill the church. Probably the best solution to the problem would be to place the choir in a tribune to one side of the sanctuary. The area could be elevated above the level of the sancutary and enclosed by a grill, so that the acoustics would not be affected, and so that the choir would not be open to the view of the faithful. Whatever arrangement is made, the singers should be able to see all the rites in the sanctuary area, and they should sense that they are intimately involved in the sacred actions of the liturgy.

Place for the Organ

As the instrument of accompaniment, the organ should normally be placed near the choir. As has already been pointed out, the Instruction of the Congregation of Sacred Rites on September 3, 1958, specifies that "unless ancient custom or some special reason approved by the local ordinary recommend otherwise, the organ should be located in the most suitable place near the altar."[22] Since the primary function of the organ in the liturgy is that of accompanying the chants, and not, as in the classical period, of rendering solos in the course of the liturgical prayers, or to fill up

[21] Gelineau, *loc. cit.*, 81.
[22] N. 67, AAS, L (1958), 651.

moments of silence in the liturgy, the position of the organ should be determined by the position of the choir, and not vice versa.

In large churches there is often a concert organ for special organ solos. It also serves to accompany very large choirs or congregations. In all cases, since the organ has a proper and an important place in the liturgy, provision should always be made for its location in the design of the church. Even if the organ is not to be acquired immediately, a specific location should be set aside for its future installation. This often prevents insoluble problems from arising once the organ is purchased.

THE AREA FOR TRANSITION AND PREPARATION

Although the entrance to the church and the narthex are not really part of the nave, nevertheless, they are so closely associated with the nave and with the assembly that they will be briefly discussed in concluding this chapter.

In the early centuries of the Church, when the catechumenate and public penance were normal institutions in the Church, the non-baptized and the penitents were not admitted to the nave, which was reserved for the faithful. They remained outside of the edifice in a narthex or portico, where they listened to the readings, chants, and prayers from the first part of the Mass. Although the ancient discipline has fallen into desuetude, there is still a need for an area of transition from the street to the church. As the

[23] O'Connell, *Church Building and Furnishing*, p. 88; Gelineau, *loc. cit.*, pp. 82–83.

Directives for the Building of a Church issued by the German hierarchy states:

> It is not desirable that the church edifice, except in cases of necessity, be located directly on a street filled with the noise of business and traffic, even though the people of our times who are so immersed in earthly things do greatly need a distinct reorientation of their mind toward God on high. It would be a commendable thing if the people assembling for divine worship might traverse a zone of quiet, a bordered fore-court, a formal atrium, and so be inwardly disposed and attuned to the divine atmosphere of the sacred interior. . . .
>
> In planning the entrances to the church building the chief considerations should not be simply protection from wind and weather and the orderly coming and going of the congregation.
>
> The portals of the church, and especially the main portal, should by their impressive design suggest to the faithful the symbolism of church portals as representing gates of heaven.[24]

The Church exists not in a civilization which is Christian, but in a world which is visibly secularized and pagan. The faithful do not easily leave this atmosphere behind them when they walk through the door of a church. Since it is only with a heart well prepared that man can take part in the mysteries of faith, an area of transition and preparation should be a normal part of the church structure. What is needed is a modern version of the ancient Christian atrium. An entirely open porch is not satisfactory, for if the area of transition is to fulfill its function of recollection, it should be enclosed and generously proportioned.[25]

Besides preparing the people for worship, the narthex or entrance hall has an essential place in various liturgical rites. For example, the ceremonies preliminary to the administra-

[24] P. 11.

[25] Filthaut, *Contemporary Church Art*, p. 60.

tion of baptism take place there,[26] and also the rites preceding the blessing of a mother after childbirth.[27] The narthex is also a place for the parish bulletin board and book stalls. In fact, the hall could be developed to such proportions that it could contain the shrines for popular devotion. The baptistry could be designed as a part of it, and it might also contain the confessionals.[28] The baptistry and the confessionals, however, will be discussed in greater detail in the next chapter.

What should be emphasized here is the fact that the entrance to the church should be prominent and significant of the sacred mysteries which are reenacted within. To dispose the souls of the faithful for the liturgy, there should be an area of transition from the outside world to the sacred space within. Generously proportioned and utilized to meet the needs of the faithful, this area should share the atmosphere of peace and reverence which is proper to the church itself.

SUMMARY

In the course of the present chapter, an attempt has been made to demonstrate that the nave is not simply an indifferent space filled with pews and people. It is rather the area destined to accommodate the people of God assembled for worship. Since the people must sense their solidarity, the dimensions and the orientation of the nave must be adapted

[26] *Rituale Rom.*, tit. II, c. 2, *Ordo baptismi unius parvuli*, nn. 1–9.

[27] *Rituale Rom.*, tit. VIII, c. 6, *Benedictio mulieris post partum*, n. 1.

[28] Filthaut, *loc. cit.*

to the assembly which gathers there. Provision must be made for the various kinds of assemblies which will change with the nature of the liturgical function. The community at the parish Mass on Sunday will be different from the assembly at a wedding. Therefore, the nave should be designed to permit modification, or a small chapel should be constructed to accommodate limited assemblies.

The Christian assembly must participate in the liturgical function. The participants, one and all, must see clearly and without strain, and so the relationship of the sanctuary and nave must be designed accordingly. The people must also hear plainly and without strain, and so the acoustics must be given due consideration. Furthermore, the people must be able to move around in the nave. A large, central aisle is essential for the entrance procession of the sacred ministers, but a proper provision must also facilitate the dignified procession of the faithful to and from Communion and on other occasions.

The Christian assembly needs a choir or *schola*. Its function is to lead the people in singing, and so its place is at the head of the assembly. It also sings the more difficult chants by itself. In this role, the choir interprets the prayer of the whole assembly, and so its place is near the sanctuary.

Finally, the Christian people need an area for transition between the secular world and the church. The entrance is not just a functional access to the church, but it is a passage from the profane to the sacred. To pass from earth to heaven, the people need a place of quiet and recollection. They should find this in the entrance hall or narthex.[29]

[29] Conclusions of the Sessions of the Centre de Pastorale Liturgique held at Versailles, August 30 to September 1, 1960, devoted to a study of "Le Lieu de la Celebration." *La Maison-Dieu*, No. 63 (1960), 236–37.

8

The Other Functions of a Church

With the recent liturgical renewal, architects have come to think of churches in terms of areas with a set purpose instead of in terms of architectural details. The spatial demands of churches are essentially demands of worship. Furthermore, the worship of the church is above all public worship which is primarily sacramental. Three sacraments especially make spatial demands on the design of a church. Consideration has already been given to the demands which the Eucharist makes, both as a sacrament and as a sacrifice; in this concluding chapter, the sacraments of baptism and penance will be treated. In addition to its acts of public worship, the Church also praises God with acts which are not strictly liturgical but which have an essential place in the Church's cult.[1] The church edifice must be designed to accommodate these acts of devotion. Since representational images have a rightful place in the church edifice, and since they influence the worship of the faithful, some consideration should be given to the role of iconography. Four topics, therefore, will be discussed in this final chapter: the baptistry, the confessionals, the space for devotions, and representational images.

[1] Cf. *Mediator Dei*, *AAS*, XXXIX (1947), 530.

THE BAPTISTRY

The significance of baptism as the means by which souls are incorporated in the Mystical Body has found striking emphasis in the architecture, location, and iconography of the baptistry from the earliest history of church architecture. The early Romans used the term *baptisterium* to designate both their bathrooms and bathtubs, but from the fourth century onward the word was used predominantly for that edifice adjoining the Christian church in which the sacrament of baptism was conferred. The very fact that a special building was erected for the administration of the sacrament indicates the importance which was attached to baptism in the early Church.[2]

Among the ancient baptistries,[3] one of the earliest and the most important from a liturgical point of view is that of the Basilica of St. John Lateran in Rome. It was erected by Pope Sixtus III (432–440) on the spot where a circular baptistry had stood from the time of Constantine the Great. The extant edifice is octagonal.[4]

Although baptistries of various shapes were constructed in the early Church, by far the greater number were octagonal. Like the eight pillars which surrounded the baptismal pool, this basic shape was linked with the mystical

[2] Righetti, *Storia Liturgica*, I, 392; Miller, *Fundamentals of the Liturgy*, pp. 120–21.

[3] Plates of a number of early baptistries and fonts may be found in Van der Meer and Mohrmann, *Atlas of the Early Christian World*, pp. 128–131.

[4] Giovanni Battista Giovenale, *Il Battistero lateranense nelle recenti indagini della Pont. commissione di archeologia sacra* (Roma: Pontificio Instituto di Archeologia Cristiana, 1929).

meaning of the number eight. The number six signified creation, after the number of days of creation; seven symbolized the rest of God and the present aeon; and eight was the number which signified the beginning of the new creation. The eighth day was the day of resurrection, the Lord's day; consequently, it became the symbol of all that was abiding, permanent, and eternal, and also of the life which sprang forth from the baptismal font.[5] The inscription found in the octagonal baptistry adjoining the church of St. Thecla in Milan and reputedly composed by St. Ambrose is striking in this regard:

> Eight-niched soars this church destined for sacred rites,
> eight corners has its font, the which befits its gift.
> Meet it was thus to build this fair baptismal hall
> about this sacred eight: here is our race reborn.[6]

Another feature of most ancient baptistries is the design whereby the pool was below the level of the floor, so that the candidate had to descend several steps to reach the pool, and then ascend several steps after the ceremony. Baptism was administered by immersion so that the candidate stood in water at least up to his waist, and at the naming of the Holy Trinity he was totally submerged three times. This gave clear expression to the Pauline doctrine that the Christian is baptized into Christ's death and burial in order that

[5] Franz J. Dölger, "Zur Symbolik des altchristlichen Taufhauses," *Antike und Christentum*, IV (1934), 153–97; Van der Meer and Mohrmann, *op. cit.*, p. 129.

[6] Octachorum templum sanctos surrexit in usus,
Octagonus fons est munere dignus eo.
Hoc numero decuit sancto baptismatis aulam
Surgere, quo populis vera salus rediit.
—Cited by Dölger, p. 155

he may rise with Christ to a new life of grace.[7] This theme has been extensively developed by the Church Fathers.[8]

The practice of erecting separate baptistries, begun during the reign of Constantine, seems to have prevailed in the West as long as baptism was administered by immersion. North of the Alps, baptism by infusion took the place of baptism by immersion sometime in the ninth century. The change may have been motivated by the cold climate.[9] In the ninth and tenth centuries, small baptismal fonts were common in the north, although in some places such fonts had been erected as early as the sixth century. South of the Alps, separate baptistries, dating from as late as the twelfth and thirteenth centuries, were built in Genoa, Pisa, Lucca, Parma, Florence, Padua, and Siena.[10]

Since it was the right of the bishop alone to administer baptism in the early Church, baptistries were attached only to the cathedral churches. The candidates for baptism had to travel to the episcopal city, where they received the sacrament from the hands of the bishop himself, or from the priest whom the bishop had delegated.[11] By the eighth century the number of Christians had increased to such a degree that the bishops alone were not able to care for so many souls spread over such large territories. Consequently,

[7] Rom. 6:3–11.

[8] Cf. Basil, *Liber de Spiritu Sancto*, XV: *PG*, XXXII, 129c; Cyril of Jerusalem, *Catechesis XX. Mystigogica* II: *PG*, XXXIII, 1081b; Gregory Nazianzen, *In Baptismum Christi: PG*, XLVI, 585; Ambrose, *De Sacramentis*, II: *PL*, XVI, 430b.

[9] Cf. Leclercq, "Baptistère," *DACL*, II, 382–469; Lucien de Bruyore, "La decoration des baptistères paleochrétiens," *Miscellanea Liturgica Cuniberti Mohlberg* (Romae: Edizioni Liturgiche, 1948), I, 189–220.

[10] Righetti, *Storia Liturgica*, I, 394.

[11] *Loc. cit.*

chapels were erected in rural districts which were served by priests and deacons who had previously been assistants in the bishop's own parish.[12] However, it was not until sometime between the tenth and twelfth centuries that this practice became universal.[13]

It was the right of the rectors of these baptismal churches to confer the sacrament on all infants and adults who lived within a certain distance from the church. Baptismal churches and their rights are explicitly mentioned by several councils. For example, a council assembled at Verneuil-sur-Oise in 755 decreed that a public baptistry was to be built only in those churches which were specially designated by the bishop.[14] The Council of Meaux legislated in 845 that no priest was to presume to confer baptism unless the church was a baptismal church.[15] In the *Ecclesiastical Law of King Edgar* (967), it was stated that priests should baptize only in baptismal churches.[16] Similar legislation was enacted at the Council of Limoges (1032).[17] Gratian's *Decree* contains a canon from a certain Council of Toledo, of unknown date, which declared that there should not be several baptismal churches in the same area.[18]

Baptismal churches were first erected in the rural areas and later in the cities themselves. As the number of such churches increased, their territorial limits grew smaller until

[12] Jules Corblet, *Histoire dogmatique, liturgique, et archéologique de baptême* (Paris, 1881–1882), II, 83–86.

[13] Bertrandus Kurtscheid, *Historia Iuris Canonici, Historia Institutorum*, I (Romae: Officium Libri Catholici, 1941), 282.

[14] Canon 7: Mansi, XII, 581.

[15] Canon 48: Mansi, XIV, 830.

[16] Canon 15: Mansi, XVIII, 515.

[17] Sessio II: Mansi, XIX, 543.

[18] C. 16, C. LVI, q. 1.

most of the churches were recognized as parishes with full parochial rights. With the development of parochial rights, the proper place for administering baptism was no longer limited to the cathedral.[19]

As the number of parishes with baptistries increased, the principle was more and more acknowledged that in every parish the pastor should baptize his own subjects.[20] Despite this developing relationship between the parish church and the proper place for baptism, the two were not always recognized as identical. For example, Pignatelli (ca. 1600–1675) stated that the children of one parish could be baptized in another parish, since he did not consider the font essential to every parish church.[21] Schmalzgrüber (1663–1735) simply stated that baptism should be administered in a church where there is a font; he did not indicate that the church should be a parish church.[22]

The Council of Aix in 1585 decreed that there should be a baptismal font erected in every parish within the province, but made no distinction between parochial and non-parochial churches.[23] Fagnani (1598–1678) stated that the proper church for baptism was the parish church. Without giving a complete reference, he declared that the Congregation of the Council desired a font to be erected in every parochial church.[24] In the seventeenth, eighteenth, and

[19] Kurtscheid, *loc. cit.*

[20] Joseph Waldron, *The Minister of Baptism* (Washington, D.C.: The Catholic University of America, 1942), p. 48.

[21] *Consultationes Canonicae* (Coliniae Allobrogum, 1700), Tome IV, Consultatio III, n. 13.

[22] *Ius Ecclesiasticum Universum*, III, 42, n. 50.

[23] Tit. VI: Mansi, XXXIV(2), 943.

[24] *Commentaria in Quinque Libros Decretalium* (Venetiis, 1709), III, tit. *De decimis*, c. XXIX, n. 59.

nineteenth centuries, several provincial councils decreed that the parochial church is the proper place for administering solemn baptism,[25] and on August 29, 1891, the Sacred Congregation of the Council finally decreed that baptismal font should be erected in every parish church.[26]

From an early date it was customary to bless baptismal water on Holy Saturday and on the Vigil of Pentecost in the cathedral or collegiate churches or in certain special parochial churches.[27] The water was then carried from these churches to other parishes. In 1892, the Congregation of Sacred Rites decreed that this custom could no longer be tolerated in the case of parochial churches, but the custom could continue in the case of baptismal churches, if such churches were still in existence.[28] The same Congregation in 1899 explicitly stated that baptismal water should be blessed on Holy Saturday and on the Vigil of Pentecost in all parish churches and in all other churches in which a baptismal font had been lawfully erected.[29] In determining the suitable place for the administration of solemn baptism, the Code of Canon Law decreed primarily that the baptistry

[25] Prov. Council of Naples (1699), tit. III, c. 2, *Coll. Lac.*, I, 180; Prov. Council of Sens (1850), tit. II, c. 2, *Coll. Lac.*, IV, 889; Council of Prague (1860), tit. IV, c. 2, *Coll. Lac.*, V, 490; Provincial Council of Avignon (1849), tit. IV, cap. 2, *Coll. Lac.*, IV, 337.

[26] *ASS*, XXIV (1891), 358.

[27] Walter J. Conway, *The Time and Place of Baptism* (Washington, D.C.: The Catholic University of America Press, 1954), p. 53.

[28] S.R.C., *Spalaten.*, June 7, 1892: *Decr. Auth.*, n. 3776.

[29] S.R.C., *Utinen.*, Jan. 13, 1899: *Decr. Auth.*, n. 4005. The blessing of baptismal water on the Vigil of Pentecost has been suppressed by the restored Holy Week Order.—*Instructio de Ordine Hebdomadae Sanctae Instaurato Rite Peragendo*, II *Adnotiones ad quasdam rubricas Ordinis Hebdomadae Sanctae*, n. 16.

in a church or public oratory is the proper place for conferring the sacrament.[30] The Code further provided that every parish church should have a font, but it does not prohibit the erection of a font elsewhere.[31]

Throughout the history of the baptistry, infant baptism has been greatly responsible for the shape of the font itself. When a small child is to be baptized, a tank or pool is scarcely necessary. Stone or metal basins began to appear as early as the sixth century, and with the established custom of baptism by immersion, large basins gave way to small structures that resemble the ordinary holy water fonts now found at the church entrance.[32] Possibly for hygienic reasons, it became customary not to baptize with water which had been used for others; consequently the font became little more than a receptacle for the baptismal water, since another basin and a shell-like dish were regularly used in the actual baptismal ceremony.[33]

In the IV Provincial Council of Milan (1576), St. Charles Borromeo gave certain norms to be followed concerning the custody of the baptismal font. Among these norms, which have served as the basis for later legislation on the font, he decreed that the font was to be made of marble or stone. It was to be located normally at the entrance of the church and was to be protected at least by a wooden gate.[34]

In general, ecclesiastical legislation concerning the bap-

[30] Canon 773.

[31] Canon 774, §§ 1, 2.

[32] O'Connell, *op. cit.*, p. 123; Miller, *op. cit.*, p. 123.

[33] Eisenhofer-Lechner, *The Liturgy of the Roman Rite*, p. 135; Miller, *loc. cit.*

[34] Pars II, c. II: Harduin, *Acta Concilium et Epistolae Decretales ac Constitutiones Summorum Pontificum* (Paris, 1715), X, 839.

tistry is rather undeveloped. The Code treats the subject in only four canons: in canon 773, the proper place for the solemn administration of the sacrament is the baptistry in a church or public oratory; in canon 774, every parish church must have a baptismal font, although the ordinary may permit a baptismal font to be erected in other churches or public oratories, within the limits of the parish; and finally in canons 775 and 776, there are specific instances when baptism may be administered in non-parochial churches or private houses. These canons are supplemented by the *Rituale Romanum,* which simply states that the font "should be kept in a proper place and is to be of a suitable shape. It should be made of solid material which can hold water, and it should be fittingly decorated. It should be surrounded with a railing, closed with a lock and key, and so well covered that dust and dirt cannot enter it. On it or at least near it (therefore some place in the baptistry) there should be a representation of St. John the Baptist baptizing Christ."[35]

The rubrics for the design and appointment of the baptistry are indeed skeletal, and of necessity they must be supplemented by norms taken from custom. However, in constructing a baptistry today, one must not be satisfied with reproducing more or less the dispositions of the ancient baptistries. One must take into account the meaning of the baptismal mystery. This significance is expressed especially in the newly restored Paschal Vigil, which in a

[35] Tit. I, c. 1, *De sacramento Baptismi rite administrando,* n. 46. A description of the font is also found in the *Memoriale Rituum,* tit. VI, c. 2, § V, n. 9, which has been replaced by the New Holy Week Order.

sense is new but is also a vital part of the Church's tradition.

In the first place, the baptistry is not to be treated as an ordinary piece of furniture nor a mere accessory to the church, as are the pews or kneeling benches. The baptistry is a sacred place. There is now no special blessing of the baptistry, but it shares in the consecration or blessing of the church of which it now regularly forms a part.[36] Although distinct baptistries are not common these days, there is no prohibition against them. The rubrics of the *Rituale Romanum* assume that the baptistry is part of the church, but the rubrics of the restored Easter Vigil take into account distinct baptistries and provide for the blessing of the baptismal water within the baptistry itself.[37] If the baptistry is within the church, one should always conceive of it as a distinct place in the church, possessing its own structure. The baptismal font should never be arbitrarily placed in an empty spot in the church.

Since it is through baptism that one gains entrance into the Church, it seems that the most logical place for the baptistry is near the main entrance of the church edifice. In the Paschal Vigil service, the rubric directs that the baptismal water to be blessed should be placed in a container on the epistle side of the sanctuary, so that the faithful may see it.[38] After the water is blessed, it is carried in procession

[36] The Roman Pontifical of 1596 did not contain a formulary for the blessing of the baptistry, but there is a form of blessing in the twelfth century Roman Pontifical (cf. Andrieu, *Le Pontifical Romain*, I, 289) and also in the thirteenth century Pontifical of Durandus of Mende (cf. Andrieu, *op. cit.*, III, 533).

[37] *Ordo Hebdomadae Sanctae Instauratus*, Sabbato Sancto, tit. *De benedictione aquae baptismalis*, n. 23.

[38] *Ordo Hebdomadae Sanctae Instauratus*, Sabbato Sancto, tit. *De benedictione aquae baptismalis*, n. 20.

to the font.[39] This arrangement seems to presuppose that the baptistry is at the back of the church, where it cannot be seen by the people assembled in the nave. If the baptistry is in the narthex, it should not block the entrance. Both the entrance and the baptistry need their own properly defined spaces. The two areas are related, but they should not coalesce, since they fulfill different functions.[40] If the baptistry stands in the narthex of the church, the candidate comes up from the font in full view of the altar where he will share in the Eucharistic Sacrifice.

The rubrics of the *Rituale Romanum* give certain precise indications of the positions in which the sacrament of baptism is to be conferred. As indicated in the rite for the baptism of adults, the preliminary ceremonies take place at the entrance to the church. In other words, these rites take place in the narthex or entrance hall of the church.[41] The priest stands at the threshold of the nave, while the candidate stands in the narthex.

After the preliminary rites have been performed, the priest leads the candidate into the nave of the church, that is, into the church itself.[42] As they are entering the church, the priest addresses these words to the candidate:

[39] *Ibid.*, n. 22.

[40] Cloud Meinberg, "The Baptistry and Other Spaces," *Worship*, XXXV (August–September, 1961), p. 593.

[41] Fortesque and O'Connell, *The Ceremonies of the Roman Rite Described*, p. 361. "Sacerdos procedit ad fores ecclesiae, et stat in limine: catechizandus vere extra limen." *Rituale Romanum*, tit. II, c. 4, *Ordo baptismi adultorum*, n. 5.

[42] Fortesque and O'Connell, *loc. cit.* "His peractis, sacerdos sinistra manu apprehendens dexteram electi prope brachium, vel ei porrigens extremem partem stolae, ex humero sinistro pendentem, introducit eum in ecclesiam." *Rituale Romanum*, tit. II, c. 4, *Ordo baptismi adultorum*, n. 29.

Enter the temple of God that you may receive the blessing of our Lord Jesus Christ and may have part with him and his saints.[43]

It is quite clear, then, that the Creed and the Our Father are recited within the church itself, but the exorcisms which follow take place at the gates of the baptistry.[44] After the renunciation of Satan and the anointing with the oil of catechumens, the priest changes his stole from violet to white, and only then does he lead the candidate into the baptistry.[45] It is interesting to note that the priest and the candidate enter the gates of the baptistry only for the baptism properly so considered, which begins with the dialogue between the priest and the candidate: "What is your name?"[46] Formerly this dialogue constituted part of the very form of the sacrament; it is not, as is commonly thought, a preparatory examination.[47] It is at this point that the baptismal rites at the Paschal Vigil begin, for the preparatory rites are usually completed in the morning outside of the vigil service itself.[48]

As is clear from the rubrics, the baptistry should be en-

[43] *Rituale Romanum*, tit. II, c. 4, *Ordo baptismi adultorum*, n. 29.

[44] *Rituale Rom.*, tit. II, c. 4, *Ordo baptismi adultorum*, n. 33. If the baptistry itself is in the narthex, the priest and the candidate must return from the nave of the church to the narthex.

[45] *Rituale Rom.*, tit. II, c. 4, *Ordo baptismi adultorum*, n. 37. "Stans ibidem extra cancellos, sacerdos deponit pluviale ac stolam coloris violacei, et sumit stolam ac pluviale albi coloris. Tunc ducitur electus ad baptisterium. . . . Et cum fuerit prope fontem, sacerdos interrogat electum. . . ."

[46] *Loc. cit.*

[47] Roguet, "Le baptistère," *La Maison-Dieu*, No. 63 (1960), 129.

[48] *Instructio de Ordine Hebdomadae Sanctae Instaurate Rite Peragendo*, II, n. 14; *Ritus Pontificalis Ordinis Hebdomadae Sanctae Instaurati*, Sabbato Sancto, c. I, n. 40.

closed by means of a gate secured with lock and key.[49] This is a sign of its dignity and its sacred character. For the actual ceremony of baptism, only the priest, the candidate, and the sponsors necessarily enter the baptistry, but the area should be large enough to accommodate a number of candidates and their sponsors as well as relatives and friends who might be present to witness the sacramental rites. Solemn baptism is not a private ceremony; it should be of interest to the whole parochial community. If the baptistry is relatively small, there should be enough space at its entrance for bystanders in addition to those who must enter for the actual rites.[50]

Although the ancient baptismal pools usually stood in the center of an octagonal structure, Christians today are no longer aware of the symbolism of the octagon; consequently, the architect has greater liberty in the design of the baptistry. The dignity of the font, however, requires that it should be free-standing and that it should be the focal point of the structure. Furthermore, there should be several steps leading down to the font, so that the venerable scriptural significance of the sacrament should not be contradicted.

The baptistry should contain nothing that does not pertain to the administration of the sacrament. After the font, the most important object is the ambry containing the oil of catechumens and the holy chrism. There is also need for a small cabinet to hold the other articles used in the administering of the sacrament—the salt, the candle, the

[49] *Rituale Rom.*, tit. I, c. 1, *De sacramento Baptismi rite administrando,* n. 46.
[50] Roguet, *loc. cit.*, pp. 126–29.

ritual, the stoles, and the white garment. There should also be a table to hold what is necessary during the rite. In some parishes, it is customary to place the paschal candle in the baptistry from the feast of the Ascension until the following Holy Saturday. This candle, which has played an important role in the blessing of the baptismal water,[51] is lighted before the baptism, and from this candle symbolizing Christ the Light and the small candle given to the neophyte at the end of the ceremony is lighted.

As has already been noted, the *Rituale Romanum* prescribes that, where it is possible, a representation of the baptism of Christ should surmount the font or be placed nearby.[52] Other baptismal scenes might well be depicted in the windows or on the walls of the baptistry, for example, the baptism of the eunuch of the queen of Ethiopia, the baptism of the centurion, Cornelius, or the baptism of St. Paul. New Testament figures of baptism might also be represented: the wedding feast of Cana, the encounter of Christ with the Samaritan woman at the well of Jacob, the cure of the paralytic at Bethsaida or of the blind man at the pool of Siloe, the resurrection of Lazarus or of the daughter of Jairus, or the burial and resurrection of Christ. Old Testament figures of baptism might also provide an interesting catechesis, for example, the creation of water, the ark floating on the flood waters, the passage across the Red Sea, the water rushing from the rock of Horeb, or Jonas and the whale. There is less reason for the use of representations of other animals such as the peacock, the phoenix, or the pelican, since they derive their symbolism from me-

[51] *Ordo Hebdomadae Sanctae Instauratus*, Sabbato Sancto, n. 21.
[52] Tit. I, c. 1, *De sacramento Baptismi rite administrando*, n. 46.

dieval legends which mean little or nothing to contemporary Christians.[53]

Although the baptistry and its decoration are important, the architect should always give primary consideration to the font itself. In this regard, the two symbolic aspects of the sacrament of baptism often find no corresponding expression in the design of the font. Baptism is above all an immersion, but this method of administering the sacrament is no longer customary, although it is still provided for in the *Rituale Romanum.*[54] The sacrament also recalls the symbolism of living water, a symbolism which is now usually absent from the baptismal font. At best the font contains a quantity of stagnant water. Generally the font is divided into two sections: the one compartment holds the water, and the other serves as a drain for the used water. The *Rituale Romanum* speaks of this latter compartment as the *sacrarium.*[55] The rubrics also provide for two other utensils in the administration of the sacrament: a vessel or ladle made of silver or other metal, from which the water is poured on the head of the candidate, and a basin or cup to receive the water which flows from the head of the baptized.[56] More commonly, however, the water is allowed to flow into the drain or *sacrarium.*

Regardless of the current method of baptizing, the font nevertheless should be designed to give better expression to the sacramental sign. To portray the Pauline doctrine of

[53] Roguet, *loc. cit.*, p. 131.

[54] Tit. II, c. 4, *Ordo baptismi adultorum*, n. 45.

[55] Tit. II, c. 4, *Ordo baptismi adultorum*, n. 40; cf. *Memoriale Rituum*, tit. VI, c. 2, § V, n. 9.

[56] *Rituale Rom.*, tit. I, c. 1, *De sacramento Baptismi rite administrando*, nn. 59, 60.

baptism as a mystical descent into the death of Christ and a corresponding resurrection with Him into the Easter life,[57] there should be several steps of descent toward the font. It is also possible to design the font in such a way that the basin of baptismal water rests in the center of the font; running water may be kept in the outer portion of the font as a symbol of the living waters of baptism. This outer portion may also serve as a *sacrarium* for the used baptismal water.[58]

In keeping with its importance, the lines of the font should be strong and dignified, with a certain suggestion of massiveness. From looking at the font and the baptistry as a whole, Christians should realize that baptism is a bath of regeneration administered at a font of life-giving water.

THE CONFESSIONALS

A subject which should be treated in conjunction with the baptistry is that of the confessional. According to St. Jerome (ca. 347–420)[59] and Tertullian,[60] the sacrament of penance may be considered a second baptism, since confession readmits the penitent to the sacramental life of the Church. The confessional, however, is a relatively late invention. The early rituals and penitentials treated the questions the confessor should ask the penitent, the penance to

[57] Cf. Rom. 6:4; Col. 2:12.

[58] This is the design of the font in the new Abbey Church of St. John's in Collegeville, Minnesota. A picture and description of the font are in *Worship*, XXXV (August–September, 1961), n.p.

[59] *Epistola CXIII ad Demetriadem de virginitate*, IX: *PL*, XXII, 1115.

[60] *De Poenitentia*, IV: *PL*, I, 1343.

be imposed, and the counsel to be given, but they did not discuss explicitly the place for hearing confessions.

During the Middle Ages, when the majority of laymen received the sacraments only once or twice a year, confessions were usually heard by the priest sitting in the chancel of the church.[61] The *Liber de Divinis Officiis*, attributed to Alcuin (ca. 735–ca. 804), states that the confessor should make the penitent sit down at his side, and indicates that the confessions were heard in the church itself.[62] The abundant conciliar legislation on the place for hearing confessions, dating from the ninth to the seventeenth centuries, emphasizes that sacramental confession should be made in the open church without any attempt to hide either the confessor or the penitent.[63]

The confessional, as it is known today, originated in its basic elements with St. Charles Borromeo. In the Fourth Provincial Council of Milan (1576), he decreed that every church should have a confessional constructed according to the design described in his *Liber Instructionum ad Aedificandam Ecclesiam*.[64] Until this time, such a structure was apparently unknown, since it sufficed that a confessional seat be located in some convenient but public place in the church.

St. Charles indicated that the confessional should be made of walnut or some other wood. It was to be closed on three sides, left, right, and rear, and also covered

[61] Anson, *Churches: Their Plan and Furnishing*, p. 159.
[62] *PL*, CI, 1196–1199.
[63] Francis J. Fazzalaro, *The Place for the Hearing of Confessions* (Washington, D.C.: The Catholic University of America Press, 1950), pp. 2–12.
[64] *Acta Ecclesiae Mediolanensis* (Lugduni, 1682–83), I, 11.

on the top. The floor of the confessional was to be made of wood, and in the middle of the confessional there was to be a seat and an armrest for the priest. The penitent was to kneel on a prie-dieu, separated from the confessor by a wooden partition, in the middle of which was to be cut a small window, divided into three equal parts by two small columns of wood. The window was to be covered with an iron grating on the penitent's side and with a cloth on the confessor's side.[65]

The same Provincial Council of Milan directed that such confessionals should be set up in all churches, both parochial and non-parochial. Cathedral and collegiate churches were to have as many confessionals as were needed, but parochial churches were to have only two, one for men and one for women. In small parochial churches, where there were fewer than five hundred souls, one confessional was sufficient.[66]

In all churches, the confessionals were to stand on the sides of the church, not too close to the main altar, but in an open place. When the confessor occupied the confessional on the epistle side, the penitent was to be at his left, and when he sat in the confessional on the gospel side, the penitent was to be on his right. In each confessional there was to be a crucifix, the list of cases reserved to the Holy See, the list of cases reserved to the bishop, the form of absolution, and the prayers to be said before hearing confessions.[67]

Although the legislation of St. Charles Borromeo was merely particular, other dioceses, especially in France and

[65] *Acta Ecclesiae Mediolanensis*, I, 386, 531, 588.
[66] *Ibid.*, I, 11.
[67] *Ibid.*, I, 486.

Italy, adopted the Milanese rules on the confessional.[68] On June 17, 1614, Paul V published the first edition of the *Rituale Romanum* by means of the constitution *Apostolicae Sedis.* According to the Ritual, priests were to hear confessions in church, unless they had a good reason for acting otherwise. The confessionals which were to be icae Sedis. According to the Ritual, priests were to hear forated screen.[69] The use of the *Rituale Romanum* was earnestly exhorted, but not imposed as were the other Roman liturgical books.[70]

These prescriptions concerning the place for the hearing of confessions remained unchanged until the promulgation of the Code of Canon Law, which insists that the proper place for confessions is a church or a public or semi-public oratory.[71] The Code further decrees that the confessional for women's confessions is always to be placed in an open and conspicuous place, generally in a church or in a public or semi-public oratory set aside for the confessions of women.[72] The Code further prescribes that all confessionals should have a screen separating the penitent and the priest.[73] The typical edition of the *Rituale Romanum* published in 1925 adopted the present wording of the Code.[74]

The present legislation on the confessional is limited. Norms for the design and the location of the confessionals

[68] Cf. Fazzalaro, *op. cit.*, pp. 12–16.

[69] *Rituale Rom. Pauli V Pont. Max. Iussu Editum* (Romae, 1658), tit., *De sacramento penitentiae.*

[70] The Brief of Paul V merely stated, "hortamur in Domino . . . ut in posterum utantur. . . ."

[71] Canon 908.

[72] Canon 909, § 1.

[73] Canon 909, § 2.

[74] Tit. III, c. 1, *De sacramento poenitentiae*, nn. 7–8. The same wording is retained in the 1952 typical edition of the *Rituale Romanum.*

within the church must be derived from sources other than the positive laws.

First of all, since the sacrament of penance is closely related to baptism, the confessionals might well be placed near the baptistry to express this relationship. If the narthex or entrance hall is reasonably large, as it should be, the baptistry might well stand in the center of the narthex and the confessionals might form part of the wall separating the narthex from the nave. With such an arrangement, the confessionals should open into the narthex, not into the nave. Furthermore, the confessionals should be designed so that they express the meaning of the sacrament of penance. It is thus unsuitable that the confessionals should look like closets. Privacy is essential, but the closet-image is an unfortunate association for the sacrament. Penance is essentially a merciful judgment made by a judge who sits on a judicial throne or bench. An easy chair is therefore out of place in the confessional. The confessor should sit on a seat with a simple sturdy back. If his bench is slightly raised above the level of the church floor, it will resemble a judgment seat by reason of its very form. Above the bench or perhaps on the door of the confessional, some symbol of Christ's mercy might well be placed, possibly the Good Shepherd, the return of the prodigal son, or the cure of the man sick with palsy. When the confessional is not in use, the door could be left open, so that the symbolism of the judgment seat would be apparent to all. This policy might also help to dispel some of the ignorance that non-Catholics have about the confessional.[75]

Above all, the confessionals must be functional. They

[75] Cloud Meinberg, *loc. cit.*, p. 540.

should be properly ventilated, heated, and lighted. In large churches, confessionals are usually double-sided, so that the confessor may hear penitents on both sides. A covering over the grille is not prescribed by general law, although it does add to the privacy of the penitent. In this regard, M. Duhamel has advocated an arrangement whereby the penitent and confessor can clearly see one another, since the confessor is taking the place of Christ himself.[76] This opinion, however, would not be supported by the many penitents who prefer to remain anonymous in the confessional.[77] Although it is not desirable for the priest to be able to identify the penitent, nevertheless he should be able to determine whether the penitent is a man, woman, or child. Likewise, the penitent should be able to see the figure of the ministering priest and the sign of the cross given in absolution.[78]

On the penitent's side of the confessional, there should be no step, but the confessional should be equipped with a curtain or a self-closing door, a wide kneeler, and an armrest placed at a convenient height. The area should be slightly lighted so that the penitent can see where he is to kneel.[79]

In recent years the functional problems of the confessional have been rather satisfactorily solved by church architects. The placement and the design of the confes-

[76] "Les confessionnaux," *La Maison-Dieu*, No. 63 (1960), 154–57.

[77] Gordon, "Synodus Romana de Locis Sacris," *Periodica*, L (1961), 277.

[78] Meinberg, *ibid.*, p. 542.

[79] O'Connell, *op. cit.*, pp. 74–75; Anson, *Churches: Their Plan and Furnishing*, pp. 163–66.

sional, however, are rarely determined on theological grounds. Contemporary studies in sacramental theology have stressed the relation of the sacraments to the Church. This tendency is also seen in the historical and theological studies of penance, the ecclesial nature of which has been rediscovered.[80] If artists and architects come to understand the full nature of the sacrament of penance, they should be able to give better expression to the sacramental sign in the design of the confessional. With an appreciation of penance as a second baptism, which readmits the Christian to the eucharistic assembly, the architect should be able to place the confessionals in such a way that they are properly related both to the baptistry and to the eucharistic altar.

PLACE FOR DEVOTIONS

The recent liturgical renewal has resulted in a better liturgical formation and education of the faithful; consequently, greater emphasis has been placed on the sacramental life of the Church. Christians who base their spiritual lives on the official worship of the liturgy do not have a great need for popular devotions. Nevertheless, as Pius XII pointed out in his encyclical on the sacred liturgy, devotional practices which are not strictly liturgical do have a valid role in attracting and directing souls to God.[81] If these practices are in accord with the spirit of the liturgy,

[80] Cf. E. H. Schillebeeckx, *Le Christ, Sacrament de la Recontre de Dieu* (Paris: Editions du Cerf, 1960); A. M. Roguet, *Christ Acts through the Sacraments* (Collegeville, Minnesota: The Liturgical Press, 1954); George McCauley, "The Ecclesial Nature of the Sacrament of Penance," *Worship*, XXXVI (March, 1962), 212–22.
[81] *Mediator Dei—AAS*, XXXIX (1947), 584.

they "develop a deeper spiritual life in the faithful, they prepare them to take part in sacred public functions with greater fruit, and they lessen the danger of liturgical prayers becoming an empty ritualism."[82]

The devotional practices of the faithful may imitate public worship or they may represent a simple expression of personal piety.[83] Devotions that imitate public worship are not public worship, that is, not official worship, although they may be celebrated by the priest and the community within the church edifice. Pius XII was very specific on this point: "They do not strictly belong to the sacred liturgy."[84] Collective devotions of this type would include the public recitation of the rosary, the holy hour, novenas, triduums, stations of the cross, and various other pious exercises. Since these services are so varied, they present numerous problems for the church architect. If the community taking part in the devotions is large, the logical place for the people is the nave of the church. But if the community is relatively small, it is better if the faithful assemble in a small chapel or oratory, so that they will be more closely united as an assembly. A Blessed Sacrament chapel might well be used in accommodation of such small congregations.

The liturgical life of the Church leaves a wide margin for these devotions, which are expressions of personal piety; nevertheless, these devotions must be properly oriented to the official worship of the Church. A norm for these devotions may be found in the official letter addressed by the Vatican Secretariate of State to the Italian National Litur-

[82] *Ibid.*

[83] Gabriel Braso, *Liturgy and Spirituality* (Collegeville, Minnesota: The Liturgical Press, 1960), p. 191.

[84] *Mediator Dei—op. cit.*, 586.

gical Week held at Vicenza in July, 1954. In this letter the Holy See pointed out the proper direction for devotion to the Mother of God:

> May the devotion to the Blessed Virgin, recalled where necessary to purity of purpose, once again find its proper function as a way to Jesus Christ, through the most careful, complete, and loving transformation of the old man into the man of justice and of Christian holiness. Any other form of devotion to Mary, not sufficiently oriented in this direction, would necessarily be defective and less pleasing to the heavenly Mother, who cannot have anything closer to her heart than our renewal in the life of her divine Son.[85]

Above all, then, a proper perspective and a correct hierarchy of values must be maintained in the matter of devotions. Not infrequently one enters churches in which numerous objects of private devotion are scattered throughout the entire edifice, with the result that there is confusion in design and lack of theological perspective. Worshipping in the midst of such a complex devotional milieu, the faithful often lose sight of the sacraments and the Mass as the primary sources of Christian life, with the result that the sacraments and devotions are put on an equal plane. As the German "Directives for the Building of a Church" states: "Everything really superfluous should be eliminated, and such details as are indispensable should be placed as inconspicuously as possible, perhaps in a lower chapel. Whatever must remain in the main area should be so designed and placed as not to interfere with the lines converging on the altar."[86]

The problem of the proper placement of various images

[85] *L'Osservatore Romano*, July 23, 1954, p. 4.
[86] "Directives for the Building of a Church," *loc. cit.*, p. 15.

and shrines in churches is easier to solve in a negative manner than in a positive one. In general, the sanctuary and the baptistry are not places for such shrines and devotional images. By reason of their dignity, these areas should be reserved exclusively for those furnishings which are necessary for the strictly liturgical functions which take place there. The best solution to the problem of placing shrines and images for private devotion is possibly a special area in the church set aside for the private devotions of the faithful. It is quite possible that some devotional images may be incorporated into the Blessed Sacrament chapel, but care should be taken that these objects do not detract from the tabernacle or the altar. Murals and statues of our Lady and of the saints do not have a proper place above the Blessed Sacrament altar, where the iconography should be exclusively eucharistic. The Blessed Sacrament chapel might also provide a quiet place for private meditation, as well as for the public recitation of prayers in the presence of a small community. It might even be used for conferences to parish groups, such as sodalities and confraternities.

The stations of the cross might well be located in the Blessed Sacrament chapel. All too often the way of the cross terminates in more or less complete forgetfulness of the resurrection; made in this light, the devotion seems contrary to Christian spirtuality.[87] If the stations are arranged in such a way that at the conclusion of the fourteenth station one comes face to face with an image of the triumphant Christ, possibly above the Blessed Sacrament altar, the devotion is seen in its proper Christological dimension.

[87] P. Amédée De Zedelgem, "Aperçu historique du chemin de la croix," *Collectanea Franciscana*, XIX (1949), 44–142.

At any rate, the stations of the cross are a permanent feature of almost all churches and oratories; consequently, the architect must take account of them in planning the edifice. If they are placed in the nave of the church, they should not break the lines of the edifice, nor should they detract from the sanctuary. Although it is customary to have an image representing each scene which is contemplated in the passion of Christ, the way of the cross is legitimately constituted by fourteen simple wooden crosses duly erected in such a way that one walks from one station to another.[88] In comparision with the twelve consecration crosses which are erected throughout the church,[89] the stational crosses are subordinate. It would seem that the stations may be placed in their proper perspective if the simple wooden crosses are inlaid at fourteen different places on the floor of the church.

Other devotional shrines and images which are placed in churches need not have a permanent character. Just as a crib is erected during the Christmas season and then removed after the liturgical period is over, so also statues of saints may be put in a place of honor outside the sanctuary during novenas or triduums.

In concluding this article on the devotional practices of the faithful, the writer will venture a few remarks concerning the holy water stoups which are regularly found at the entrance to the church. Righetti links the use of holy water as taken from these stoups with the practice of sprink-

[88] *Rituale Rom.*, Appendix, tit. *Ritus erigendi stationes viae crucis.*

[89] S.R.C., *Senien.*, May 4, 1882: *Decr. Auth.*, n. 3545; *Nitrien.*, July 13, 1883: *Decr. Auth.*, n. 3584; *Barcinon.*, Jan. 16, 1886: *Decr. Auth.*, n. 3651.

ling the faithful during the Sunday Asperges.[90] The custom of the faithful taking holy water upon entering the church certainly antedates the introduction of the Asperges; therefore, it seems more probable that this use of holy water is derived from the *cantharus* or fountain in the early Latin basilicas, where the faithful were accustomed to wash themselves before entering the church.[91] When the atrium ceased to be a normal part of the church structure, the fountains were replaced with smaller vessels placed inside the church door.

Regardless of the origin of the fonts at the entrance to the church, the holy water stoups are certainly counterparts of the baptismal font. In the Book of Exodus,[92] Aaron and his sons were required to bathe before approaching the altar. Psalm 50 also refers to the rite of purification: "Sprinkle me with hyssop and I shall be cleansed; wash me and I shall be made whiter than snow." John the Baptist preached a baptism of water and repentance.[93] Christ willed to continue this symbolic rite, but he infused into it a supernatural purification of the soul through the sacrament of baptism. Tertullian reported that the Christians of his time washed before prayer.[94] Clement of Alexandria noted the same practice, but he insisted that a genuine spiritual purity of heart must be sought along with the ritual.[95] The present custom of taking blessed water upon entering the

[90] Righetti, *op. cit.*, 484; cf. Eisenhofer-Lechner, *op. cit.*, p. 109; O'Connell, *op. cit.*, p. 84.

[91] Cf. Leclercq, "Benitier," *DACL*, II, 758–71; Miller, *op. cit.*, p. 112.

[92] Exod. 30:18–20.

[93] Luke 3:3; John 1:25–26.

[94] *De oratione*, XIII: *PL*, I, 1271.

[95] *Stromata*, IV, 22: *PG*, VIII, 1351.

church is a continuation of this practice. As the Christian enters the church, he signs himself with the sign of the cross and holy water as a renewal of his baptism. This use of blessed water should help to maintain in the Christian the spirit of baptism, in which, through the instrumentality of water, God cleansed the soul from original sin and adorned it with sanctifying grace.

The Easter Vigil is in a special way the occasion for the celebration of baptism. Every Sunday in turn is meant to be a renewal of the Easter mystery. This connection between blessed water and the baptismal font is evident in the rubric from the new edition of the *Missale Romanum:* "Where there is a baptismal font, on Easter Sunday the Asperges is made with water blessed at the Easter Vigil, but which has been separated before the infusion of the oils."[96]

In churches where the baptismal font stands in the narthex, the connection between the font and the holy water stoups may receive emphasis through the placing of holy water fonts in close proximity to the baptistry.

REPRESENTATIONAL IMAGES

In comparison with the churches of the Gothic, Renaissance, and baroque periods, well-designed contemporary churches offer little place for painted or sculptured images. In former periods, sculpture had an important place in the design of the high altar, the choir stalls, the pillars, and the numerous side chapels. But in the modern church the altar is often reduced to a simple table without any reredos, and

[96] Carolus Braga, "Ordinationes ad librorum liturgicorum editores circa novas Missalis Romani editiones," *Ephemerides Liturgicae,* LXXV (1961), 426.

the pillars and side chapels give way to the unity of a church interior centered on the sanctuary. Consequently, there is sometimes the complaint that the artist finds little outlet for his talents in the decoration of the modern church. However, if church builders would adopt the concept of art as the well-making of anything that needs to be made, contemporary artists would find ample opportunity to exercise their skill in executing the various objects which have a legitimate place in the church edifice.

The great surfaces of a contemporary church may be treated artistically, either with representational art or otherwise, but in general,

> The decoration of the church should be simple, organic, and unpretentious. All deceit and false enrichment of the basic structure are to be strictly avoided. The structural qualities of the architecture should carry the weight of beauty and purpose. Art works and furnishings of the church must find their proper place in the higher order of the architectural structure. The architect and artist should be united in purpose.
>
> Traditional Christian symbolism should be utilized in church decoration with understanding and significance. The sign of the cross, to cite one example, ought not to be employed as mere decoration on church furnishings or woven indiscriminately into architectural elements of the church, i.e., masonry, window frames, doors, etc. Such use is unbecoming the sacred character of the Christian symbol.[97]

In spite of its simplicity, the altar itself is still a subject worthy of the artist's serious attention. Reduced to its basic sculptural form, the altar frequently achieves its artistic value not by way of applied ornamentation but rather through the relationship between the surface and the lower

[97] "Diocesan Church Building Directives," Diocesan Liturgical Commission, Superior, Wisconsin.

structure. The canopy or baldachin and the tabernacle are also worthy subjects of artistic attention. The work in textiles which has been so successfully developed in the design of vestments can also be applied to the tabernacle veil. Likewise the candlesticks, the sanctuary lamp, and the liturgical vessels are subjects for artistic design, which should be included in the overall plan of a church; they should not be left to chance. Although these objects are essentially functional rather than symbolic, nevertheless the artist may embellish functional forms with symbols and inscriptions, provided these additions remain within the stylistic limits of the basic design of the object itself. In reality, there is nothing in the church which does not deserve the careful attention of the artist, whether it be a holy water stoup, the furniture for the sanctuary, or simply the casing for the organ.

The rubrics explicitly recommend only two specific representational images in the church: the one is mandatory, namely, the figure of Christ on the altar crucifix; the other is only exhorted namely, the representation of the baptism of Christ, which is to be placed in the baptistry. This reserved recommendation suggests the sobriety which is traditionally associated with the liturgy. It is a sobriety which is at the same time joyful, for the tradition of the Church in sacred images has been one which expresses the fulness of the mystery of salvation. Perhaps its finest representation is to be found in the apsidal art of the primitive basilicas, for in these sanctuary images the Church gave eloquent expression of its mission and its goal in Christ.

In the early basilicas, the central idea which determined the inconography of the sanctuary was the reality of the Eucharist. It was the task of the artist to visualize the sacred mysteries which intimately involved the sacrificing community itself. As a result, there were produced powerful frescoes and mosaics representing the Church in heaven and the Church on earth. These images were thought of as extensions of the Eucharist itself, for they portrayed the community which the Mass was in the process of sanctifying, as well as the heavenly community on the last day.

In the lower part of the fresco or mosaic, the Church was regularly represented in the person of the apostles and other saints who had sprung from the community. Bearing their instruments of human achievement such as books, keys of office, or priestly vestments, these figures bore witness to the fact that the Christian life honors whatever is worthy of human dignity.[98]

In the upper part of the representation, one finds the figure of the triumphant Christ. Although he is pictured sitting in eternity, Christ is still mindful of men, for he bears man's wounds in his hands and feet. He is the great high priest of the heavenly liturgy, as he bears the marks of his earthly sacrifice. He is the beginning and the end, the victor over death and sin.[99]

The rhythm and form of these early images are clear expressions of the fact that Christ is still in the midst of human life, for the texts which often surround the images are words of courage and hope. They remind men of Christ's victory already won, but they also warn men that the fullness of Christ's triumph awaits man's acceptance of the victor. The victory of Christ cannot emerge in full splendor without the final response of men. This response

[98] Daniel Berrigan, "The Catholic Dream World and the Sacred Image," *Worship*, XXXV (1961), 551–52.
[99] *Loc. cit.*

is made by the Christian through a full life in the living Church.[100]

The iconography of the primitive basilicas, essentially sacramental, mystical, and eschatological, is far removed from the representations often found in churches today. The space behind the altar is frequently occupied by a large crucifix. Although the crucifix is required by the rubrics, and the Mass is the unbloodly renewal of the sacrifice of Calvary, nevertheless a large crucifix dominating the entire church seems to place an overemphasis on the historical details of the crucifixion to the detriment of the mystery of the sacrifice of the altar itself.[101]

If an image is to adorn the apsidal wall of the church, it would seem desirable to return to a representation of the triumphant Christ. An eschatological presentation of this type sums up the whole of Christian dogma, in which the past, present, and the future are all one in Christ. However, this recommendation certainly does not mean that the style or materials of execution should be copied from past ages. Above all, the terminal wall of the church should never be adorned with figures that have no direct relation to the eucharistic sacrifice, nor should the wall be pierced by windows, lest the clear vision of the sanctuary be obscured. If the sanctuary is properly designed, the altar and

[100] Apsidal mosaics delineating this description are to be found in the Roman churches of St. John Lateran, St. Pudentiana, St. Praxedes, Sts. Cosmas and Damian, and St. Laurence in Lucina. Similar mosaics also existed in the primitive basilicas of St. Peter and of St. Paul outside the Walls.—Cf. Armellini, *Le Chiese di Roma*. This theme in the early Church is extensively treated by F. van der Meer, *Majestas Domini* (Roma: Pontificio Instituto di Archeologia Cristiana, 1938).

[101] Meinberg, *loc. cit.*, p. 547.

the empty throne will stand as symbols of Christ.[102] As Romano Guardini has written, the very absence of superfluous images in a place dedicated to worship is itself an image of the invisible God.[103]

The role of iconography and decoration in a church may be summarized in terms of the German "Directives for the Building of a Church":

> It would be a mistake to arrange and decorate the interior of the church in such a way as to create the atmosphere of a comfortable and cozy bourgeois residence; and a mistake, also, to wish to imitate the poverty of a proletarian dwelling.
>
> The church interior should be neither bourgeois nor proletarian. It should bespeak forcibly the grandeur of God which surpasses all earthly measure, so that it may exalt the worshipper above the sphere and atmosphere of his daily private life; and yet, it must still leave one with the friendly feeling of "the goodness and kindness of our Savior" (Titus, 3:4).
>
> It would be a mistake, and it is one that is often made in our times, to entrust the decoration of the church, in painting and sculpture, in the designing of its furnishings, above all in the artistic treatment of the main portal, of the sanctuary, the altar, the baptismal font, and the pulpit, to the arbitrary action of a transient pastor or of a donor, or to the risk of mere haphazard.
>
> In our efforts to erect an exemplary church edifice it is necessary to work out not only a structural plan, but also a well thought out plan, of artistic expression which will be theologically and pedagogically correct. Such a plan will recognize that the decorative scheme of the finished house of God should present to the view of the congregation an ensemble of the theme of our holy faith, not in a fragmentary way, but with a certain completeness and in significant proportions and with a right placing of accents.[104]

[102] *Ibid.*, p. 549.

[103] "Sacred Images and the Invisible God," *The Furrow*, VIII (June, 1957), 353.

[104] Pp. 16–17.

Bibliography

Agnel, Arnaud d'. *L'Art religieux moderne*. Grenoble: B. Arthaud, 1936.

Alce, V. "Architettura sacra contemporanea in Germania," *Chiesa e Quartiere*, No. 13 (1960), 31–51.

Anson, Peter. *Churches: Their Plan and Furnishing*. Milwaukee: Bruce Publishing Co., 1948.

———. "Mass Facing the People," *Liturgical Arts*, XXIV (1955), 2–4.

Armellini, Mariano. *Le Chiese di Roma dal secolo IV a XIX*, 2 vols. Roma: Typografia Vaticana, 1891.

Auvert, Guy-Jean. *Défence et illustration de l'art sacré*. Paris: Nouvelles Éditions Latines, 1956.

Baldoni, D. "La liturgia pastorale nel pensiero di Papa Giovanni XXIII," *Ephemeredes Liturgicae*, LXXV (1961), 384–387.

Bardet, Gaston. "La Maison de Dieu," *Témoignages de la Pierre-Qui-Vire*, XXXVI (1953), 50–56.

———. "Una Polemica se allarga," *Arte Cristiana*, XXXVIII (1951), 129–130.

Barron, Mark. "The Sacramental Character of Christian Art," *Liturgical Arts*, XXVII (1959), 32–34.

Bartoli, Luciana. *L'Arte nella casa di Dio*. Turin: Società Editrice Internazionale, 1950.

Baumstark, Anton. *Comparative Liturgy*, revised by Bernard Botte, English edition by F. L. Cross. Westminster, Md.: Newman Press, 1958.

Berrigan, Daniel. "The Catholic Dream World and the Sacred Image," *Worship*, XXXV (1961), 549–560.

Berrigan, Daniel. "The New Spirit of Modern Sacred Art," *The Critic*, XX (1962), 30–33.

Bethune, A. "Acoustics, Light, and Seating for the People's Participation in the Mass," *Liturgical Arts*, XXX (1962), 62–64.

———. "Tabernacle and Altar," *Liturgical Arts*, XXIX (1961), 30–33.

Biedrzynski, R. *Kirchen unserer Zeit*. München: Hirmer, 1958.

Bishop, Edmund. "Fear and Awe Attaching to the Eucharist," *The Liturgical Homilies of Narsai*. Cambridge: University Press, 1909, 92–97.

———. *Liturgica Historica*. Oxford: Clarendon Press, 1918.

Bonnette, R. W. "The Primacy of the Liturgy in Church Art," *Liturgical Arts*, XXVIII (1960), 28–29.

Bouman, Cornelius. "The History of the Architectural Setting of the Interior of the Church," *Participation in the Mass*. Washington, D.C.: Liturgical Conference, 1960, 85–94.

Bourke, John. *Baroque Churches of Central Europe*. London: Faber & Faber, 1958.

Bourniquel, Camille. "La Querelle de l'art sacré," *Esprit*, XIX (1951), 563–572.

———, and Guichard-Meili, Jean. *Les Créatures et le sacré*. Paris: Editions du Cerf, 1956.

Braga, Carolus. "Ordinationes ad librorum liturgicorum editores circa novas Missalis editiones," *Ephemerides Liturgicae*, LXXV (1961), 401–448.

Brasó, Gabriel. *Liturgy and Spirituality*. Collegeville, Minn.: Liturgical Press, 1960.

Braun, Josef. *Der christliche Altar in seiner geschichtlichen Entwicklung*, 2 vols. München: Karl Widman, 1924.

Brehier, Louis. *Les Basiliques chrétiennes*. Paris: Bloud et Cie, 1905.

Brenson, Theodore. "Abstract Art and Christianity," *Liturgical Arts*, XXII (1954), 76–78.

Brion, Marcel. *Ces palais où Dieu habite*. Paris: Librairie Arthème Fayard, 1960.

Burkart, A. "La Chiesa e la sintesi delle arti," *Chiesa e Quartiere*, No. 15 (1960), 27–35.

Cahill, Daniel. *The Custody of the Holy Eucharist*. Washington, D.C.: Catholic University of America Press, 1950.

Carey, Graham. *Art in Time*. Newport, R.I.: John Stevens, 1939.
———. "Distortion in Art," *Catholic Art Quarterly*, XV (1952), 132–141.
———. *The Majority Report on Art*. Newport, R.I.: John Stevens, 1937.
———. *Pattern*. Newport, R.I.: John Stevens, 1938.
———. *Thoughts and Things*. Newport, R.I.: John Stevens, 1937.
Carrière, Paul. "J'ai une église a aménager," *La Maison-Dieu*, No. 63 (1960), 159–189.
Cassou, Jean. "Paris: Controversy and Quintessence," *Art News*, L (1951), 18–19, 57–58.
Cavanaugh, W. J. "L'Acustica nella chiesa," *Chiesa e Quartiere*, No. 13 (1960), 80–90.
Cerfaux, Lucien. *Christ in the Theology of St. Paul*. English translation by Geoffrey Webb and Adrian Walker. New York: Herder & Herder, 1959.
———. *The Church in the Theology of St. Paul*. English translation by Geoffrey Webb and Adrian Walker. New York: Herder & Herder, 1959.
———. "Regale Sacerdotium," *Revue des Sciences Philosophiques et Théologiques*, XXVIII (1939), 5–39.
Chelini, Jean. *La Ville et l'Église*. Paris: Les Éditions du Cerf, 1959.
Conant, Kenneth J. *Carolingian and Romanesque Architecture*. Baltimore: Penguin Books, 1959.
Congar, Yves Marie. *Lay People in the Church*, translated by Donald Attwater. Westminster, Md.: Newman Press, 1956.
———. *The Mystery of the Temple*. Westminster, Md.: Newman Press, 1962.
———. *La Tradition et les Traditions*. Paris: Librairie Arthème Fayard, 1960.
———. *Vrai et fausse réforme dans l'Église*. Paris: Éditions du Cerf, 1950.
Conway, Walter. *The Time and Place of Baptism*. Washington, D.C.: Catholic University of America Press, 1954.
Coomaraswamy, Ananda K. *Christian and Oriental Philosophy of Art*. New York: Dover Publications, 1956.
———. *The Transformation of Nature in Art*. New York: Dover Publications, 1956.
———, and Carey, Graham. *Patron and Artist, Pre-Renaissance and Modern*. Norton, Mass.: Wheaton College Press, 1936.

Cope, G. "Building a New Church," *Anglican World*, I, No. 4 (1961), 45–51.

Corblet, Jules. *Histoire dogmatique, liturgique, et archéologique du sacrement de baptême*, 2 vols. Paris: V. Palme, 1881–1882.

Cory, Herbert Ellsworth. *The Significance of Beauty in Nature and Art*. Milwaukee: Bruce Publishing Co., 1947.

Costantini, Celso. "Circa l'arte figurative," *L'Osservatore Romano*, August 3, 1952.

———. "Competenza della Santa Sede," *L'Osservatore Romano*, July 25, 1952.

———. "Dell'architettura sacra," *L'Osservatore Romano*, July 30, 1952.

———. "Dell'arte sacra deformatrice," *L'Osservatore Romano*, August 1, 1952.

———. "Epurazione artistica della chiesa," *L'Osservatore Romano*, August, 1, 1952.

———. "L'Instruzione del Santo Uffizio sull'arte sacra–Modernità e Tradizione," *L'Osservatore Romano*, August 13, 1952.

———. "Per la Cultura artistica del clero," *L'Osservatore Romano*, August 13, 1952.

———. "Réponse à diverses critiques, *L'Osservatore Romano*, August 20, 1951.

———. "Signore ho amato il decors della tua casa," *Fede e Arte*, II (1954), 33–63.

Costantini, Giovanni. "Accordo e collaborazione fra artisti e clero," *Fede e Arte*, I (1953), 258–263.

———. "Norme pratiche per l'ordinazione e l'escuzione della opere d'arte sacra," *Fede e Arte*, I (1953), 149–151.

Couturier, Marie-Alain. *Art et catholicisme*. Montreal: Éditions de l'Arbe, 1945.

———. "Historique de l'église d'Assy," *L'Art Sacré*, No. 1–2 (1950), 2–7.

Crichton, J. D. "The Church – The House of God's People," *Liturgy*, XXVIII (1959), 43–47.

Cullmann, Oscar. *Le Culte dans l'Église primitive*. Paris: Delachaux & Niestlé, 1948.

———. *La Tradition: Problème exégétique, historique et théologique*. Paris: Delachaux & Niestlé, 1953.

Denis–Boulet, Noële-Maurice. "L'Autel dans l'antiquité chrétienne," *La Maison-Dieu*, No. 29 (1952), 40–59.

———. "La Leçon des églises de l'antiquité," *La Maison-Dieu*, No. 63 (1960), 24–40.

Dijk, S. J. P. van, and Walker, J. Hazelden. *The Myth of the Aumbry*. London: Burns & Oates, 1957.

Dix, Gregory. *A Detection of Aumbries*. Westminster: Dacre Press, 1942.

———. *The Shape of the Liturgy*. Westminster: Dacre Press, 1945.

Documents for Sacred Architecture. Collegeville, Minn.: Liturgical Press, 1957.

Dölger, Franz J. *Sol Salutis*. Münster: Aschendorff, 1925.

———. "Zur Symbolik des altchristlichen Taufhauses," *Antike und Christentum*, IV (1934), 153–197.

Donck, E. van der. "Kerkbouw nu, vanuit haar historisch perspectief," *Tijdschrift voor Liturgie*, VL (1961), 424–444.

Doncoeur, Paul. "L'Architecture de l'église," *Études*, Vol. 275 (1952), 83–92.

———. "Au service de l'art sacré," *Études*, Vol. 252 (1947), 110–115.

———. "Confusions et clarités dans le débat sur l'art sacré," *Études*, Vol. 272 (1947), 29–39.

———. "Lessons of Eucharistic History," *Orate Fratres*, XXIII (1949), 409–417.

———. "La Querelle de l'art sacré," *La Vie Intellectuelle*, XI (1951), 3–48.

Duchesne, Louis. *Origine du Culte Chrétien*. Paris: Thorin & Fils, 1902.

Dumas, A. "Image de Dieu invisible," *Notes de Pastorale Liturgique*, No. 35 (1961), 36–39.

Eisenhofer, Ludwig, and Lechner, Joseph. *The Liturgy of the Roman Rite*. Translated by A. J. and E. P. Peeler, edited by H. E. Winstone. New York: Herder & Herder, 1961.

Evans, I. "St. John's Abbey Church: An Appraisal," *Worship*, XXXV (1961), 515–521.

———. "Tradition and Traditionalism," *Liturgical Arts*, XXIX (1961), 79–81.

Fallani, G. "L'Altare nell' architettura sacra contemporanea," *Fede e Arte*, VIII (1960), 84–116.

———. "Liturgia e arte nel prossimo Concilio Ecumenico," *Rivista Diocesana di Roma*, II (1961), 630–636.

Fazzalaro, Francis J. *The Place for the Hearing of Confessions.* Washington, D.C.: Catholic University of America Press, 1950.

File, M. Jeanne. *A Critical Analysis of Current Concepts of Art in American Higher Education.* Washington, D.C.: Catholic University of America Press, 1958.

Fortesque, Adrian, and O'Connell, J. B. *The Ceremonies of the Roman Rite Described.* Westminster, Md.: Newman Press, 1958.

Frank, Karl B. *Kernfragen kirchlicher Kunst.* Vienna: Herder, 1953.

Freestone, W. H. *The Sacrament Reserved.* London: A. R. Mowbray & Co., 1917.

Geiselmann, J. R. *Die lebendige Überlieferung als Norm christlichen Glaubens.* Freiburg: Herder, 1959.

Gelin, Albert. "L'Autel dans L'Ancien Testament," *La Maison-Dieu,* No. 29 (1952).

Gelineau, Joseph. *Chant et musique dans le culte chrétien.* Paris: Éditions Fleurus, 1962.

———. "L'Église, lieu de la célébration," *La Maison-Dieu,* No. 63 (1960), 41–52.

———. "La Nef et son organisation," *La Maison-Dieu,* No. 63 (1960), 69–85.

———. "Le Sanctuaire et sa complexité," *La Maison-Dieu,* No. 63 (1960), 53–68.

Gieselmann, Reinhard, and Aebli, Werner. *Kirchenbau.* Zürich: Girsberger, 1960.

Gilbert, Katherine, and Kuhn, Helmut. *A History of Esthetics.* Bloomington: Indiana University Press, 1954.

Gill, Eric. *Art.* New York: Devin-Adair, 1950.

———. *Beauty Looks After Herself.* New York: Sheed & Ward, 1933.

———. *It All Goes Together.* New York: Devin-Adair, 1944.

———. "The Priesthood of Craftsmanship," *Blackfriars Magazine,* XX (1940), 107–113.

Gilson, Etienne. *Painting and Reality.* New York: Pantheon Books, 1957.

Giovenale, Giovanni Battista. *Il Battistero lateranense nelle recenti indagini della Pont. commissione di archeologia sacra.* Rome: Pontificio Instituto di Archeologia Cristiana, 1929.

Goettelmann, Paul. *The Baptistery of Frejus.* Washington, D.C.: Catholic University of America, 1933.

Gordon, Ignatius. "Quaestiones Recentiores de Locis Sacris et Legum Universalium Deregationes in Prima Synodo Romana," *Periodica de Re Morali, Canonica, Liturgica*, L (1961), 267–307.

Grabar, André. *Martyrium: Recherches sur le Culte des Reliques et l'Art Chrétien Antique*, 2 vols. Paris: Collège de France, 1946.

Grassi, L. "Tradizione e problematica dell'architettura sacra," *Chiesa e Quartiere*, No. 15 (1960), 67–91.

Greene, Theodore. *The Arts and the Art of Criticism*. Princeton: Princeton University Press, 1940.

Grisar, Hartmann. *History of Rome and the Popes in the Middle Ages*, Vol. III. London: Kegan Paul, Trench, Trübner & Co., 1911.

Gromier, Leon. *Commentaire du Caeremoniale Episcoporum*. Paris: La Colombe, 1959.

Grossi Gondi, Felice. *I Monumenti Cristiani*, Vol. II. Rome: Università Gregoriana, 1923.

Guardini, Romano. *The Church and the Catholic and the Spirit of the Liturgy*. Translated by Ada Lane. London: Sheed & Ward, 1935.

———. "Sacred Images and the Invisible God," *The Furrow*, VIII (1957), 350–363.

Guerrisi, Michele. "L'Arte religiosa e la crisi del gusto contemporaneo," *Fede e Arte*, I (1953), 77–84.

———. "Dalla porta del paradiso e quella dell'inferno," *Fede e Arte*, IX (1961), 154–193.

Hammond, Peter. *Liturgy and Architecture*. London: Barrie & Rockliff, 1960.

——— (ed.). *Towards a Church Architecture*. London: Architectural Press, 1962.

Heisenberg, A. *Grabeskirche und Apostelkirche*. Leipzig, 1908.

Henze, Anton. *Neue kirchliche Kunst*. Recklinghausen: Paulus-Verlag, 1958.

———, and Filthaut, Theodor. *Contemporary Church Art*. Translated by Cecily Hastings, edited by Maurice Lavanoux. New York: Sheed & Ward, 1956.

Hertling, Ludwig, and Kirschbaum, Engelbert. *The Roman Catacombs and Their Martyrs*. Translated by M. Joseph Costelloe. Milwaukee: Bruce Publishing Co., 1956.

Herwegen, Ildefons. *The Art-Principle of the Liturgy*, Collegeville, Minn.: Liturgical Press, 1931.

Hess, Robert. *Moderne kirchliche Kunst in der Schweiz*. Zürich: NZN Buchverlag, 1951.

Hitchcock, Henry Russell. *Architecture, Nineteenth and Twentieth Centuries*. New York: Pelican Books, 1958.

Holstein, Henri. "La Tradition Catholique," *Études*, Vol. 301 (1959), 346–354.

Javier, Benjamin P. "Living Tradition," *Liturgical Arts*, XXVII (1958), 30–32.

Johnston, Mary. *Roman Life*. Chicago: Scott, Foresman & Co., 1957.

Journel, Pierre. "L'Enseignement inconographique du premier millénaire chrétien," *La Maison-Dieu*, No. 63 (1960), 138–146.

Journet, Charles. *The Church of the Word Incarnate*, Vol. I, *The Apostolic Hierarchy*. Translated by A. H. C. Downes. London: Sheed & Ward, 1955.

Jungmann, Josef A. "Church Art," *Worship*, XXIX (1955), 68–82.

———. *The Early Liturgy to the Time of Gregory the Great*. Translated by Francis A. Brunner. Notre Dame: University of Notre Dame Press, 1959.

———. *Des lois de la célébration liturgique*. Traduction de l'allemand par Marc Zemb. Paris: Éditions du Cerf, 1956.

———. *Der Gottesdienst der Kirche*. Innsbruck: Verlagsanstalt Tyrolia, 1955.

———. *The Mass of the Roman Rite*. 2 vols. Translated by Francis A. Brunner. New York: Benziger, 1951–1955.

———. *Pastoral Liturgy*. New York: Herder & Herder, 1962.

———. *Public Worship*. Translated by Clifford Howell. London: Challoner Publishers, 1957.

Kammerer, Louis. "J'ai une église à construire," *La Maison-Dieu*, No. 63 (1960), 190–208.

Kaufmann, Carlo. *Manuale di archeologia cristiana*. Roma: F. Pustet, 1908.

Kenny, J. P. "Reflections on Contemporary Religious Art," *America*, CIV (1961), 698–700.

Kirsch, J. P. "Die christlichen Cultusgebäude in der vorkonstantinischen Zeit," *Festschrift zum elfhundertjahrigen Jubiläum des deutschen Campo Santo in Rom*. Freiburg: Herder, 1897, 6–20.

———. *Die römischen Titelkirchen im Altertum*. Paderborn: F. Schöningh, 1918.

———. *Die Stationskirchen des Missale Romanum*. Freiburg: Herder, 1926.

Kirsch, P. "La 'Domus ecclesiae' cristiana del III sec. a Dura Europos in Mesopotamia," *Studi dedicata alla memoria di Paulo Ubaldi*. Milan: Società editrice "Vita e Pensiero," 1937, 73–82.

Klauser, Theodor. "Die liturgischen Austauschbeziehungen zwischen der römischen und der fränkischdeutschen Kirche vom 8. bis zum 11. Jh.," *Historisches Jahrbuch der Görresgesellschaft*, LIII (1933), 169–189.

———. *The Western Liturgy and its History*. Translated by F. L. Cross. London: Mowbrays, 1952.

Kramkreiter, R. "Architettura religiosa contemporanea in Austria," *Fede e Arte*, VIII (1960), 316–354.

Küng, Hans. *The Council, Reform and Reunion*. New York: Sheed & Ward, 1961.

LaFarge, John. "Private Opinion and Church Authority," *Liturgical Arts*, XVI (1948), 124–125.

Lanotte, A. "L'Art vivant et la communauté chrétienne," *Revue Nouvelle*, XXXVI (1962), 30–56.

Lauck, Anthony. "Modern Sacred Art? Rome Speaks," *Ave Maria*, VIII (1954), 206–211.

Laurent, Marie-Céline. *Valeur chrétienne de l'art*. Paris: Librairie Arthème Fayard, 1959.

Lavanoux, Maurice. "L'Architettura sacra negli Stati Uniti," *Chiesa e Quartiere*, No. 15 (1960), 49–55.

———. "The Authentic Tradition in Art," *Liturgical Arts*, XXII (1954), 122–125.

Lawler, Justus George. "The Idea of a Christian Art," *Thought*, XXIV (1949), 309–320.

Leader, R. "Living Expression and a Living Faith," *Participation in the Mass*, Washington, D.C.: Liturgical Conference, 1960, 94–99.

Leclercq, Henri. *Manuel d'archéologie chrétienne*, Vol. I. Paris: Letouzey & Ané, 1907.

Leclercq, Jean. "Le Mystère de l'autel," *La Maison-Dieu*, No. 29 (1952), 60–70.

Lefrançois-Pillion, L. *Abbayes et Cathédrales*. Paris: Librairie Arthème Fayard, 1956.

Lemaire, D. "Humanisme classique et symbolisme liturgique," *La Maison-Dieu*, No. 42 (1955), 134–136.

Lemaire, Raymond. *L'Origine de la basilique latine.* Paris: Vromant & Cie, 1911.

Lercaro, Giacomo. "Building the House of God," *Liturgical Arts,* XXVIII (1960), 2–3.

———. "The Christian Church," *The Furrow,* VI (1957), 341–349.

———. "La Participation active, principe fondamental de la réforme pastorale et liturgique de Pie X," *La Maison-Dieu,* No. 37 (1954), 16–24.

———. "Rapporto su Bologna – Chiese," *Chiesa e Quartiere,* No. 19 (1961), 11–37.

———. "Il Senso del mostero," *Chiesa e Quartiere,* No. 19 (1961), 19–32.

Leroy, Alfred. *Naissance de l'Art Chrétien.* Paris: Librairie Arthème Fayard, 1956.

Louvel, François. "Le Mystère de nos églises," *La Maison-Dieu,* No. 63 (1960), 5–23.

Mâle, Émile. *The Early Churches of Rome.* Translated by David Buxton. Chicago: Quadrangle Books, 1960.

Malraux, André. *The Voices of Silence.* Translated by Stuart Gilbert. Garden City, N.Y.: Doubleday & Co., 1953.

Mariani, Goffredo. *La legislazione ecclesiastica in materia d'arte sacra.* Rome: Ferrari, 1945.

Marier, T. H. "Choir and Congregational Participation," *Bible, Life and Worship.* Washington, D.C.: Liturgical Conference, 1961, 142–146.

———. "Organ Design and Placement," *Participation in the Mass.* Washington, D.C.: Liturgical Conference, 1960, 73–79.

Maritain, Jacques. *Art and Scholasticism and Other Essays.* Translated by J. F. Scanlon. New York: Charles Scribner's Sons, 1930.

———. *Creative Intuition in Art and Poetry.* New York: Pantheon Books, 1953.

———. *The Philosophy of Art.* Ditchling (Eng.): O'Connor, 1923.

———. *The Responsibility of the Artist.* New York: Charles Scribner's Sons, 1960.

Martimort, A.-G. (ed.). *L'Église en prière.* Tournai: Desclée & Cie, 1961.

———. "Place du siège du célébrant," *La Maison-Dieu,* No. 63 (1960), 135–137.

———. "Le Rituel de la consécration des églises," *La Maison-Dieu*, No. 63 (1960), 86–95.

———, *et al. The Liturgy and the Word of God*. Collegeville, Minn.: Liturgical Press, 1959.

Mary of the Compassion. "Sacred Art and Stylism," *Journal of Arts and Letters*, II (1950), 69–70.

Mascall, E. L. *The Recovery of Unity*. New York: Longmans, 1958.

McCall, Robert. "The Metaphysical Analysis of the Beautiful and the Ugly," *Proceedings of the American Catholic Philosophical Association*, XXX (1956), 137–146.

McCarthy, E. "An Analysis of the *Instruction* with Regard to Church Structure," *Participation in the Mass*. Washington, D.C.: Liturgical Conference, 1960, 80–85.

McCauley, George. "The Ecclesial Nature of the Sacrament of Penance," *Worship*, XXXVI (1962), 212–222.

McDonnell, Kilian. "Liturgy and Sacred Art," *Sponsa Regis*, XXXI (1960), 157–161.

McKenzie, J. L. "The Dynastic Oracle: II Sam. 7," *Theological Studies*, VIII (1947), 187–218.

McManus, Frederick. *Handbook for the New Rubrics*. Baltimore: Helicon Press, 1960.

———. "Mass Facing the People," *Worship*, XXXIII (1958–1959), 123–125.

———. "Some Principles for Church Planning," *Worship*, XXXV (1961), 657–660.

McNaspy, C. J. "The Priest as Patron," *Liturgical Arts*, XXIX (1961), 65–66.

Meer, F. van der. *Maiestas Domini*. Rome: Pontificio Istituto di Archeologia Cristiana, 1938.

———, and Mohrmann, Christine. *Atlas of the Early Christian World*. Translated and edited by Mary F. Hedlund and H. H. Rowlet. London: Thomas Nelson & Sons, 1958.

Meinberg, Cloud. "The Baptistry and Other Spaces," *Worship*, XXXV (1961), 536–548.

———. "The Meaning of Sacred Art," *Sponsa Regis*, XXXI (1960), 148–156.

———. "The New Churches of Europe," *Worship*, XXXI (1957), 68–77.

Miller, John. "Altar Facing the People: Fact or Fable?" *Worship*, XXXIII (1958–1959), 83–91.

———. *Fundamentals of the Liturgy*. Notre Dame: Fides Publishers Ass., 1959.

Mollerfeld, Johannes. "Der Altar ist Christus: Gedanken zur Altar- und Tabernakelfrömmigkeit," *Geist und Leben*, XXXIV (1961), 261–271.

Montague, G. F. "Structure of the Altar: Cross or Crucifix," *Irish Ecclesiastical Record*, VIIC (1960), 405–407.

Montrond, Henri de. "Art sacré et théologie," *Etudes*, Vol. 271 (1951), 314–321.

Morel, G. "La Nature du symbole," *La Maison-Dieu*, No. 42 (1955), 98–105.

Muehlberger, R. C. "Sacred Art – A Critique of the Contemporary Situation," *Liturgical Arts*, XXVIII (1960), 69–72.

Mumford, Lewis. *The Culture of Cities*. New York: Harcourt, Brace & Co., 1938.

Nabuco, Joachin. *Jus Pontificalium: Introductio in Caeremoniale Episcoporum*. Tournai: Desclée & Cie, 1956.

Nemetz, Anthony. "Art in St. Thomas Aquinas," *New Scholasticism*, XXV (1951), 282–289.

Ochsé, Madeleine. *Un Art sacré pour notre temps*. Paris: Librairie Arthème Fayard, 1959.

———. *La Nouvelle querelle des images*. Paris: Édition du Centurion, 1952.

O'Connell, J. B. *Church Building and Furnishing, The Church's Way*. Notre Dame: University of Notre Dame Press, 1955.

O'Donohoe, James. "Administrative Aids to the Bishop," *The Jurist*, XX (1960), 13–29.

Paissac, Hyacinthe. "L'Athéisme des Chrétiens," *Supplément de la Vie Spirituelle*, I (1947), 5–28.

Paluzzi, Oreste. "Il Papa agli artisti," *Fede e Arte*, I (1953), 115–116.

Parmoissin, R. *Mystère de l'art sacré*. Paris: Nouvelles Éditions Debresse, 1957.

Perkins, John Ward. "Constantine and the Origins of the Christian Basilica," *Papers of the British School at Rome*, XXII (1954), 69–90.

Pichard, Joseph. *L'Art sacré moderne*. Paris: B. Arthaud, 1953.
———. *Les Églises nouvelles à travers le monde*. Paris: Éditions des Deux-Mondes, 1960.
Pinsard, Pierre. "Ce que les architectes demandent aux curés," *La Maison-Dieu*, No. 63 (1960), 209–216.
———. "Les Églises modernes en France," *Chiesa e Quartiere*, No. 15 (1960), 36–44.
Pratelli, G. "Ubicazione dell'edificio religioso e nuovi confini territoriali per le comunità rurali d'oggi," *Chiesa e Quartiere*, No. 18 (1961), 66–76.
Quasten, Johannes. "The Conflict of Early Christianity with the Jewish Temple Worship," *Theological Studies*, II (1941), 481–487.
———. "Mysterium tremendum: Eucharistische Frömmigkeitsauffassungen des vierten Jahrhunderts," *Vom Christlichen Mysterium*. Düsseldorf: Patmos-Verlag, 1951, 66–75.
Racz, André, "Tradition: Fertile Soil for Growth," *Liturgical Arts*, XVII (1949), 108–112.
Radó, Polycarpus, *Enchiridion Liturgicum*. 2 vols. Rome: Herder, 1961.
Rambusch, R. E. "Art: The Visible Bible," *Bible, Life and Worship*. Washington, D.C.: Liturgical Conference, 1961.
Ramelli, A. Cassi. *Edifici per il culto*. Milan: Edizione Vallardi, 1953.
Régamey, Pie-Raymond. "Architecture de l'autel et exigences liturgiques," *La Maison-Dieu*, No. 29 (1952), 71–87.
———. *Art sacré au XXe siècle?* Paris: Éditions du Cerf, 1952. English adaptation: Religious Art in the Twentieth Century. New York: Herder & Herder, 1963.
———. "La Chapelle et la forêt," *L'Art Sacré*, No. 3–4 (1961), 11–12.
———. "Christianity or Paganism in Modern Architecture," *Journal of Arts and Letters*, II (1950), 82–94.
———. "Cinq tendances dominantes," *Cahiers de l'Art Sacré*, III (1951), 40–62.
———. "Les Conditions de l'art sacré dans le monde moderne," *La Vie Intellectuelle*, No. 12 (1948), 8–34.
———. "Débat sur l'art non figuratif," *La Vie Intellectuelle*, XIX (1951), 40–62.

Régamey, Pie-Raymond. "L'Éducation artistique du clergé," *Cahiers de l'Art Sacré*, No. 9 (1946), 4–30.

———. "Les Étapes de l'académisme," *L'Art Sacré*, No. 10 (1947), 245–287.

———. "Gardez le mesure . . . ," *L'Art Sacré*, No. 5–6 (1953), 28–31.

———. "Liturgy, Architecture, and the Arts," *Irish Ecclesiastical Record*, VC (1961), 299–305.

———. "Les Lois de l'église sur l'art sacré," *Cahiers de l'Art Sacré*, No. 1 (1945), 6.

———. "Note sur l'orientation," *Cahiers de l'Art Sacré*, No. 1 (1945), 30.

———. "Les Possibilités chrétiennes des artistes incroyants," *La Vie Intellectuelle*, XIX (1951), 4–23.

———. "The Present State of Religious Art," *Journal of Arts and Letters*, I (1949), 106–127.

———. *Les principes d'un véritable renouveau des arts sacrés*. Liège: La Pensée Catholique, 1948.

———. "La Querelle de l'art sacré," *La Vie Intellectuelle*, XIX (1951), 3–48.

Reinhold, H. A. "The Architecture of Rudolf Schwarz," *Architectural Forum*, VI (1939), 25–28.

———. "Celebration of Baptism and the Eucharist," *Bible, Life and Worship*. Washington, D.C.: Liturgical Conference, 1961, 157–159.

———. "Copyrighted Churches," *Orate Fratres*, XX (1946), 464–467.

———. "Liturgy and Church Architecture," *Jubilee*, IX (1962), 17–19.

———. "Liturgy, Sacred Art and the Bourgeois Mind," *Journal of Arts and Letters*, II (1950), 97–103.

———. *Speaking of Liturgical Architecture*. Notre Dame: University of Notre Dame Liturgical Programs, 1952.

Ricciotti, Giuseppe. *The History of Israel*. Translated by Clement della Penta and Richard T. Murphy. 2 vols. Milwaukee: Bruce Publishing Co., 1955.

Righetti, Mario. *Manuale di Storia Liturgica*. 4 vols. Milan: Editrice Ancora, 1950–1956.

Robb, C. J. "Shrines in Churches," *Irish Ecclesiastical Record*, VIIC (1960), 362–363.

Rogues, P. "Signification du baroque," *La Maison-Dieu*, No. 26 (1951), 125–142.

Roguet, A. M. "L'Autel," *La Maison-Dieu*, No. 63 (1960), 96–113.

———. "Le Baptistère," *La Maison-Dieu*, No. 63 (1960), 125–134.

———. "Le lieu de la réserve," *La Maison-Dieu*, No. 63 (1960), 114–124.

———. "Liturgical Renewal and the Renewal of Preaching," *The Assisi Papers*. Collegeville, Minn.: Liturgical Press, 1957, 91–94.

———. "La Pastorale liturgique et l'autel," *La Maison-Dieu*, No. 29 (1952), 5–8.

Rousseau, Olivier. "Le Christ et l'autel: note sur la tradition patristique," *La Maison-Dieu*, No. 29 (1952), 32–39.

———. *Histoire du mouvement liturgique*. Paris: Éditions du Cerf, 1945.

Rubin, William. *Modern Sacred Art and the Church of Assy*. New York: Columbia University Press, 1961.

Sadlowski, Erwin L. *Sacred Furnishings of Churches*. Washington, D.C.: Catholic University of America Press, 1951.

Saviolo, A. "Il Dono gratuito della bellezza," *Chiesa e Quartiere*, No. 14 (1960), 43–49.

Schädel, H. *Katholische Kirchen, Kappellen und Gemeindezentren*. Stuttgart: Krämer, 1956.

Schillebeeckx, E. H. *Le Christ, Sacrement de la recontre de Dieu*. Paris: Éditions du Cerf, 1960.

Schleck, Charles, A. "The Integration of Dogmatic Theology with the Liturgy," *Yearbook of Liturgical Studies*, ed. by John H. Miller, I (1960), 41–64.

Schmidt, Hermanus. *Introductio in Liturgiam Occidentalem*. Rome: Herder, 1960.

Schmitt, Joseph. "Petra autem erat Christus," *La Maison-Dieu*, No. 29 (1952), 18–31.

Schnell, H. "Church Architecture in Post-war Germany," *Catholic Mind*, LIX (1961), 345–349.

Schwarz, Rudolf. *The Church Incarnate*. Translated by Cynthia Harry. Chicago: Henry Regnery Co., 1958.

———. *Kirchenbau, Welt vor der Schwelle*. Heidelberg: Kerle, 1960.

Shewring, Walter. *Art in Christian Philosophy*. Matawan, N.J.: Sower Press, 1950.

Short, Ernest. *A History of Religious Architecture.* 3rd ed. New York: W. W. Norton and Co., n.d.

Silli, A. "L'Architettura sacra e l'epoca moderna," *Fede e Arte,* VIII (1960), 242–255.

Steiss, Albert J. "Outline of a Philosophy of Art," *The Thomist,* II (1940), 14–58.

Stenzel, Alois. *Die Taufe.* Innsbruck: Verlag Felizian Rauch, 1958.

Stevenson, F. R. "Architecture and Liturgy," *Scottish Journal of Theology,* XIV (1961), 390–402.

Stoddard, W. S. *Adventures in Architecture: Building the New St. John's.* New York: Longmans, Green and Co., 1958.

Streignart, Joseph. "Deux documents ecclésiastiques en matière d'art religieux," *Nouvelle Revue Théologique,* LXXIV (1952), 944–958.

Tavard, George H. "The Recovery of an Organic Notion of Tradition," *The Liturgy and Organic Unity in Christ.* Washington, D.C.: Liturgical Conference, 1961, 122–129.

Tegels, Aelfred. "The Church: House of God's People," *Worship,* XXXV (1961), 494–501.

Testini, Pasquale. *Archeologia Cristiana.* Rome: Desclée & Co., 1958.

Torres, R. "La Legislación de la Iglesia sobre el tabernáculo," *Liturgia,* XV (1960), 221–225.

Trebbi, G. "Architettura per la comunità," *Chiesa e Quartiere,* No. 15 (1960), 45–48.

Tucker, D. "Church Art in the Service of Praise," *National Liturgical Week* (1942), 148–160.

Vagaggini, Cyprian. *Theological Dimensions of the Liturgy.* Translated by Leonard J. Doyle. Collegeville, Minn.: Liturgical Press, 1959.

Vaumas, Guillaume de. "L'Église dans la cité," *La Maison-Dieu,* No. 63 (1960), 217–233.

Veronesi, G. "Chiese nuove in Francia," *Chiesa e Quartiere,* No. 14 (1960), 85–89.

Vielliard, René. *Les origines du titre de Saint-Martin aux Monts à Rome.* Rome: Pontificio Instituto di Archeologia Cristiana, 1931.

Wagner, Johannes. "Liturgical Art and the Care of Souls," *The Assisi Papers,* Collegeville, Minn.: Liturgical Press, 1957, 57–73.

Warnach, Walter. "Rom und die moderne Kunst," *Wort und Wahrheit,* VII (1952), 927–932.

Watkin, E. I. *Catholic Art and Culture.* Rev. ed. London: Hollis & Carter, 1947.

Webb, Geoffrey. *The Liturgical Altar.* New York: Benziger, 1939.

Weyers, Willy. *Neu Kirchen im Erzbistum Köln.* Düsseldorf: Schwann Verlag, 1957.

———, Bartning, Otto, *et al. Kirchen: Handbuch für den Kirchenbau.* München: Verlag Georg D. W. Callwey, 1959.

White, J. F. "Some Contemporary Experiments in Liturgical Architecture," *Religion in Life*, XXX (1961), 285–295.

Wilpert, Joseph. *Die römischen Mosaiken und Malereien der kirchlichen Bauten vom IV bis XIII Jahrhundert.* 2 vols. Freiburg: Herder, 1916.

Wind, Edgar. "Traditional Religion and Modern Art," *Art News*, LIII (1953), 18–23, 60–63.

Winninger, Paul. *Construire des églises.* Paris: Éditions du Cerf, 1958.

Wulf, Friedrich. "Gedanken zu einer Theologie des Altars," *Geist und Leben*, XXXIV (1961), 337–347.

Wulf, Maurice de. *Art and Beauty.* Translated by Mary Gonzaga Udell. St. Louis: B. Herder, 1950.

Xydis, Stephen. "The Chancel Barrier, Solea, and Ambo of Hagia Sophia," *The Art Bulletin*, XXIX (1947), 1–24.

Zander, G. "Chiesa e simmetria centrale: introduzione all'iconografia di oggi," *Fede e Arte*, VIII (1960), 34–69.

Zedelgem, P. Amédée de. "Aperçu historique du chemin de la croix," *Collectanea Franciscana*, XIX (1949), 44–142.

Index